New Approaches to Comparative Politics

GLOBAL ENCOUNTERS: STUDIES IN COMPARATIVE POLITICAL THEORY
Series Editor: Fred Dallmayr, University of Notre Dame

This series seeks to inaugurate a new field of inquiry and intellectual concern: that of comparative political theory as an inquiry proceeding not from the citadel of a global hegemony but through cross-cultural dialogue and critical interaction. By opening the discourse of political theory—today largely dominated by American and European intellectuals—to voices from across the global spectrum, we hope to contribute to a richer, multifaceted mode of theorizing as well as to a deeper, cross-cultural awareness of the requirements of global justice.

Border Crossings: Toward a Comparative Political Theory, edited by Fred Dallmayr
Race and Reconciliation in South Africa: A Multicultural Dialogue in Comparative Perspective, edited by William E. Van Vugt and G. Daan Cloete
Gandhi, Freedom, and Self-Rule, edited by Anthony J. Parel
Beyond Nationalism? Sovereignity and Citizenship, edited by Fred Dallmayr and José M. Rosales
Conversations and Transformations: Toward a New Ethics of Self and Society, by Ananta Kumar Giri
Comparative Political Culture in the Age of Globalization: An Introductory Anthology, edited by Hwa Yol Jung
Hinterlands and Horizons: Excursions in Search of Amity, by Margaret Chatterjee
New Approaches to Comparative Politics: Insights from Political Theory, edited by Jennifer S. Holmes

New Approaches to Comparative Politics

Insights from Political Theory

Edited by Jennifer S. Holmes

LEXINGTON BOOKS
Lanham • Boulder • New York • Oxford

LEXINGTON BOOKS

Published in the United States of America
by Lexington Books
A Member of the Rowman & Littlefield Publishing Group
4501 Forbes Boulevard, Suite 200, Lanham, Maryland 20706

PO Box 317
Oxford
OX2 9RU, UK

British Library Cataloguing in Publication Information Available

Library of Congress Cataloging-in-Publication Data

New approaches to comparative politics : insights from political theory / edited by Jennifer S. Holmes.
p. cm.
Includes bibliographical references and index.
ISBN 0-7391-0462-4 (cloth : alk. paper)
1. Comparative government—Study and teaching. I. Holmes, Jennifer S.

JF130 .N48 2003
320.3—dc21 2002154018

Printed in the United States of America

∞™ The paper used in this publication meets the minimum requirements of American National Standard for Information Sciences—Permanence of Paper for Printed Library Materials, ANSI/NISO Z39.48–1992.

To Robert T. Holt, scholar, mentor, and friend

Contents

Introduction

Comparative Politics with Political Theory

Jennifer S. Holmes

This collection promotes a new approach to comparative politics that transcends the old debate about the future of the discipline and the rigid division of labor, proposed by some within the discipline. Historically, the field has been divided into camps with quantitatively driven, universal-scope work and a more qualitative, area studies approach. Underlying this divide are fundamental issues of the philosophy of science, brought to the forefront during the behavioral movement in political science. The unifying theme of all the chapters is theoretically informed comparative analysis. The scholars, in different ways, draw upon political theory to craft arguments which are then analyzed comparatively. The results are fruitful linkages of political theory with comparative politics that provide fresh insights into an old debate and new answers to innovative questions. In addition, this collection is relevant to political theorists. Political theory, when comparative, and comparative politics that takes into account questions from political theory, offer a great possibility for collaboration across the lines of these two subdisciplines. Political theory has great relevance for comparative politics and vice versa.

Michaelle Browers, in "The Reconciliation of Political Theory and Comparative Politics," examines the histories of the subfields of political theory and comparative politics. She begins with a brief assessment of the history of the study of politics, follows up with a discussion of the division of political science into separate subfields, and concludes with some remarks about future relationships between them. She calls for reconciliation and collaboration. Since the beginning of the twentieth century, the study of politics has been contested, with some promoting a division of labor with comparative politics being the empirical partner to political theory. However, according to this vision, political theory has not lived up to its role, instead slipping into historicism. This view of the relationship among different subfields epitomizes the disagreements among comparativists and political theorists. What, if any, division of labor should exist? Has political theory become alienated within political science? Is comparative politics as a subfield hopelessly divided between the large sample size, broadly comparative studies and the small sample size area studies? Browers surveys the recent surge of interest in democracy and democratization that has linked the concerns of comparative political scientists and political theorists. She also discusses the work of a number of political theorists who are trying to reestablish "comparative political theory" as an integral component of political theorizing. She believes that many of these studies lack a perspective on the interaction, contention, and negotiation that occurs between and among different cultural or national contexts and within our increasingly global context. Browers' vision of a future relationship between the two subfields can offer a response to the challenge of the "Perestroika" movement within political science to combine diverse theoretical perspectives with a concern for real-world problems and puzzles. To achieve this, the work needs to be truly interdisciplinary, both within and outside of political science and across cultures.

Ann Davies, in "Modernity and the State: Enlightenment, Liberalism, and Political Development in the United States," provides an example of how political theory benefits from the study of practical politics. Davies discusses the relationship between enlightenment thought and the American Founding, then turns toward a consideration of the degree to which political power arises within the aegis of liberal Enlightenment or remains outside of it. In the process, she compares accounts of the American and French Revolutions and how they were influenced by the Enlightenment and the American liberal Enlightenment. They have influenced accounts of the development of the centralized state within the liberal tradition. Prominent aspects of the American liberal tradition tend to be viewed as working against the kind of authoritative action necessary to establish a centralized "autonomous" ruling apparatus, promoting a deep skepticism toward public action and the authoritative use of distinctive public power and discouraging candid—or even coherent—discussion of their necessity or possibility. While remaining aware of liberal skepticism toward the extension of government power, she argues that a concomitant strand of the Enlightenment and liberalism calls for, and reinforces, the construction of a powerful state. In the process, she considers the theoretical underpinnings of a model of the interactions between democracy and the state that has implications for students of political development, liberalism, and the state. She provides an example of a dynamic process in which theory informs practical politics which then informs theory.

Zeric Kay Smith, in "Relationships between Poverty Reduction Approaches and Donor Support for Democracy: The Case of Mali," discusses how democratic theorists have long debated the normative nature of democratic politics. Many take a substantive view of democracy, imputing its value to its capacity for producing ancillary goods (justice, human rights, economic growth, equity). Others argue for a minimalist definition of democracy, saying that to burden the definition with the goods democracy can (but does not always) produce, risks a tautology. Instead, under this view, democracy should be valued because the process of democratic self-governance is itself ennobling and consistent with human good. Some have tried to articulate a middle road with process and outcome taking coequal status in terms of normative preference for democracy.[1] This theoretical debate has been mirrored in practice within the international development community over the past fifteen years as well. Some practitioners have pursued democracy explicitly because of its assumed positive impact on economic growth or other goods, while others focus on the against each other whether they are democratic or not, while frequently waging war against their own populations. They conclude that until a more satisfying theoretical foundation for the causal linkage between democracy and peace is presented, the democratic peace will remain unconvincing. The critical perspective utilized by Bowman and Eudaily stresses the importance of historical and regional contexts, the nature of the capitalist world system, and the intertext of internal militarization, democracy, and peace.

Robert A. Kahn, in "Imagining Legal Fairness: A Comparative Perspective," develops an idea of the legal imaginary to operationalize competing images of legal fairness or competing political theories of the law. To do so, Kahn examines the different legal systems in Germany, France, Canada, and the United States in regard to a shared legal problem of whether or not to prosecute Holocaust deniers under hate speech and group libel laws. In addition, he briefly overviews the history of comparative inquiry across legal systems, including the study of doctrinal variation, the study of comparative public law, the study of the influence of legal systems on culture, the study of federalism and constitutions, and the study of legal fairness. He challenges scholars to rise above typically static "old constitutionalism" to capture more dynamic legal doctrines and guiding legal values. To do so, he comparatively conceptualizes how societies assess legal fairness, using the ideal type of legal imaginary. Here he focuses on the difference between inquisitorial and adversarial legal systems and differences in legal cultures. The relationship between the norms of free speech and criminal procedures gains clarity by the inclusion of political theory to comparative research. Kahn demonstrates that there is no single political theory of legal imaginaries and concludes that an understanding of these legal differences has payoffs that go beyond the study of Holocaust denial.

These chapters, in different ways, demonstrate the fruitfulness of collaboration between political theory and comparative politics. The result of these works is not a unified style of theoretically informed comparative analysis, but a smorgasbord of different perspectives, theories, and approaches that entwine theory and comparative analysis in useful ways. The point of these disparate chapters is to demonstrate the potential of a collaboration between political theory and comparative politics. These chapters offer examples of the value of the incorporation of Aristotelian, radical, democratic, and legal imaginary to comparative politics. Collaboration offers fresh insights and answers to comparative questions of democratic stability, development, legal systems, democratic peace. Moreover, the chapters by Ann Davies and Zeric Kay Smith highlight that this productive collaboration also works the other direction, from comparative politics to political theory.

Note

1. See Ian Shapiro, *Democratic Justice* (New Haven, Conn.: Yale University Press, 1999).

Chapter One

The Reconciliation of Political Theory and Comparative Politics

Michaelle Browers

When the systematic study of politics emerged in ancient Greece it was both theoretical in nature and comparative in scope. In fact, many of the greatest figures in the history of political thought viewed their enterprise comparatively, from Plato and Aristotle in ancient times, to Machiavelli during the Renaissance, Montesquieu during the Enlightenment, and numerous thinkers of the nineteenth century, such as Tocqueville, Marx, and Mill. Nonetheless, by the beginning of the twentieth century, political theory had become less comparative and comparative politics had become less focused on generating theory. All the more puzzling is that, although the attempt to overhaul comparative politics in American institutions in the postwar period was aimed at making it more theoretical, the outcome was its increasing alienation from the subfield of political theory. However, recent discussions over the state of political science may offer the possibility for the renewal of relationships among the subfields within the discipline. Beginning in 2000, a loosely formed group going by the name of "Perestroika" began to challenge many of the institutions and practices of the American Political Science Association (APSA), most significantly, the domination of theoretical approaches claiming "scientific" status in the profession. By late 2001, one of the most prominent suggestions for reform offered by this group involved the restoration of "political philosophy to a central place in political studies."[1]

The aim of this paper is to assess the histories of the subfields of comparative politics and political theory—where we have been, where we stand now—as a way of pointing toward where we might go together. Certainly, the time is ripe for collaboration, even reconciliation. The recent surge of interest in democracy and democratization has linked the concerns of comparative political scientists and political theorists: Both fields are seeing a resurge of interest in such topics as civil society, citizenship, sovereignty, constitutionalism, and liberalism. So too, a number of political theorists, intent on combating the perceived provincialism of their study and equally concerned with addressing the increasingly global and interdependent context of contemporary politics, are attempting to reestablish "comparative political theory" as an integral component of political theorizing.

Since my specialization falls within an area of political theory—albeit with focus on Arab political thought—most of the comments that follow reflect my interest in assessing the ways in which political theory may benefit from a comparative and/or nonwestern focus and what political theory can offer comparative politics. I conclude with an assessment of the promise and shortcomings of these recent trends. I argue that, although the current scholarship may succeed in bolstering the quality of comparative studies of parallel developments of the concepts, theories, and practices of politics—that is, for the delineation of similarities and differences among civil society, liberalism, or democratization found, for example, in the Arab region and western Europe—what many such studies lack is a perspective on the interaction, contention, and negotiation that occur between and among different cultural or national contexts and within our increasingly global context.

History of a Relationship

It is commonplace to begin introductions and overviews to comparative politics by affirming that its "pedigree reaches back as far as Aristotle."[2] The common starting point for political theory and comparative politics is not surprising since most of the social sciences, and especially political science, trace their origins to ancient Greece in one way or another. In addition, most of those works that have achieved status as "classics" in political science are notable for both their theoretical character and comparative approach. For example, in his *Politics*, Aristotle studied around 150 political constitutions from among the Greek city-states and beyond, and the socioeconomical and political-cultural conditions shaping and determining those forms, in order to account for the stability and instability of different types. In *The Spirit of the Laws*, the eighteenth century French philosopher, Montesquieu, used a comparative approach in studying the climate, religion, laws, maxims of government, morals, and customs toward discerning the national character or "general spirit" permeating various nations. Tocqueville wrote *Democracy in America* as part of a project to understand the significance of the new world for the old, with the aim of aiding early nineteenth century France's difficult transition from aristocracy to democracy.

Certainly the emergence of political science as a discipline was both a result of and contributed to the increasing professionalization and specialization in modern American institutions of higher learning.[3] As comparative politics and political theory developed into distinct subfields in political science, their relationship began to take on more of a "division of labor" character.[4] For example, comparativist David Apter suggests that "from the start, comparing has been a particular way of connecting ideas derived from political philosophy and theory to empirical events and phenomena."[5] Yet, in referring to modern political science, Apter maintains that "comparative politics, insofar as it goes beyond mere description, can be said to be the empirical side of political philosophy or political theory."[6] The problem with the "division of labor" understanding of the subfields in political science is that not all—and certainly not many political theorists—agreed upon how or even whether such a division might form the basis of the common discipline of political science.

As a result, by 1953 David Easton charged leading scholars in political theory with, in essence, not doing their job, with permitting their field to decline into historicism and, hence, into irrelevance for contemporary political science.[7] Easton, and others engaged in the "behaviorist revolution" at the time, sought "scientific" and "empirical" theory, which they understood as the search for and articulation of uniformities in political behavior that could then be verified or tested by reference to relevant behavior and which aimed at providing a unifying framework for all political inquiry.[8] What came to be known as a "behaviorist credo" involved a series of tenets that aimed at explicitly differentiating these "new theoretical aspirations" from "traditional" political theory.[9] In the words of another prominent political scientist, "political theory [as an intellectual activity which pervades the entire discipline] waxed and Political Theory [as a separate field in political science] waned as the behavioral perusal gained ground in the profession."[10] In other words, just as the rest of political science was seeking to become more theoretical—so the argument goes—political theory began to seek refuge in the history of political thought.

Many political theorists argued that rumors of their subfield's death were premature, and the publication of Rawls' *Theory of Justice* in 1971 was put forth by many as an indication of political theory's "revival." Others would point to "the return of grand theory," albeit in a more "skeptical" form, apparent not only in Rawls' work, but also the writings of Gadamer, Derrida, Foucault, Habermas, and others.[11] In many other quarters there was little concern—and perhaps some sense of relief—to be found in the intellectual distance afforded by estrangement from more mainstream political science. Yet, concern about the health of the subfield of political theory has remained until the present time. Throughout the 1980s, John Gunnell expressed alarm over the "alienation" of political theory from substantive political problems and questions.[12] More recently, Terence Ball has reiterated and extended Gunnell's argument. While continuing to worry about "political theory's increasing isolation from its own subject-matter . . . namely, politics," Ball has further expressed unease with political theory's alienation *within* political science. According to Ball, if theorists are "to speak knowledgably about and intervene intelligently in the crises of our time, we will need at least some of the sensibilities of those among our fellow political enquirers who are conventionally classified as 'empirical' political scientists."[13]

At the same time that many began lamenting the decline or death of political theory in the 1950s and 1960s, comparative politics was witnessing what some consider the "golden age" of their field. The ascendance of comparative politics is said to have begun with the research programs initiated by Gabriel Almond and others affiliated with the American Social Science Research Council's Committee on Comparative Politics (founded in 1954), which was very much a part of the behaviorist revolution of the time. The Committee sought to extend the range of comparative politics to developing nations and to establish as the core of the subfield a focus on "large-scale comparisons," ambitiously global in scope and involving a high level of abstraction.[14]

It is within the context of comparative politics that the "behaviorist credo" began to show its earliest—and what would be its most sustained—fissures. By the 1980s, one could hear grumbling over the "division, fragmentation, and atomization in the field . . . [and the lack of] clear direction, leadership, or a commonly held and agreed-upon set of theoretical underpinnings,"[15] such that in 1997 comparative politics would be characterized as a field whose "promise . . . has not been fulfilled," but rather "has lost its way."[16] Not all comparativists share this concern with unity and (scientific) progress in the subfield. In fact, most of the participants in the 1996 *World Politics* symposium on "The Role of Theory in Comparative Politics" seemed content to be part of a "messy center" that combines "diverse conceptual lenses"[17] and is driven not by method but by "real-world puzzles."[18]

In the past few decades, contemporary politics has undergone a narrowing of the scope of comparison and seen a corresponding rise in area specialists, which has contributed to the proliferation of approaches and questions. Much contemporary research in comparative politics tends to be restricted by region and limited to only a very small number of cases or to an in-depth understanding of one particular case. Area specialists tend to view field research as a central component of serious scholarship and many are multidisciplinary in their approach to politics, often drawing upon extensive knowledge of history, language, literature, and social and intellectual traditions of an area. Yet, according to Robert Bates, a prominent comparativist, such studies are *untheoretical*—and outside the domain of a political *science* as a result.[19] The argument advanced by Bates and other such scholars is not that comparativists need to be more attuned to the approaches employed and the substance offered by their colleagues in political theory, but that they need to fulfill the promise and aspirations of comparative politics in the postwar period—that is, to look to the sorts of theory that a presumably more scientific core of mainstream social scientists are engaged in.

Yet, it is precisely my hope that these two subfields, comparative politics and political theory—the former accused of abandoning theory for description, the latter of neglecting practical politics from the heights of metatheoretical disputes—can reestablish a long and meaningful relationship. There are many signs that the time is ripe for such an intra-disciplinary coupling. In the 1996 *World Politics* symposium, Peter Evans suggested that there is a "growing need to erase the barriers between comparative politics—of which American politics is a part—international relations, and political theory."[20] At a panel at the 2001 American Political Science annual meeting in San Francisco, entitled "Perestroika: Undisciplined, Unpunished," Anne Norton reported that the time had come to retrieve traditional political theory from the "ghetto" it had been placed in by "formal" (rational-choice) theory. At that same meeting, Rogers Smith reported a "hopeful suspicion" that "political theory as practiced in political science departments" was beginning to "engage work in empirical social science, including quantitative, historical, institutional, and policy analyses, more deeply and pervasively than was customary from roughly 1970 through 1995."[21] The Foundations of Political Theory section of the American Political Science Association has attempted to encourage this suspicion by establishing a new book prize, appropriately called the David Easton Award, with the aim of encouraging work that is both empirical and philosophical.

At the same time, the form this renewed relationship will take seems unlikely to either correspond to the "division of labor" ideal advocated by some in the past, or contribute to the aspirations that many continue to hold for a political science united under a political theory—unless by "political theory" we mean the wide variety of intellectual activities that currently take place under the subfield heading of political theory. Rather, the new form of the relationship between political theory and mainstream political science might best be conceived in the manner suggested by Ball: where political theorists adopt at least some of the "sensibilities of those among our fellow political enquirers who are conventionally classified as 'empirical' political scientists."[22] As such, we may see more productive interactions based on common concerns accompanied by a greater plurality of approaches to the study of politics. There are already a few indications that some political theorists are developing an appreciation for context, comparison, and even sustained "field research."

Fruitful Linkages between Political Theory and Comparative Politics

Rogers Smith points to a number of recent studies in political theory that exemplify empirically engaged theorizing, singling out in particular David Miller's *Principles of Social Justice* and Ian Shapiro's *Democratic Justice.*[23] Smith praises Miller for his "critical engagement with sophisticated, contextually sensitive empirical research into popular beliefs" about justice. Shapiro is lauded for his "Deweyan choice to begin [his study] with current felt problems and the conflicting claims and interests they involve, and his quest to find the most democratically just accommodation of those interests."[24] In Smith's view both theoretical works are exemplary not only for their use of empirical evidence, but also for their ability to speak to some of the main political concerns of both more-empirical political scientists and the broader citizenry. To Smith's two favorites, I would add two of my own, though for slightly different reasons. Like Miller and Shapiro's books, the recent study of European liberalism by Richard Bellamy[25] and the edited collection on the role of lawyers in the emergence of western liberalism by Terence Halliday and Lucien Karpik[26] have the merit of engaging empirical research and political issues of contemporary significance. Yet, the latter two works capture historical *and* comparative aspects in their analyses of liberalism that are missed by the former.

Halliday and Karpik bring together sociologists and historians to examine how lawyers, over the past three centuries, have been variously committed to the building of liberal political society in France, Germany, Great Britain, and the United States. In the introductory essay, entitled "Politics Matter," the authors argue that their project departs from other theories of legal professions, which neglect politics, and advances a comparative political theory of collective action by demonstrating lawyers' influence on the historical emergence and development of western political liberalism. The editors argue that although lawyers in one country may espouse models of liberalism that differ perceptibly from those of other countries, collectively they have contributed in various ways to three core elements of liberal politics: the development of the moderate state, the creation of civil society, and the expansion of citizenship. The editor's "Postscript" elaborates an additional theory that "national lawyers' movements around liberal politics are thus part of a political globalization whose singularity can be captured by its differences with the dynamics of economic globalization."[27] The various contributors to the study demonstrate that lawyers' politics are much more entangled in localism than they are with the market. Whereas markets universalize, politics particularize, such that this movement has uniquely contributed to a global political liberalization. Nonetheless, the authors conclude that "more and more contemporary national professionals are becoming willingly or not, part of transnational economic exchanges that have most dramatically expanded in the past twenty years."[28]

Combining political theory with institutional analysis, Bellamy offers four national studies of political development in Britain, France, Italy, and Germany. Through an examination of late nineteenth and early twentieth century liberal ideas in their national contexts, Bellamy provides a historical account of the overcoming of ethical liberalism by economic liberalism. According to Bellamy, understanding these ideas in context "reveals the historically contingent nature of many of liberalism's key propositions. When the favorable constellation of social forces linking the bourgeois class with liberal institutions and values was absent, the philosophical assumptions of ethical liberalism proved unstable and had to be drastically rethought."[29]

The book's fifth chapter analyzes contemporary liberal theories, which Bellamy shows continue to rely on the traditional social assumptions of ethical liberalism. In light of the erosion of the social conditions necessary for tying bourgeois interests to liberalism that is demonstrated in the course of the book's preceding chapters, Bellamy argues that contemporary liberal philosophy remains untenable within today's postmodern, postindustrial societies. Bellamy concludes that "to cope with this situation, liberalism must transform itself from an ethical to a political theory, in which the central place is occupied, not by liberal values, but by institutions or procedures capable of giving expression to a plurality of points of view and arranging agreements between them,"[30] and then provides the outlines of such a theory. Whether or not one agrees with Bellamy's normative claims, his work is notable for demonstrating the importance of understanding political ideas in context in any attempt to link political thought to contemporary political practice.

Each of these studies is important and suggests fruitful linkages between the questions and problems addressed by political theory and mainstream political science. In regard to comparative politics, although Miller and Shapiro's books are not comparative in nature, but focus more generally on "western" understandings of justice, like the contributors to the Halliday and Karpik study and Bellamy's work, which offer a more explicitly comparative focus on liberalism, each contributes concepts and theories that are of interest to scholars of comparative politics. While especially the latter two are exemplary in providing a "thick description" of ideas in context, it is notable that each of these studies limits their purview to western political thought and the contexts of modern North American and Europe. Whereas comparative politics (and international relations) have expanded their focus well beyond the western world, political theory exhibits—usually rather unself-consciously—a distinct provincialism in regard to the questions, concepts, and contexts they engage.

Comparative political scientists in particular have an interest in understanding traditions of political thought in non-Western contexts and in assessing the extent to which such ideas as democracy, liberalism, civil society, and justice—to name just a few possibilities—resonate and/or are applicable there. A number of recent works by area specialists in comparative politics have grappled with contemporary political thought.[31] The present volume (in which, it is worth noting, authors from comparative politics vastly outnumber those who are primarily political theorists) is also an excellent example. But perhaps the most promising—and most overdue—movement toward a fruitful linkage between comparative politics and political theory can be found—albeit still somewhat uncomfortably—situated in the latter subfield. That is, despite the long history of provincialism in political theory, a number of promising recent studies have demonstrated a concern with understanding "nonwestern" political ideas comparatively and in context.

Comparative Political Theory

While "comparative philosophy" (that extends beyond western philosophy) has a bit longer history in the modern academy—dating at least back to the first East-West philosophy conference in 1939, which Larson argues was "one of the formative events for the beginning of comparative philosophy as a field"[32]—the move to open up the subfield of political theory to comparative studies of a similar scope is a more recent phenomena, perhaps not much older than the work undertaken by the scholars who came together in Fred Dallmayr's edited volume which bears the promising subtitle, "Toward a Comparative Political Theory."[33] In that work, Roxanne Euben "maps" western and Islamic critiques of modernity, Nancy Hirschmann demonstrates that western conceptions of freedom are inadequate for understanding eastern forms of veiling, and Russell Arben Fox compares communitarianism in western political thought and Confucianism. Other contributors study constitutionalism and democracy in an Islamic context;

martyrdom in Iranian; Pashtun conceptions of nonviolence; secularism in India; liberal democracy in postcolonial Taiwan; universalism in a Japanese colonialist critique; and Taoist contributions to a tolerant and non-dogmatic Enlightenment.

These studies demonstrate many of the same concerns reflected in the best work undertaken by area specialists: the pursuit of deep and sensitive knowledge of the particularities of the political, social, linguistic, and intellectual contexts they study. Yet one problem with most, though not all, of the writings in comparative political theory is that they tend to treat "non-western" works as "parallel developments" in the history of political thought.[34] One of the few works to bear the title of "comparative political philosophy," describes its enterprise as "the study of substantive equivalence or *parallelism* in the development of different traditions of political philosophy."[35] With the notable exception of Euben's chapter, and perhaps also Hwa Yol Jung's,[36] the contributors to Dallmayr's edited volume (noted above) either study a single context and posit (whether explicitly or implicitly) a comparison with the West, or study an eastern context alongside a western one. As such, comparative work tends to give the impression that the traditions compared developed independently of each other. Larson articulates a similar concern about comparative philosophy's "tendency to favor large, holistic boundaries of language, culture, and history; [and] a tendency to treat conceptual systems as 'entities' or 'things' that can be externally compared."[37] However the important "break" his volume represents in terms of "older conventional notions of what comparative philosophy represents" still underemphasizes the already existent transculturality of the works and ideas compared. The solution Larson suggests for the two tendencies he identifies consists not in looking at influences and exchanges of ideas *across* cultures or languages, but in highlighting the differences *within* the "wholes" of language, culture, and conceptual schemes. This criticism is not unique to political theory. On the contrary, one finds parallel arguments in comparative political and international relations, for example, regarding problems with using states (or other cultural or political wholes) as the unit of analysis. However, here too political theory, comparative politics, and international relations might find reading across subfields productive for thinking through these issues.

A few recent works attempt to be not only comparative, but also cross-cultural. For example, Parel focuses on "cross-cultural understanding in the threatening context of modernity."[38] A work comparing "western" liberal democracy and Confucianism aims at "build[ing] bridges across a cultural gap."[39] Similarly, Dallmayr's most recent work seeks to articulate "the proper modes of living and sharing together,"[40] amidst the "alternative visions"[41] that occupy our increasingly "global village." Such works do at times manage to incorporate the transportation and appropriation of ideas across cultures into their analysis, despite their claim to be "comparative" or the stated goal of articulating an "ethic" to guide interactions between "alternative visions." One good example is found in Euben's discussions of Arab-Islamic "rationality" in the thought of Sayyid Qutb, which suggests a conscious, if not always direct, influence or interaction between "eastern" and "western" theorists of rationality.[42] Euben's most recent work, *Enemy in the Mirror,* even more clearly presents Sayyid Qutb's political thought as "a rebuttal of and antidote to [western] rationalist discourse."[43] Similarly, Dallmayr's discussion of democracy in India suggests the existence of a cross-cultural response on the part of a number of thinkers.[44]

Part of the difference between the sort of approach I am encouraging here and these very promising works in the most recent comparative political theory seems to lie in the different ways in which the "encounter" is conceptualized—which itself has implications for the approach in that it influences what is taken into account or looked for in a comparative analysis. This is seen most clearly in Dallmayr's work, entitled *Beyond Orientalism*, in which he identifies seven "modes of cross-cultural encounter": conquest, conversion, assimilation/acculturation, partial assimilation/cultural borrowing, liberalism/minimal engagement, conflict/class struggle, and dialogical engagement.[45] Dallmayr characterizes the first three (conquest, conversion, assimilation) as starkly hegemonic or hierarchical. Assimilation, in particular, resembles comparative studies that attempt to apply "ready made" concepts to new or foreign contexts such that what the research finds must be assimilated into preconceived notions of what is worth finding. The third, partial assimilation or selective borrowing, takes place on a more nearly equal basis, but the "outcome," Dallmayr notes, "can be greatly varied," ranging from "the melting-pot syndrome" to "an ambivalent form of syncretism" or "a precarious type of cultural coexistence" to a "movement of genuine self-transformation." The fourth mode (liberalist/minimal engagement) tends toward isolationism; while the fifth (conflict/class struggle) is overly contentious and unstable. The final mode, that of dialogical engagement, becomes Dallmayr's mode of choice once he succeeds in redescribing it as a deconstructive dialogue which respects otherness beyond assimilation.

Ideally, the cross-cultural interactions involved in comparative analyses would consist of each culture viewing the others from their own point of reference and thus acting as both the subject and object of study in turn. However, due to the uneven social, political, and economic status accorded various "cultures," such a situation seldom, if ever, ensues. Conflict rather than cooperation is more often the norm. Studies focused on achieving cross-cultural, mutual understanding are only relevant to those discursive interactions that actors enter into with the intention of achieving agreement. More often, what takes place is that the intellectuals of the less-powerful, the "observed" cultures, themselves incorporate the concepts—categories and standards of intelligibility—of the dominant culture in their observation, understanding, and critique of their own cultures.

This is not to say that cross-cultural interactions need be characterized as the more hegemonic forms that Dallmayr identifies (conquest, conversion, assimilation). Rather, the nature of conceptual change is such that cross-cultural encounters most closely resemble what Dallmayr calls "partial assimilation" when social and political concepts are involved; and the outcomes of such encounters can be as varied as Dallmayr describes. At the same time, what is often missed in many accounts of "[partial] assimilation" is the other half of this cultural borrowing: the activity and efforts on the part of those who translate and transport concepts cross-culturally, and in a way that leaves neither the concept or its new home unchanged.

It is this "agency" that I sought to highlight in my doctoral thesis, entitled "The Politics of Translation: Civil Society's Travels and Travails in Arab Political Thought."[46] In contrast to previous studies which focus on assessing the extent to which "civil society" is empirically present or absent in Arab countries, this work addresses the question of what happens when such a political concept crosses "cultures" or "languages." To answer this question, I examined the history of the concept of civil society in Anglo-European political thought and the more recent emergence of a discourse on civil society in Arab political thought. The goal of the study was to analyze the transformations that have occurred in Arab political thought over the past decade as a result of Arab forays into an international discourse about "civil society." The research presented aims to demonstrate that the "translation" required to talk about "civil society" in Arabic is not so much a hindrance to understanding, as an opportunity for *different understanding*—that is, for political and conceptual transformation and contestation in Arab political thought. The work identifies three competing discourses in the civil society debate that are taking place in Arabic. For Arab liberals "civil society" is most importantly tolerant and democratic. For Islamists, it is most important that society be Islamic and that an Islamic civil society be independent from the existing uncivil (secular) state. Finally, Arab leftists seek to construct a civil society that provides a progressive force able to contribute toward the creation of a leftist counterhegemony.

What Dallmayr terms "partial assimilation" has much in common with what others refer to as "transculturation." According to Pratt, the term "transculturation" has been used by ethnographers "to describe how subordination or marginal groups select and invent from materials transmitted to them by a dominant or metropolitan culture."[47] Pratt further notes that "while subjugated peoples cannot readily control what emanates from the dominant culture, they do determine to varying extents what they absorb into their own and what they use it for."[48] This phenomenon is what I describe in my thesis through an analysis of the internal and external factors that contributed to the recent Arab focus on the civil society idea, and the outcomes of this transcultural encounter.

However, there is another important facet of "partial assimilations," which lies in the fact that especially the initial encounter with a new concept is the freest, most fluid, and perhaps also the most authentic. Gadamer tells us that "we understand in a *different* way, *if we understand at all*."[49] One might also add that conceptual innovation is, in a sense, often the offspring of such "different understanding." When communication is impeded between different conceptual schemes, cultures, or languages; when concepts are "translated" (intentionally or unintentionally), new opportunities ensue. Or, to return to the analogy introduced in the introductory chapter, new opportunities arise when a new concept, like new technology, is put to different use in a new context, or when an old concept, like old technology, is put to new use.

As is apparent from the first discussions of civil society, Arab intellectuals did not feel tied to any particular school of western political thought, and seldom felt compelled to "drop names" of particular theorists of civil society in making their points. Rather, they made use of concepts that they had come into contact with in a "partial" or undeveloped way and then looked to their own intellectual context and heritage for ideas that resonated with the new ones. As a result of this "partial assimilation," Arab liberals, such as Wajih Kawtharani[50] and Burhan Ghalyun,[51] were able to begin to develop theories about how a pluralistic and democratic movement could draw strength from or incorporate elements of traditional society; Arab leftists, such as Sadiq Jalal al- Azm,[52] could present an alternative vision of the way in which an Islamic ideology had been broken down and was being replaced by a bourgeois civil society, which, he argues, would have to be superceded by something else; Arab Islamists, such as Hasan Turabi[53] and Rachid al-Ghannouchi[54] could conceptualize the Islamic *umma* [community] as both a broader concept in the sense of a public sphere in which both moral and democratic political authority would be invested and, at the same time, as the locale of a political strategy delineated by the context of an existing nation-state; and a female Arab Islamist, Heba Raouf Ezzat,[55] could both further expand and further delineate that Islamic community that, respectively, encompasses the family as an important element in social change and women as integral political actors in that social sphere.

Perhaps it is at least in part result of the Arab Left's rather late entry into the civil society debate that their assimilation of the concept appears less "partial" (in the sense that it is conceived in connection with Gramsci) and less incorporated as part of an actual political strategy (in comparison to the Islamists). Certainly when "civil society" is discussed as Gramsci's idea or Tocqueville's idea, one becomes bound to a particular notion. "Authentically" presenting Gramscian civil society can both enable and burden the presentation of authentic Arab or Islamic civil society. So too, opposing "civil societies" may run the risk of clashing over Gramsci and Tocqueville, for example, rather than clashing over the way in which civil society is really being used.

What is understood differently across cultures very often becomes a point of contestation. As one scholar has rightly pointed out, the real "clash of civilizations" in our time is not "between the West and some homogenous 'other' but between rival carriers of tradition within the same nations and civilizations."[56] Gaining a truly cross-cultural perspective on the exchange of political and social ideas—that is, a perspective not only on the way in which one culture is "dealt with" by and deals with another or one aimed at articulating a better "ethic" for to guide future interactions, but one that explores the travels and travails of political ideas as they cross boundaries of language and culture and are put to use in a new context—requires that we work in between not only comparative politics and political theory, but also in between political-theoretical contexts.

In light of the considerable political upheaval in the last few decades and the increasingly global climate that characterizes our present, comparativists can and should benefit from the insights and categories of analysis of both contemporary political theory and the history of political thought. Recent transformations within political science (such as the perestroika movement) and within the political world (such as increasing globalization) suggest the need and opportunity for comparativists and theorists to not only cross the subfield divides within political science, but to engage to incorporate a greater interdisciplinary perspective in general. This sentiment is strongly stated in the form of a "maxim" by a comparativist and one of the most prominent members of the perestroika movement in political science, James Scott:

> If half your reading is not *outside* the confines of political science, you are risking extinction along with the rest of the subspecies. Most of the notable innovations in the discipline have come in the form of insights, perspectives, concepts, and paradigms originating elsewhere. Reading exclusively within the discipline is to risk reproducing orthodoxies or, at the very least, absorbing innovations far from the source.[57]

Scholars and students of comparative politics and political theory need to further heed the call to pursue fruitful linkages in studies of the contemporary political world.

Notes

1. Gregory J. Kasza, "Perestroika: For an Ecumenical Science of Politics," *PS: Political Science and Politics* 34 (2001): 598.

2. Harry Eckstein, *Regarding Politics: Essays on Political Theory, Stability and Change* (Berkeley: University of California Press, 1992), 60; Jan-Erik Lane and Svante Ersson, *Comparative Politics: An Introduction and New Approach* (Cambridge, Mass.: Polity Press, 1994), xiii; Peter Mair, "Comparative Politics: An Overview," in *A New Handbook for Political Science*, ed. Robert E. Goodin and Hans-Dieter Klingmemann (Oxford, Oxford University Press, 1996), 309.

3. See Dorothy Ross. *The Origins of American Social Science*, (Cambridge, UK: Cambridge University Press, 1991), esp. 282–300.

4. Accordingly, a 1957 political science textbook described political theory as the branch of political science which "attempts to arrive at generalizations, inferences, or conclusions to be drawn from the data gathered by other specialists, not only in political science, but throughout the whole range of human knowledge and experience." C. C. Rodee, T. J. Anderson, and C. Q. Christol, eds. *Introduction to Political Science* (New York: McGraw-Hill, 1957), 11.

5. David E. Apter, "Comparative Politics: Old and New," in *A New Handbook for Political Science*, ed. Robert E. Goodin and Hans-Dieter Klingmemann (Oxford, UK: Oxford University Press, 1996), 372.

6. Apter, "Comparative Politics," 273.

7. David Easton, *The Political System: An Inquiry Into the State of Political Science* (New York: Knopf, 1953).

8. David Easton, *A Framework for Political Analysis* (Englewood Cliffs, N.J.: Prentice-Hall, 1965), 7

9. Easton, *Framework*, 7–9.

10. Marian Irish, "Introduction: Advance of the Discipline?" *Journal of Politics* 30 (1968): 298.

11. Quentin Skinner, *The Return of Grand Theory in the Human Sciences* (Cambridge, UK: Cambridge University Press, 1985).

12. John G. Gunnell. *Between Philosophy and Politics: The Alienation of Political Theory* (Amherst, Mass.: University of Massachusetts Press, 1986). More recently, Gunnell has identified a similar, more "paradoxical" tension between empirical theory and the social relevance it seeks:

> The idea of an empirical theory of politics was always conceived as part of a program for intervening in political life, but, paradoxically, the basis of that intervention was understood to be the epistemological independence of such a theory. This paradox involved a simultaneous search for practical authority and scientific purity that led political science at once to distance itself from politics and to conceive of theory in a manner that reflected its practical aspirations.

John G. Gunnell, "Paradoxos Theoretikos," in *Contemporary Empirical Political Theory*, ed. Kristen R. Monroe (Berkeley, Calif.: University of California Press, 1997), 47.

13. Terence Ball, *Reappraising Political Theory: Revisionist Studies in the History of Political Thought* (Oxford, UK: Clarendon Press, 1995), 53, 60.

14. Mair, "Comparative Politics," 312.

15. Sidney Verba, "Comparative Politics: Where Have We Been, Where Are We Going?" in *New Directions in Comparative Politics*, ed. Howard J. Wiarda and Douglas A. Chalmers (Boulder, Colo.: Westview, 1985), 28.

16. Mark Irving Lichbach and Alan S. Zuckerman, "Preface," in *Comparative Politics: Rationality, Culture, and Structure*, ed. Mark Irving Lichbach and Alan S. Zuckerman. (Cambridge, U.K: Cambridge University Press, 1997), ix.

17. Atul Kohli, Peter Evans, et al., "The Role of Theory in Comparative Politics: A Symposium," *World Politics* 48 (1996): 2.

18. Kohli et al., "Role of Theory," 46.

19. While president of the Comparative Politics section of the APSA, Bates charged that "within the academy, the consensus has formed that area studies has failed to generate scientific knowledge." Robert H. Bates, "Area Studies and the Discipline," *APSA-CP: Newsletter of the APSA Organized Section in Comparative Politics* 7 (1996): 1; and Bates, "Area Studies and the Discipline," *PS: Political Science and Politics* 30 (1997), 166.

20. Kohli et al., "Role of Theory," 11.

21. Rogers M. Smith, "Reconnecting Political Theory to Empirical Inquiry, or, A Return to the Cave?" Paper presented at the annual meeting of the American Political Science Association, San Francisco, September 2001.

22. Terence Ball, *Reappraising Political Theory*, 60.

23. David Miller, *Principles of Social Justice* (Cambridge, Mass.: Harvard University Press, 1999). Ian Shapiro, *Democratic Justice* (New Haven, Conn.: Yale University Press, 1999).

24. Rogers M. Smith, "Reconnecting Political Theory."

25. Richard Bellamy, *Liberalism and Modern Society: A Historical Argument* (University Park, Pa.: Pennsylvania State University Press, 1992).

26. Terence C. Halliday and Lucien Karpik, eds., *Lawyers and the Rise of Western Political Liberalism: Europe and North America from the Eighteenth to Twentieth Centuries* (Oxford, UK: Oxford University Press, 1997).

27. Halliday and Lucien, *Lawyers*, 351.

28. Halliday and Lucien, *Lawyers*, 367.

29. Bellamy, *Liberalism and Modern Society*, 4.

30. Bellamy, *Liberalism and Modern Society*, 8.

31. At the risk of omitting a great number of these important works, I will confine myself to two areas I know best due to my own interests in political theory. Works by comparativists that grapple with contemporary theories of democracy and civil society include Gideon Baker, *Civil Society and Democratic Theory: International Perspectives* (New York: Routledge, 2002); Anthony Butler, *Democracy and Apartheid: Political Theory, Comparative Politics and the Modern South African State* (New York: St. Martin's Press, 1998); John A. Hall, ed., *Civil Society: Theory, History, Comparison* (Cambridge, UK: Polity Press, 1995); Chris Hann and Elizabeth Dunn, eds. *Civil Society: Challenging Western Models* (London: Routledge, 1996); Adrian Leftwich, ed., *Democracy and Development: Theory and Practice* (Cambridge, UK: Polity Press, 1996). A number of comparative works have been influenced by and/or contributed to debates in contemporary feminist theory, including Vicky Randall and Georgina Waylen, eds., *Gender, Politics and the State* (London: Routledge, 1998) and Dorothy M. Stetson, *Abortion Politics, Women's Movements, and the Democratic State: A Comparative Study of State Feminism* (Oxford, UK: Oxford University Press, 2001).

32. Gerald James Larson, "Introduction," in *Interpreting Across Boundaries: New Essays in Comparative Philosophy*, ed. Gerald James Larson and Eliot Deutsch. (Princeton, N.J.: Princeton University Press, 1988), 6.

33. Fred R. Dallmayr, ed., *Border Crossings: Toward a Comparative Political Theory* (Lanham, Md., Lexington Books, 1999).

34. One of the great works of comparative philosophy written by a non-western author, Hajime Nakamura, takes this phrase as his title: *Parallel Developments—A Comparative History of Ideas* (New York: Harper & Row, 1975).

35. Anthony Parel and Ronald C. Keith, eds, *Comparative Political Philosophy: Studies under the Upas Tree* (New Delhi, India; Newbury Park, Calif., Sage, 1992), 7, my italics.

36. Euben's contribution to *Border Crossings* examines both "Islamic" and "western" thinkers that "simultaneously abolish, transcend, preserve, and transform modernity" (p. 30), suggesting a transcultural dimension to critiques of modernity, though perhaps, problematically conceiving both "fundamentalists" and "postmodernists" as somehow outside of "modernity." Jung's contribution seems to aim at articulating a cosmopolitan

perspective that emerges out of what he refers to as "lateral universals" or "mutual influence" between contemporary postmodernism and aspects of Chinese thought.

37. James Larson, "Introduction."

38. Parel and Keith, *Comparative Political Philosophy*, 8.

39. Chenyang Li, *The Tao Encounters the West: Explorations in Comparative Philosophy* (Albany: State University of New York Press, 1999)

40. Fred R. Dallmayr, "Introduction: Toward a Comparative Political Theory," *The Review of Politics* 59 (1997): 421–7 and Dallmayr, *Border Crossings*, 1.

41. Fred R. Dallmayr, *Alternative Visions: Paths in the Global Village* (Lanham, Md.: Rowman & Littlefield, 1998).

42. Roxanne Euben, *Enemy in the Mirror: Islamic Fundamentalism and the Limits of Modern Rationalism, A Work of Comparative Political Theory* (Princeton, N.J.: Princeton University Press, 1999).

43. Euben, *Enemy in the Mirror*, 155.

44. Fred R. Dallmayr, *Beyond Orientalism: Essays on Cross-Cultural Encounter* (Albany: SUNY Press, 1996).

45. Dallmayr, *Beyond Orientalism*, 3–37.

46. Michaelle L. Browers, "The Politics of Translation: Civil Society's Travels and Travails in Arab Political Thought," Doctoral Thesis in Political Science, University of Minnesota, 2001.

47. Mary Louise Pratt notes that "'transculturation' was coined in the 1940s by Cuban sociologist Fernancdo Oritz" and that "Uruguayan critic Angel Rama incorporated the term into literary studies in the 1970s," in *Imperial Eyes: Travel Writing and Transculturation* (London: Routledge, 1992), 228.

48. Pratt, *Imperial Eyes*, 6. I am aware of one theorist who tries to incorporate "transculturation" into contemporary political theory. In a recent article, Greg Nielsen seeks to develop Habermas' communicative action and Bakhtin's concept of dialogue to explain the discursive process of transculturation and develop what he refers to as a "transcultural ethics." Nielsen, "Backhtin and Habermas: Toward a Transcultural Ethics," *Theory and Society* 24 (1995): 803–36.

49. Hans-Georg Gadamer, *Truth and Method* (New York: Continuum, 1993), 297.

50. Wajih Kawtharani, "al-Mujtama` al-madani wa al-dawla fi al-ta'rikh al-`arabi [Civil Society and the State in Arab History]," in *al-mujtama` al-madani fi al-watan al-'arabi wa dawruhu fi tahqiq al-dimuqratiyya* [Civil Society in the Arab World and Its Role in the Realization of Democracy], ed., Center for Arab Unity Studies (Beirut: Center for Arab Unity Studies, 1992), 119–31.

51. Burhan Ghalyun, "al-Mujtama` al-madani fi al-watan al-`arabi wa dawruhu fi tahqiq al-dimuqratiyya [Review of Civil Society in the Arab World and Its Role in the Realization of Democracy]," *al-mustaqbal al-`arabi* 179 (1994): 139–45; and Ghalyun, "Bina` al-mujtama` al-madani al-`arabi: dur al-`awamil al-dakhiliyya wa al-kharijiyya [Constructing Arab Civil Society: The Role of Internal and External Factors]," in *al-mujtama` al-madani fi al-watan al-'arabi wa dawruhu fi tahqiq al-dimuqratiyya* [Civil Society in the Arab World and Its Role in the Realization of Democracy], ed., Center for Arab Unity Studies (Beirut: Center for Arab Unity Studies, 1992), 733–55.

52. Sadiq Jalal al-`Azm, *al-`Almaniyya wa al-mujtama` al-madani* [Secularism and Civil Society] (Cairo: markaz al-dirasat wa al-ma`lumat al-qanuniyya li-huquq al-insan, 1998).

53. Hasan Turabi, Hiwarat fi al-Islam, al-dimuqratiyya, al-dawla, al-Gharb [Dialogues on Islam, Democracy and the West] (Beirut: Dar al-Jadid, 1995) and Hasan Turabi

and Arthur L. Lowrie, *Islam, Democracy, the State and the West: A Roundtable with Dr. Hasan Turabi* (Tampa, Fla.: World & Islam Studies Enterprise, 1993).

54. Rachid al-Ghannouchi, *al-Hurriyyat al'ammah fi al-dawlat al-Islamiyya* [Public Liberties in the Islamic State] (Beirut: Center for Arab Unity Studies, 1993).

55. Heba Raouf Ezzat, "al-Usra wa al-taghyir al-siyasi: ruya islamiyya [The Family and Political Change: An Islamic View]," *islamiyyat al-ma`rifa* 191 (1995): 11–47.

56. Robert W. Hefner, "Multiple Modernities: Christianity, Islam and Hinduism in a Globalizing Age," *Annual Review of Anthropology* (1998): 27.

57. Kohli et al, "Role of Theory," 37.

Chapter Two

Modernity and the State: Enlightenment, Liberalism, and Political Development in the United States

Ann Davies

While some of the other chapters in this volume use political theory as a vehicle for understanding particular situations encountered in comparative politics, I attempt to suggest in the following pages that the relationship between political theory and comparative politics is certainly not uni-directional: Just as comparative politics may benefit from theory, theory in turn benefits from the study of practical politics. While my study is limited to the United States and the interaction between the Enlightenment and political development, I think that my conclusions hold implications for political scientists' assumptions in general as they situate themselves around some of the more dominant theoretical paradigms regarding revolutions and political development.

Although theorists and politicians of the Enlightenment often invoked metaphors of light-shedding clarity and mechanical necessity, the Enlightenment's approach to political development seems anything but straightforward and clear. First, while a chronological connection exists between the development of modern politics and the Enlightenment, many of its thinkers did not develop full-bodied political theories, and we cannot always be certain of the relation between those theories and the political situations at hand. However, the shadows around the Enlightenment's relationship to politics may involve more than incomplete theories or the usual challenges of determining the nexus between theory and practice, for enlightenment theory itself seems to have an apolitical aspect. As Judith Shklar argues, the Enlightenment in some of its forms offered a politics to end all politics. If reason could govern, society would be self-regulating and force would be unnecessary.[1] This point implies an accusation against Enlightenment thinking, because for all their claims of clarity and investigation, Enlightenment thinkers seem, to many of their interpreters, to have been incredibly blind to the dynamics and structure of political power, as well as to the fundamental conflicts and intransigent problems of political life.

As a result, the Enlightenment sometimes seems simultaneously blamed for the disasters of modern political life and rendered politically inconsequential. A comparison of accounts of the American and French revolutions is revealing in this regard. On the one hand, the Enlightenment is sometimes blamed for an abstract idealism that contributed to the French Terror, either because it didn't adequately circumscribe the limits of politics, providing a seductive portrait of reason and equality, the pursuit of which could justify nearly any means, or because it remained blissfully aloof from the inevitable forces of tradition, resistance, and coercion within politics. Thus it could neither fully anticipate, nor coherently respond to, the unleashing of revolutionary and reactionary forces. Conversely, the American case is praised for its temperance, its realism, and the aversion of its own political disaster.[2]

Yet this "good United States–bad France" seems to practice its own form of abstraction, downplaying the significant contextual differences between the two revolutions. One could easily argue that France suffered not from the ideals of the *philosophes* but from the limits of democratic development. From this perspective, the Terror resulted from the inadequate institutionalization of popular rule, which allowed the cynical manipulation of the mob by the political elite, rather than from an excess of democracy and idealism. If political development occurred more successfully in the early American republic, much of this had to do with the separate histories of France and the United States, with the new states, and ultimately the union, having a richer experience of liberty and self-government upon which to draw.

Embedded in this defense of the Enlightenment's political effects, however, are several qualifications, and possible ironies. First, while the argument about institutionalization may divert those accusations which seek to tie *philosophes* theories directly to the extremes of the Revolution, it still leaves open the question of whether the Enlightenment provides, leaves room for, or discourages a realistic construction of political power. Second, is the Enlightenment "saved" from linkage to the Terror by citing the American case? The degree to which political development succeeded in the early republic of the United States seems to lie not so much in the Enlightenment, per se, but in the traditions and institutions of the English republic that predated it. Further, enlightenment rhetoric in the United States may have clouded more than clarified political debates, for while accounts of the successful construction, limitation, and evolution of government power may begin with bold discussions of "rational" principles and institutional "mechanics," those discussions often seem ultimately to end in obfuscation, the invocation of tradition, and a general "muddling through." In the United States government power seems often constructed not by systematic analysis or justification but rather by the denial of its presence, by falling back upon appeals to the past, or simply by talking about something else. Thus, despite Hamilton's declaration in Federalist 1 that the ratification of the Constitution would determine "whether societies of men are really capable or not of establishing good government from reflection and choice, or whether they are forever destined to depend for their political constitutions on accident and force," the powers of our central government might seem to be more the product of accident than reflection, something that happened when we were not looking.[3]

The strength of this observation has influenced both accounts of the past and the contextualization of the development of the centralized state within the liberal tradition. Hegel, Tocqueville, Santayana, and Weber all remarked on the absence of the state—in both an institutional and conceptual sense—in the United States. This need not be a surprise; since the American state could not replicate the prototypical European state's bureaucracy and army arising from the vestiges of its feudal and royal past, it was unlikely to take that form or to produce theories intended to mold or justify it. However, the claims of such theorists seem to reach deeper into the American mind-set for, in their view, prominent aspects of the American liberal tradition—which I take to be integrally associated with aspects of the Enlightenment—work against the kind of authoritative action necessary to establish a centralized "autonomous" ruling apparatus and especially promote a deep skepticism toward public action and the authoritative use of distinctive public power. Later students of political development, including Louis Hartz, Samuel Huntington, Stephen Skowronek, and Theodore Lowi, have echoed such views. As many of their accounts suggest, the absence of a sense of the state holds implications for the course of U.S. political development and the legitimacy of its political institutions.

This observation in turn points to a second irony in the relationship between the Enlightenment and political development, namely that even in the aftermath of the French Revolution, its violence, social unrest, and short-lived constitutions, France (along with much of the rest of continental Europe) is viewed as having a more coherent and cohesive concept of the state than the United States, with the authoritative action of a centralized state recognized, justified, and rationalized.[4] Yet again, this results not so much from the Enlightenment as from practices and theories that predate it, the inheritance of feudal armies, the bureaucracies associated with absolutism, and the theories of Bodin and Richelieu.

Thus the options for the Enlightenment in its interaction with politics are not particularly appealing and are perhaps paradoxical as well. It either bears the weight of the political horrors of modernity, beginning with the Terror, or prevents, obscures, or muddies the construction of "rational" political power in the United States, or seems to have little or no political relevance at all. The implication of the last possibility in particular is that the political phenomena so associated with modernity, the centralized nation-state, seems largely disconnected from the philosophical phenomena so often linked with modernity, the Enlightenment. This seems particularly strange given that one of the dominant political ideologies of modernity—liberalism—has such close ties to the Enlightenment.

I will argue that it may be helpful to re-evaluate the interaction between the Enlightenment and political power, first by considering the role of rationalism in the strands of the Enlightenment that seemed to hold force in the United States and, second, by evaluating the ways in which these discourses provided or left room for the incorporation of the institutional (and possibly corrosive) demands associated with political rule. In approaching these issues, I assert a close tie between central notions of enlightenment thought and liberalism in the United States, particularly in their focus upon individual autonomy, its conditions and limitations, as well as the rights and responsibilities it carries. I will then argue that, although this outlook qualifies, and promotes skepticism toward, the extension of government power, a concomitant strand of the Enlightenment and liberalism calls for, and reinforces, the construction of a powerful state.

Rationalism and the Liberal State

Many of the factors most closely associated with the purported absence, fragmentation, or incoherence of the liberal state seem integrally related to facets of the Enlightenment.[5] With its emphasis on rationalism, the Enlightenment worked to promote the individual to the center of the political universe and contributed to liberalism's emphasis on individual rights, as well as the limitation and de-mystification of authority. The progression is marked well by Locke's works, with his *Essay Concerning Human Understanding, Letter Concerning Toleration,* and *Second Treatise on Government* combining to advance a notion of the individual set free politically, intellectually, economically, and morally.[6] However, while this aspect of the Enlightenment rationalized and limited power by basing it in calculation and consent, the main blow was struck against *de*centralized, traditional, non-political authorities. Churches, guilds, and kin could not lay claim to legitimate coercive authority over individuals. The state, on the other hand, becomes the sole source of legitimate power.[7]

Occupying this lone seat of authority and armed with the collective power of the community, the state held the potential to be "infinitely more awesome and frightening to individuality than its predecessors."[8] Yet liberal enlightenment thinkers tamed this entity by delimiting its realm of activity as well. First, liberals posited the notion of a collectivity of individuals that existed prior to the state, made a community by each member's possession of individual rights, prior to any political organization. As Charles Taylor has argued, "to the extent that a society is defined by its political organization, to that degree it is in principle permeable by political power. It lacks a principle of resistance to the invasive force of sovereign political authority."[9] Rather than essentially *creating* society, the liberal sovereign is instead brought into being by that society of individuals. In the United States, opening the Constitution with "We the People" drew the (at the time) revolutionary conclusion that the people have an identity and will outside of any political structure and as a result may make and unmake political structures for their own purposes.[10] Empowered to protect individuals and their rights, the state becomes an agent for the preservation of order and protection against harm. Its functions, then, are specific, limited, and essentially negative, and its activities become predictable and manageable.

Yet the world posited by the framers of the Constitution was full of unknown and unknowable demands and threats, and seeking to secure predictability and manageability in a world of flux and change in turn requires dynamism and flexibility. A theme that emerges from the constitutional debates of 1787–1789 is that *over*limitation of power may result in its arbitrary exercise. Thus the bestowal of more power may actually result in the exercise of less, because a government with inadequate power will either be unable to impose order, resulting in anarchy (and the "vibration" toward the opposite pole of tyranny), or the government will simply usurp the powers necessary to impose order. In either case, liberty is lost. Many supporters of the Constitution argued that providing the constitutional means for the exercise of necessary powers prevents their usurpation in emergencies and provides means for accountability. Conversely, their arguments also held the implication that a government with limited powers benefits from the perception of its legitimacy and also possesses a flexibility which allows it to adapt to changing situations. It can be an effective, not necessarily a weak, government. At the Constitutional Convention, Hamilton stated flatly, "Establish a weak government, and you must at times overleap the bounds," and his Federalist 23 offers perhaps the most straightforward argument regarding the necessity—and consequent manageability—of adequate powers. In his view law should be structured in a way that allows adaptability and authority to respond to emergencies. A weak or overly stringent constitution inculcates a culture of violation; emergencies inevitably lead to the overstepping of bounds, and once the law is overstepped out of necessity, it becomes easy to justify its violation in other instances as well.

Others picked up on the "more power is less" theme. John Marshall, for example, argued that it is essential in times of peace to give government the power which will be indispensable in times of war because otherwise, "When danger shall come upon us, may we not do what we were on the point of doing once already—that is, appoint a dictator? . . . if we defer giving the necessary power to the general government till the moment of danger arrives, we shall give it then and with an *unsparing* hand."[11] In thinking about rationalism and the modern state, we see here, on the one hand, a kind of attempt to rationalize the state, to keep it within the bounds of written law. On the other hand, the framers accomplish this through vague language (e.g., "necessary and proper") and a sense that the various branches' actions would be monitored and checked by the other branches as well as by the voting public. What is important to Hamilton and Marshall is that this negotiation occur within the legal framework rather than outside of it. While such an approach might be labeled a muddle, one could alternatively argue that the framers toed a line between legalism and a hard-nosed assessment of the exercise of political power, that this is not the failure of the Enlightenment in connecting with realism but rather its realization.

This attempt to combine realism with rationalism permeated other aspects of the constitutional debate as well. Madison and Hamilton both made the case that a federal government that could prevent the states from warring against each other would prevent an imbalance in executive power. Arguing that the United States should seek to imitate England by being a (united) island, Madison depicted the distortion of European nations living under military threat: "Constant apprehension of war has . . . the tendency to render the head too large for the body. A standing military force, with an overgrown Executive will not long be safe companions to liberty. The means of defense against foreign danger, have been always the instruments of tyranny at home."[12] Thus Madison (and Hamilton elsewhere) appealed to the fear of one form of power in order to argue in favor of power of a different kind. A government strong enough to sustain the union would prevent a decline into wars between the states and the eventual imposition of armies strong enough both to provide protection and to oppress.

Does such a claim amount to a politics to end all politics? I would answer no, although Madison's metaphor of the head and the body does suggest the framers' fascination with balance and proportion and the idea of a "science" of politics that could secure stability even in the face of uncertainty and change. Newtonian physics made its appearance in these Enlightenment discussions of political order, along with the obligatory "state as machine" metaphors. Two aspects of this perspective should be noted, however. First, assumptions of rationality should not be overemphasized. While the framers of the Constitution expressed confidence in "laws" of human behavior and the possibility of constructing institutions that took such dynamics into account, the paradigm upon which they relied emphasized our decidedly mixed natures, in which passion threatened always to outweigh reason and narrower interests often outweighed the public interest. Nonetheless, if we were not—and could never be—fully rational, our behavior could be rationalized; institutions could be constructed that promoted the balance of passions and interests, approximating rationality, if not exactly achieving it, through the mechanisms of our political institutions. While attempting to avoid a coercive bureaucratic apparatus, Madison and the other framers of the Constitution did not expect society to be wholly self-regulating. As Federalist 10 makes clear, they expected that the political system they designed would contribute to social cohesion by shaping how the majority perceives itself and acts and would also, by protecting minorities, limit the incentive for sabotage. Madison's solution is often labeled as pluralism, and the idea of the government as a neutral umpire certainly incorporates some of the essential characteristics of pluralism. However, his formulation of the relationship between government and interests should be distinguished from some of the connotations associated with interest group politics, namely, that the government only adjusts a preexisting equilibria rather than contributing to the construction of those forces. Madison's solution is more self-consciously engineered: Groups' perceptions and actions are affected by the structure of the republic and the government.

However, mechanical analogies can only go so far, and this points to the second qualification of the state-as-machine metaphor, particularly in the parallels drawn between the Constitution and Newton's cosmos. Newton's physics points to harmony and stability in a relatively static physical universe. While the tree itself may grow taller, the forces at work upon the apple when it falls do not themselves change. A constitution, on the other hand, must maintain structural harmony in the face of flux and change, economic development, geographic expansion, and shifting moral perceptions.[13] Change will inevitably occur, and as a result the fundamental law will change its profile and even substance.

One of the larger questions about our political development and its relation to the Constitution is the question of whether such change is approached systematically or rationally or is simply "patched in." I would find it difficult to deny that our political tradition does not include its share of inconsistencies, overlays, and compromises. However, I think one can viably ask whether this must inevitably lead to a conclusion of incoherence or malfunction. The framers left the Constitution vague in part due to political exigency. Where they could not reach agreement, they found ways to duck the issues (e.g., vesting "executive power" in the President). At the same time, such vagueness has solid theoretical foundations as well. It allows flexibility in the face of change without an overt return to first principles. The sense of our mixed natures again returns to the fore: A sense of the limits of our rationality becomes manifest in the notion that debates about fundamentals will be marred by passions and interests; yet the framers of the Constitution also appear confident in our rationality over time. They seem most concerned about "momentary" passions, but they view the more permanent public will of the community (filtered through the proper institutions) as necessarily rational. What seems most important to the framers are cooling mechanisms, processes that slow change, and at times perhaps even mask it. "Muddling through" takes on another aspect in this case, serving to preserve stability and predictability and to legitimize change. While irksome to political scientists who seek identifiable structures and categories, such layers need not necessarily be viewed as entirely at odds with coherent political development. While I would not want to oversell the notion, it does strike me that an argument can be made that there is a certain method to the madness. While some might argue that this represents an accession to political realities at the expense of solid theoretical underpinnings or "rational" institutions, I would argue that such attempts represent the empiricist facet of the Enlightenment, drawing conclusions and solutions from the observed reality of human experience.[14]

The reputation of the Enlightenment—for good or for ill—centers on its relentless pursuit of "the nature of man." How such knowledge should be viewed or how it should be used seems to be more ambiguous. Is nature the standard by which all else is measured or is it an entity to be controlled and manipulated? In the American case, I think that the concept of nature is multifaceted and that the Founders' approach to it varied. "Natural" rights were an immutable standard; human nature was in some ways immutable but its expression could (and should) be shaped in different ways. That which might seem most "natural," such as local attachments or religious beliefs, might, in fact, distort or threaten our most basic rights. While the idea that societal and governmental structures are human constructs carries with it notions that those entities, as well as the purposes they serve, are and should be limited, it also expresses a confidence in humans' ability to control their own destinies and to wring from nature that which they desire.

Louis Hartz's presentation of liberalism did not address the relation between that tradition and the Enlightenment, per se, although one might argue that Hartz himself is a product of the Enlightenment: What he objects to most is the *tradition* of liberalism and its blind faith. In tracing this development, he also emphasizes some of the same factors in liberalism that I take to be associated with the Enlightenment and which have the potential to fragment and delimit government power, even as, Hartz maintains, the hegemony of liberalism places its own strictures upon us. While many have sought to dismantle, or at least qualify, the Hartzian thesis that the liberal tradition has dominated American political culture from eighteenth century onward, some aspects of his arguments remain largely unchallenged. Theorists and historians parse the republican and liberal threads, but they tend to pass without comment Hartz's claim that

"American liberal language" does not "understand the meaning of sovereign power."[15] In his view, the framers of the Constitution paid lip service to sovereignty but then constructed a structure of government that basically qualified it out of existence. This "innocence of mind" ultimately becomes, in Hartz's mind, a velvet trap. We do not even see or feel the power to which we fall prey. For Hartz, this is more an ideological cage than an institutional one. Because we can conceive of no other political or social model, our regime perpetuates itself on the basis of blind adherence to substantively ungrounded beliefs.

Huntington, too, picks up on what he takes to be the decisive rejection of sovereignty in the American liberal model. However, in his view, this is not the product of modernity, the Enlightenment, or even liberalism but of an implicit medievalism on the part of the founders. What some take to be innovations in the political experiment Huntington views as throwbacks to the past. Popular sovereignty, for example, replaces one deity with another while defanging the potential power of the state. While the seat of power ostensibly lies in the people, "The voice of the people can be about as readily identified as the voice of God. It is thus a latent, passive and ultimate authority, not a positive and active one."[16] Further, Huntington argues that constitutionalism in the United States appeals to the notion of a "natural" law, where law is the source rather than the product of authority and the reason of law outweighs the will of the rulers. Thus the decisions of the majority and its representatives are not legitimate simply because they are actions of the majority but because they are rational and "just." While Huntington thinks that this notion hearkens back to the medieval notion of law, it also certainly parallels Enlightenment appeals to reason, to natural right or law, and the limits of political authority. Yet Huntington seeks more distant sources because his is a story not of the Enlightenment but of the adoption of somewhat anachronistic structures in the face of modernity. In his view, there was a strong whiff of the past even at the inception of American institutions. The Federalists may have boldly told a story of the new science of politics and innovation, but Huntington sees more of the past than the future there.

By playing up the thread of liberalism that they view as limiting political power, Hartz and Huntington's accounts raise questions about the legitimacy and coherence of the state. If liberalism is entirely about the limitation of power, then any increased power or activity of the government seems inherently problematic. Obviously, this is a dynamic within the American political tradition, but it is certainly not the only one. What seems clear from the political discourse surrounding the ratification of the Constitution, civil rights and the New Deal, for example, is that often the same variables that are associated with limiting government may also be invoked in order to strengthen it, and Hartz and Huntington's accounts seem one-sided in this regard. An even more disturbing aspect of the Hartz and Huntington perspectives, however, is their static quality and the deafening silence they impose. Not only is the extension and structuring of government power immediately suspect; it is essentially taboo, unable to fit within the American political vocabulary. Theodore Lowi picks up on this theme in *The End of Liberalism*, suggesting that the liberal vocabulary cannot encompass the development of the bureaucratic state and thus such power develops inexorably and circumspectly. Brought in under the table, made to conform to categories that do not fit, the ends and powers of the welfare state are neither debated nor legitimized—and apparently cannot be so debated under our existing ideological paradigm. As a result, our attitude toward the centralized state becomes more and more ambivalent, as we view it as both ineffective and tyrannical.[17]

Isaac Kramnick has made a convincing case for the presence of multiple vocabularies at the founding of the American republic, tracing out threads of republicanism, Lockean liberalism, work-ethic Protestantism, and state-centered theories of power and sovereignty.[18] I think it is useful to conceive of the "profusion and confusion" of political languages continuing beyond the framing of the Constitution and to view approaches to political development in this light. Existing alongside of arguments about the limited state may be found more statist discourse, as evidenced by Woodrow Wilson and Herbert Croly. Yet even when the state plays a more central role, it often remains cloaked in the language of representation, federalism, and rights. Nonetheless, I would like to propose that even the language of liberalism need not be viewed as utterly blind, or hostile to, the construction of coherent and authoritative political power. Central tenets of liberalism need not be viewed as strictly inimical or even skeptical toward state power. Further, such principles and institutions are also open to contestation as well as consensus. Prevailing interpretations of liberalism and the state may be challenged and changed at different times. While providing a frame for political discourse past political beliefs need not necessarily determine its outcome; in fact, they may themselves be "used," that is, recast in new light to serve new ends. The American liberal tradition (and the legacy of the Enlightenment) continues to shape how we think and talk about the state, but what we need from the state in turn may also affect what we ascribe to those traditions.

Exploration of the dynamics of liberal political discourse over time should be left to a different and larger discussion. However, here I would like to address some of the central concepts of liberalism and their relation to government power. In particular, I focus on popular sovereignty, the emphasis placed upon individual rights, the separation of powers, and the rule of law because these have been the factors most closely associated with arguments about the limited or incoherent liberal state by theorists such as Hartz and Huntington.

While popular sovereignty and the division of power between different branches of government are intended to preserve "negative" liberty, they do not in themselves amount to an attack on governmental sovereignty. Sovereignty resides in the people, but the people's consent to the national government allows it to hold the strongest claim to being the preeminent power, and it remains strong enough to repulse any other power laying claim to broad allegiance. As Edmund Morgan argues, popular sovereignty reinforces the people's status as subjects as well as rulers, "affirming the power, the authority and the rights of the people over their government even while sustaining the power, authority and prerogative of the government by virtue of their authorization of it."[19]

Further, while the separation of powers and checks and balances is most often portrayed as a means for limiting—and perhaps even entangling or confusing—power, such division and mixing can also be viewed as constructing and recognizing power. In the first place, the separation of powers represents a division of labor. It not only limits power but provides for its effective exercise, for example, providing for deliberation in the legislature while allowing for energetic action on the part of the executive. Checks and balances were meant not to stymie administration but to provide for its smooth operation by eliminating corruption. Second, the separation of powers should not be mistaken for the absence or confusion of sovereignty. As d'Entreves argues, the division of power is not only compatible with, but presupposes a clear notion of sovereignty: "Only by knowing for certain who has the power to command can that 'tranquility of mind' be attained which Montesquieu praised so highly as the condition of political liberty." A state which sought to divide power in order to protect liberty without at the same time having a clear seat of sovereignty would contradict itself; its ends could not be secured.[20]

Huntington, as mentioned earlier, is skeptical about the reality of popular sovereignty. If sovereignty clearly lies in the hands of the people, their action or even the attempt to delineate their will remains problematic. Presumably, Huntington would recognize elections as an expression of popular will. However, the problem is that their results are rarely decisive, in that mandates are easy to claim but difficult to prove. Further, the President, Congress and even the courts can in different ways claim to be the voice of the people. Political power therefore remains divided among a multiplicity of bodies which justify their authority by reference to their source in the people but none of which can conclusively demonstrate that it is more popular than the others. While latent sovereignty remains in the people, the question of what institution within the government holds "active" sovereignty remains an issue of constant contention. According to Huntington's formulation, this shared sovereignty between the people and the government and between the different branches of government inevitably results in the nearly complete inhibition of the construction of state power.

Presenting the Constitution as Tudor in character and therefore as backward-looking, Huntington himself seems infatuated by traditional notions of sovereignty and therefore misses part of the innovation of the Constitution. As Pole suggests, the diffusion of power in the Constitution amounted to a "redefinition" of sovereignty. Departing from the European tradition of the sovereign incarnate, the Americans "created a system which effectively redefined sovereignty as a *process* rather than as a person or a seat of active and visible power."[21] The give-and-take between the branches of government approximates the will of the sovereign people, or so the story goes.

While representation is often cited as the source of the permeability and reflexivity of the state and thus a signal of its limitation, the government must be adequately powerful and autonomous to allow "the people" to rule through their representatives. It should be able to resist corruption by private powers seeking to gain control of it in order to use it for their own purposes, and an effective framework of procedures must be constructed in order to give voice to the true will of the majority and to enact its edicts. "The people" require institutional channels—elections, the modes of representation, and administration—which can form and focus the sovereign will as well as carry out its wishes.

That the framers and supporters of the Constitution anticipated the institutional demands of popular sovereignty is clear from their argument regarding each branch of the government. In Massachusetts, James Bowdoin maintained, "The power of Congress, both in the legislative and executive line, is the power of the people, collected through a certain medium, to a focal point, at all times ready to be exerted for the general benefit. . ."[22] In his view, government institutions are necessary simply to gather the opinions of the people, to clarify and express them. As Madison argued, the public is not "one homogeneous mass in which every thing that affects a part will affect in the same manner the whole."[23] Diversity might mean that a majority is not immediately evident and must be pieced together or that the majority may oppress those who differ from it. While power lies with the people, their will must be discerned and perhaps tempered.

Acting on the sovereign will involves not only filtering the sometimes unreasonable, cacophonous, or inconstant demands of the public but also ensuring that a powerful private will is not mistaken for that of the public. Along with Madison's precautions against the dominance of narrow factions in Congress, Gouverneur Morris also portrayed the President as the "great protector of the mass of the people," guarding against the "great and wealthy" who might come to predominate in Congress.[24] Even at this point, the presidency suggested to some the embodiment of the people as a whole, an office strong enough to resist particular or corrupting interests. Hamilton also associated the Supreme Court with strong government and the preservation of a certain kind of popular sovereignty. By being able to strike down unconstitutional laws (even those the public supported), Hamilton saw the court as protecting the more permanent public will embodied in the Constitution. Popular sovereignty, from this perspective, requires that at least part of the government remain autonomous from the more immediate demands of the public.[25]

While Huntington argues that the competing "representativeness" of each of the branches hinders government action because each can claim but not conclusively demonstrate that it represents the people, Ackerman points out that the contest between the different branches means that no small group can be "transubstantiated" into "the people." Popular sovereignty is thus broadened, which may enhance the government's capacity for legitimate, authoritative action when no single-voice majority exists over time.

Yet, as noted earlier, Huntington thinks that sovereignty is limited not only by the problematic nature of the "voice" of the people but also by notions of "natural" law that authorize and delimit the public will. In making such a claim, Huntington seems to focus only on the juridical claim of "pure" law, which, unaffected by political power or interest, hands down its edicts from above. Yet a significant strand of legal positivism existed in the United States even before the twentieth century. The Federalists, for example, certainly recognized that rights and law were creations of, as well as limits placed upon, government. At its framing, the Constitution was not presented as the product of natural law, but as a creation of men, who praised its innovation and viewed it as a necessary state-building measure. That voluntaristic notion remains at the base of the Constitution, recognized by the power of amendment and even reinterpretation. While such changes may be criticized for violating some "higher" normative standard, such an accusation cannot short-circuit the change itself. For example, while some might argue that an amendment to prohibit flag burning expresses patriotic passion at the expense of free political expression, such arguments would not trump the decision of two-thirds of Congress and three-fourths of the state legislatures if they should choose to pass it. The people and their representatives are recognized as authors of the law and not simply as its mouthpiece or agent.

We should be careful not to overdraw the limits that concepts of natural law or natural right place upon the sovereignty of the state. As Stuart Scheingold states, "Rights are declared as absolutes, but they ripple out into the real world in an exceedingly conditional fashion. . . . [T]hat struggle is primarily coercive. When it comes to getting large numbers of people to conform to norms they oppose, power is indispensable; it is necessary although it may not be sufficient."[26] That rights or law have been at times merely recognized without actually being realized should not be denied. Yet at other points, the power of the central state has been increased in the name of rights, as the late 1780s and mid-1960s suggest.

I began this paper by arguing that a murkiness surrounds the political development associated with the Enlightenment. While some of this relates to the ideals and ideas of the Enlightenment and liberalism themselves, I have sought to argue that a good deal of it also results from the way in which we have approached those phenomena. While one certainly needs to take into consideration the way in which the American liberal Enlightenment tended to limit and decentralize power, one should also avoid overemphasizing those tendencies. Rather than juxtaposing power and liberty, political actors such as Madison and Hamilton depicted power and liberty as being tenuously complementary. The government protects as well as threatens liberty while liberty in turn may make government stronger and more effective. As Hamilton argued, giving the necessary powers to the federal government will prevent it from usurping powers or from being forced into a militaristic stance.

Embedded within the founding debates are blunt assessments of the need for political power and institutional development and its relation to central concepts such as individual rights, popular sovereignty, and the rule of law. While tradition, overlapping powers, and, yes, even confusion certainly come into play in the construction of our political institutions, I have attempted to point out ways in which these dynamics need not necessarily be viewed as either antithetical to the enlightenment project or to the construction of coherent, effective government power.

Abandoning the presupposition of the necessary juxtaposition of liberty with power and considering the ways in which familiar tenets of the liberal tradition call for, or enhance, the powers of the federal government reveals important links between the liberal tradition and the state. From this perspective, state-building which occurs within the hermeneutic of liberalism—through discussions of individual rights popular sovereignty and the rule of law, for example—need not be viewed as unconscious, unintended, or as the importation of the state by covert and perhaps self-defeating means. That we remain uneasy in the face of government power and sometimes invoke it unconsciously need not be viewed as incoherence or complete antipathy. Surely we are also uneasy with the unadulterated implications of popular rule, the workings of the market, and the power of the individual states, and yet we tend not to say that the liberal enlightenment cannot encompass democracy, the free market, or federalism. The uneasy relationship between the Enlightenment and the state may say less about the Enlightenment's limits in acknowledging and grappling with the hard realities of politics and more about the difficulty of arriving at straightforward or unqualified conclusions about any human phenomenon. One can certainly debate the degree to which various Enlightenment thinkers were willing to acknowledge the latter, but that is a different argument from the assertion that the Enlightenment, and the liberalism associated with it, cannot acknowledge, or make room for, the institutionalization and exercise of limited yet authoritative government action.

Yet the latter assertion has been an appealing lens for many as they seek to understand, compare, and evaluate the American and French cases, and for this reason I end the essay with words of caution and optimism. As someone who believes that ideas matter both as political phenomena unfold and as we seek to understand them, I firmly believe that political theory can be a useful tool for comparativists. At the same time, I think we should also approach those tools and narratives with some skepticism, aiming for a dynamic process in which theory informs the study of practical politics and that study in turn informs the theoretical paradigms. Such an exchange promises to be mutually beneficial.

Notes

1. Judith N. Shklar, *After Utopia* (Princeton, N.J.: Princeton University Press, 1957), 9.

2. Clearly, Horkheimer, Adorno, Foucault, and other critics have their own reservations about the abuses inherent in the Enlightenment even in its (apparently diluted) Americanized form.

3. Alexander Hamilton, James Madison, and John Jay, *The Federalist Papers* ed. Clinton Rossiter, (New York: New American Library, 1961), 33. In making this delineation between clarity and obscurity and emphasizing the role of rational principles in the enlightenment, I don't intend to neglect the facets of the Enlightenment that actually *downplay* the role of reason and our ability to understand and clarify our existence. For example, because Hume believes that we are ruled not by reason or intellect but by passion and instinct, he would not be at all surprised to find that our institutional structures have been influenced more by history and custom than by

deliberate choice. I consider the role of passion in the discourse of the American case later in this paper.

4. Some might argue that this divergence is not surprising at all, claiming that the *absence* of the centralized state contributed to the successful construction of a democratic regime in the United States (cf. Tocqueville and Milton Friedman, to name just two). On the other hand, as I suggest above, others will argue that the absence of a rationalized state leads to serious issues of coordination and legitimacy. While not wishing to neglect the importance of civil society to the functioning of democracy, I think that it is misleading simply to juxtapose democracy and the state. Democracy needs to "work," and a state that exists under the table, as it were, poses severe challenges for democratic legitimacy. The aim of this paper is to consider some of the theoretical underpinnings of a more dynamic and nuanced model of the interactions between democracy and the state.

5. Pointing to the fact that American colonies had from their inception an "ingrained habit of self-government" and a concern for religious liberty, J. R. Pole argues that it is "historically unrealistic" to regard American institutions as creations of Enlightenment thought. J. R. Pole, "Enlightenment and the Politics of American Nature," in *The Enlightenment in National Context,* eds. Roy Porter and Mikulas Teich. (New York: Cambridge, 1981), 194–5; cf. Arendt, *On Revolution*. However, Enlightenment thought did provide encouragement and supporting analogies for American political and judicial institutions.

6. Isaac Kramnick, *Republicanism and Bourgeois Radicalism* (Ithaca, New York: Cornell University Press, 1990.), 88–91. and *The Portable Enlightenment Reader*, ed. Isaac Kramnick (New York: Penguin, 1995), xiv–xvii. For a qualification of the Enlightenment's emphasis on the individual, at least in its relation to the Constitution, see Pole, 208–9.

7. Loius Hartz, *The Liberal Tradition in America* (New York: Harcourt, Brace, Jovanovich, 1991), 59–60. Hartz argues that the absence of feudal oppression in the United States meant that the contractual idea of organizing the state carried no implication of fortifying it and that the Federalists relied on the assumption of a self-regulating society even as they argued for a government strong enough to govern a society that they believed would be divided along class lines. I suggest that Hartz overstates the framers' assumption of a self-regulating society.

8. Kramnick, 1990, 34.

9. Charles Taylor, "Modes of Civil Society," *Public Culture* 3, no. 1 (Fall 1990), 102.

10. Taylor, 1990, 111.

11. *The Debates in the Several State Conventions, on the Adoption of the Federal Constitution,* vols. 1–4. ed Jonathan Elliott. (Philadelphia, Pa.: J. B. Lippincott Co., 1901–1911), III, 227.

12. Max Farrand, ed. *Records of the Federal Convention of 1787* vols. 1–3. (New Haven, Conn.: Yale University Press, 1966), 465.

13. Pole, 196.

14 . (cf. Meyer, 158).

15. (7; cf. Wood, 464–472).

16. Samuel Huntington, *Political Order in Changing Societies* (New Haven, Conn.: Yale University Press, 1968), 106.

17. Theodore Lowi, *The End of Liberalism: The Second Republic of the United States* Second Edition. (New York: W. W. Norton & Co., 1979) 50; cf. Skowronek 1982, vii–x, 3–46).

18. Kramnick 1990.

19. Edmund Morgan, *Inventing the People: The Rise of Popular Sovereignty in England and America* (New York: W. W. Norton & Co., 1988), 38.

20. Alexander Passerin d'Entreves, *The Notion of the State* (Oxford, United Kingdom: Clarendon Press, 1967), 118–122.

21. Pole 210–1.

22. Elliot II, 84.

23. Farrand I, 422.

24. Farrand II, 52.

25. Hamilton, 469–470.

26. Stuart Scheingold, *The Politics of Rights* (New Haven, Conn.: Yale University Press, 1974), 123.

Chapter Three

Relationships between Poverty Reduction Approaches and Donor Support for Democracy: The Case of Mali[1]

Zeric Kay Smith

Democratic theorists have long debated the normative nature of democratic politics with many taking a substantive view of democracy and imputing its value to its capacity for producing ancillary goods (justice, human rights, economic growth, equity). Others argue for a minimalist definition of democracy saying that to burden the definition with the goods democracy can (but does not always) produce, risks a tautology. Instead, under this view democracy should be valued because the process of democratic self-governance is itself ennobling and consistent with human good. Some have tried to articulate a middle road with process and outcome taking community organization coequal status in terms of normative preference for democracy.[2] This theoretical debate has been mirrored in practice within the international development community over the past 15 years as well. Some practitioners have pursued democracy explicitly because of its assumed positive impact on economic growth or other goods while others focus on the importance of the democratic process itself with minimal regard for the ancillary benefits.

It has been argued persuasively that in precolonial Africa, the most common attribute of those who suffered from enduring poverty was that they lacked access to surplus labor. This is in contrast to medieval Europe and Asia where enduring poverty tended to be a function of lack of access to land. Thus, the most vulnerable in Africa were those misfortunates who could not employ their own labor or depend on the labor of family, e.g., the widows, orphans, the handicapped, the sick, or social outcasts.[3] In fact, this class is so important in African historiography that they form an archetype among folklorists. In the founding epic of the Malian state, the figure of Sundiata Keita represents just such an archetype of the structural poor that rose to power through wit and supernatural means. He triumphs over the circumstances of his birth (fatherless and crippled) to overcome a series of challenges and then overthrows a dictatorial ruler to found the Mali Empire. The fact of Sundiata's importance as a contemporary political symbol in the context of Malian democratization during the past decade has been recognized[4] but the significant cultural link that the Sundiata figure illustrates between poverty and politics, in particular democratic politics, has not been explored. Accounting for and giving voice to the poor in the context of Mali's democratic experience has been an important political goal of Malian politicians since the People's Revolution of 1991. International donors have also given significant support to democracy promotion in Mali. This paper examines the linkages between democracy promotion on the part of one donor, the United States Agency for International Development (USAID), and current attempts at poverty reduction in Mali. The hypothesis that is tested is that democracy promotion and poverty reduction in Mali are complementary goals and in fact mutually necessary for success in either endeavor. The paper examines the links between poverty and democracy at a broad theoretical level and then focuses more concretely on the relationships between democracy promotion and poverty reduction using Mali as a case study.

In the late 1980s, after decades of lagging economic indicators and marginal success of billions of foreign aid dollars, development agencies in many nations around the world began to turn explicitly toward "democracy and governance" (DG) as a new set of tools for promoting economic development. Authoritarian and corrupt government had begun to be seen as a major impediment to efficient use of development resources and a roadblock to economic growth. It was argued that putting good governance and democracy first would assist in creating a more propitious, enabling environment for economic development by increased transparency reducing corruption, and thereby increasing governmental efficiencies. These efficiencies would result from applying market values to government service delivery, justice sector reforms to ensure human rights and efficient economic transactions, engaging the energy and creativity of civil society, and generally raising the level of state legitimacy among all citizens. In turn, this improved enabling environment would result in higher levels of economic growth and better conditions for all in the developing world. This view assumes that poor institutional (newly equated with democratic) performance is at the heart of development's failure. Thus successful development will only occur when well-functioning (read: democratic, transparent, accountable, and efficient) public institutions are in place. Relatively less common at the level of programming have been justifications of democracy aid primarily because the process of democratic decision making in and of itself holds intrinsic value. These justifications have occasionally been articulated at the level of high politics by senior policymakers, but rarely enter directly into prosaic aid programming.

A third view on the role of democratic institutions and poverty could place primacy on the poverty side of the equation. Many in the political development/modernization school have done this implicitly by arguing the paramount importance of the link between level of economic development and democracy. Przworski even identifies a GNP per capita threshold below which democracy is very unlikely. Others who have argued that democracy is a luxury that underdeveloped countries can ill afford also belie an assumption that democracy will follow, not precede, economic development. Yet GNP and other standard economic development measures are not identical to poverty and while there are ample empirical linkages that correlate democracy and development, the reasons for these correlations are still hotly debated. Classic developmentalists (Almond, Verba, Huntington) followed the lead of Moore in hypothesizing that the role of a growing bourgeoisie class imbued with both entrepreneurial motivation and cultural links to Protestantism played a key causal role in pushing for democracy. Rueshmeyer, Stephens, and Stephens argue that the emergence of working-class interests (and not bourgeoisie) and attempts by states to accommodate these interests are more predictive of democratization. In either case though the importance of poverty and attention to the interests and needs of the poor are not central factors. Arguments about the role of economic inequality and economic development get closer to the heart of a poverty-centered approach, but the macro-level political economy approaches typically do not allow for careful case specificity.

Whether resulting from middle-class or working-class movements though, democracy is seen as a by-product of economic development. Those in the United States Agency for International Development (USAID) and other international development actors with an interest in democracy promotion have tended to emphasize the role of democracy in promoting economic development. With such a macro-structural goal in mind, the early interventions of USAID in the arena of democracy assistance often tended to focus on national and sub-national democratic institutions. When serious attempts have been made to disaggregate democratic strengths and weakness (as in the "democracy and governance" (DG) Center's Democracy Assessment Framework), the role of the poor in democracy and impact of democracy on poverty have not been systematically explored. Typical approaches to programming and evaluation in the USAID democracy and governance sector currently include a process of assessment, activity design, implementation, and monitoring and evaluation that focuses on five key variables assumed to be central to democratic institutional function. These include: *consensus, rule of law, competition, inclusion,* and *governance*. As these variables are usually articulated and reflected in aid programming, they tend to ignore, or minimize questions and issues of poverty except at a very macro-level. In most instances the poor become visible only in terms of their over-representation among *other* groupings such as women, racial minorities, or regionally excluded or disadvantaged populations. The central question to be addressed by this paper is a counterfactual—what would democracy assistance, and USAID democracy and governance programming in particular, look like if poverty were explicitly taken into account? To animate the theoretical question, the paper will look at the particular country case of Mali and compare the current USAID democracy and governance strategy in Mali with strategies that might be suggested using a poverty-centered approach.

This chapter first outlines contemporary debates and academic thinking on the critical relationships between poverty (broadly defined) and democratic political health. From this literature review, the tensions between a poverty-centered approach to democracy and governance programming and one that privileges democracy as procedurally and normatively preferable seem to emerge. How can donors and development professionals balance the longer-term need for structural reforms, investment and export-oriented trade, and claims of universal human rights with the shorter-term demand to produce benefits for the at-risk populations such that democracy does not lose face—legitimacy—and maintains a level of popular support?

The chapter then explores what a greater emphasis on poverty in democracy and governance programming might look like. The implications of a poverty-centered approach could mean development activities that focus on decentralization, local empowerment, democratization of the work-place, operational rule of law and citizen security, conflict resolution, and civil society capacity building in partnership with local government. Support for democratic institution building at the national- and subnational-level might take a back seat with a de-emphasis on elections, party-building, institutional rule of law, etc. Yet the linkages between these macro-level democracy and governance activities and poverty are also considered and the trade-offs involved are explored. This is important because many current democracy and governance activities link national-level with local-level engagement. For example, in the area of anticorruption, systemic institutional reforms are often paired with civic education and local reform efforts. What would a poverty-centered approach imply for such activities?

These areas of inquiry lead into a discussion of the case of one of the world's poorest democracies, the African nation of Mali. The paper examines to what degree USAID democracy and governance activities are actively targeting the poor and the approach that is taken to do so. Strengths and weaknesses of the USAID approach to democracy and governance assistance in Mali in regards to the likely impacts on the poor are explored.

Democracy and governance support to Mali is currently being provided in circumstances where the strategies guiding international aid are poised to evolve. The government of Mali is currently deeply engaged with the Bretton Woods institutions in preparation of a Poverty Reduction Strategy Paper (PRSP) or the Cadre Stratégique de Lutte contre la Pauvreté (CSLP) as it is known in French. This document is intended to serve as the national blue-print for translating the savings that are to be derived from World Bank negotiated debt relief into a medium-term framework to support poverty reduction. The PRSP process is mandated by the World Bank but is expressly to be developed by the government of Mali. Additionally the process is mandated to include modalities in support of the participatory development of the PRSP. The PRSP process evolved largely in response to criticisms of structural adjustment programs of the 1980s and 1990s that often seemed to have unequal impact on the poorest members of society, but offered little immediate- or medium-term benefits to the poor. Because the PRSP is explicitly targeted at poverty reduction, and because the process itself is participatory by design, proponents hope that it will result in pro-poor economic growth. At the level of political democracy, the PRSP offers some hope that political power holders, often more responsive to economic or commercial interests, will become more aware of the need to efficiently attend to the voices of the poor in society. By tailoring international assistance to the new PRSP and following principles implied by a poverty focus, democracy assistance may be able to contribute to poverty reduction in both direct and indirect ways.

Poverty and Democracy—Current Debates

From the mid 1950s, the study of comparative political development has been largely animated by questions about the relationships between socioeconomic development and political democracy. Some of the most influential scholars in the discipline over the past thirty years made names for themselves by establishing the basic linkages and exploring the implications thereof (Lipset, Almond, Verba, Nie, Huntington, Weiner, Bates, Migdal, etc.) Yet while the relationships between democracy and development have been a mainstay in comparative politics, the linkages between poverty and democracy have been only rarely treated. The question of poverty has remained to a great extent the purview of development economists and more recently applied political scientists involved in the relatively new field of "democracy development." The relationship between poverty and democracy offers a potentially rich area to deal with some fundamental questions of democratic theory. Most obviously, a consideration of poverty helps to shed light on a central dilemma of democratic theory—the debate on democracy's substantive content. What is democracy for? Is democracy most usefully defined by a set of minimalist procedures (Dahl's Polyarchy) or is it more meaningfully understood in terms of the goods it is often associated with (justice, human rights, economic growth, equity)?

In the former definition, at best democracy could be thought of as a neutral institutional setting in which the poor compete with other social interests for access to resources. Thus political democracy becomes a necessary but not sufficient condition for efficient poverty reduction. Under this neutral institutional model, the political process operates to determine the particular emphasis of policymakers and the content of policy; so if the poor are successful in articulating their interests, then poor-friendly policies may emerge. Yet, the very assertion of neutrality might be suspect when differences, that by definition disempower one group (in this case, the poor), serve as a nonneutral conditioning factor. In practice, neutral institutions nearly always favor those with wealth because of their accompanying power, knowledge, and capacity to function within the institutions. The poor typically do not possess these assets in their interactions with government institutions. Further, organization by class is not the most common form of political mobilization in many developing nations. In practice the poor are often divided by other cleavages including ethnicity, religion, regional origin, etc. These identity characteristics can dilute the strength of political organizations that advocate for the poor because it is often much easier for politicians to tap the salience of other characteristics. Thus the neutrality of even the most well-designed democratic institutions is immediately suspect.

Minimalist conceptions of democracy also have the unfortunate attribute of treating average citizens with distrust. This does not bode well for the participation and impact that poor people as a subset of citizens are likely to be able to exercise in such settings. The following quote is surprising in that one could easily mistake the author as commenting on citizens in a newly established African democracy such as Mali: ". . . if the survival of the . . . system depended upon active, informed, and enlightened citizenry, then democracy in . . . would have disappeared long ago; for the masses . . . are apathetic and ill-informed about politics and public policy, and they have a surprisingly weak commitment to democratic values . . . "[5] The citizens in question are of course from the United States. If American citizens are so suspect as regards their contribution to democratic decision making under a minimalist view, the capacity for meaningful participation by poor people in Mali would be even more distrusted.

If minimalist views of democracy and institutional neutrality may downplay the contributions of and disfavor the poor as citizens, what about a definition of democracy that is more substantive? If one equates democracy with the goods it can be expected or hoped to create, would this vision of democracy hold more promise for listening to and meeting the political needs of the poor? What in turn might a more substantive vision of democracy offer for poverty alleviation? Strong democracy, or unitary democracy, claims to add to the strict freedom of formal democracy "the means and not just the right" to meaningful participation.[6] When Anatole France quipped that the poor were free to sleep under the bridges of Paris, he captured the essential difference between a substantive and minimalist conception of democracy.[7] Yet the promise of more meaningful redistributive policy in favor of equity and more universal opportunity has been both difficult to achieve at a political level (consensus on the scope of welfare state is largely absent in many countries around the world), as well as at the practical level (though poverty levels are very low in virtually all Western European and North American nations, dramatic inequality remains an important challenge to meaningful democratic freedom for many citizens even in these wealthy societies).

A very different view of substantive democracy has also recently emerged. Sen argues that substantive democratic freedoms should be valued not only for their potential in producing pro-poor policy outcomes, but as the single most important objective of development. "Development can be seen . . . as a process of expanding the real freedoms that people enjoy. . . . If freedom is what development advances, then there is a major argument for concentrating on that overarching objective, rather than on some particular means, or some specially chosen list of instruments."[8] Here Sen links liberal democratic freedoms quite explicitly with social well-being. Arguing that poverty alleviation has as its ultimate end "freedom" broadly defined, he sees liberal freedoms (and presumably their promotion) as a clear pro-poverty policy choice. In the following section an outline of a specific set of activity areas is considered and the potential impact on poverty alleviation is entertained.

Putting Poverty First—What if Poverty Alleviation Drove Democracy and Governance Programming?

Meaningful democracy for the poor relies on well-designed and efficiently functioning institutions, committed democratic actors, and engaged and active citizens. The same can be said for democracy and any other subset of the population, yet for the poor, the basic need for functioning institutions may be even more acute. Shortcomings in any of these areas can mean that the ability of democracy to serve the poor is severely compromised. Consequently, to promote democracy and good governance using a focus on the poor could mean both directly targeted activities and indirect activities. The purpose of this section is to outline how a range of possible democracy support activities may look if their relationship to the poor is explicitly considered.

The range of typical USAID democracy and governance programs (strategic objectives) can be fairly wide. Additionally they have evolved and adapted considerably over the past decade. Activities might occur in the following general sectors:

- Rule of Law/Human Rights
- Political Party Strengthening
- Legislative Strengthening
- Executive Strengthening
- Civil Society
- Local Governance/Decentralization
- Elections
- Anticorruption

Given new priorities recently identified by the administration of George W. Bush, activity areas might soon be expected to include a greater focus on conflict response in addition.

Any particular mission with a democracy and governance program normally supports activities in some subset of the above and in practice democracy and governance programs often evolve in response to shifting political circumstances (and funding). Thus, in the early 1990s, many democracy and governance programs focused on elections and political party oriented activities largely in reaction to a historical moment when many of the countries in which USAID worked were experiencing either democratic transitions (Africa, Eastern Europe, Caribbean) or consolidations of previous transitions (Latin America). As initial electoral euphoria ebbed, and the agency learned both pros and cons of democracy aid, USAID country portfolios have largely diversified moving into a host of activities related both to the areas in the bulleted list above and to the other imperatives specific to the countries in which they work.

Rule of Law/Human Rights

A cursory look at the list of activity areas above seems to reveal a subset that might have more intuitive promise in terms of their ability to impact poverty directly. The poor are clearly and directly impacted by shortcomings in rule of law/human rights as they are the most vulnerable to state abuse and least able to access legal recourse. Recent scholarship has pointed out that "the content and the administration of land law, family law, labour law and negligence, for instance, impact on the security with which poor people can hold and use assets such as land or natural resources, obtain a fair return for their labour, or develop small business opportunities."[9]

This view recognizes that the legal system is part of the state power structure which serves to manage power relations among individuals and groups having a differential impact on the poor. One remedy to this is viewing law as a public service to which all are given a right to utilize. While this should be, strictly speaking, true for the poor in a democracy, even the most efficient legal systems can only be available to a tiny fraction of potential litigants. There is a danger in promoting universal access to courts for the pursuit of social rights, namely it can create an unattainable expectation that ends in mountainous case-backlogs and ultimately cynicism on the part of those who had hoped to gain access.

Alternative methods of dispute resolution that are based on both legal practice and traditional law have been used to bring more immediate just solutions to disputes and to aid in attaining legal system efficiencies, but these too can result in less-than-just outcomes for the poor. Nader points out that dispute resolution can only be expected to reach consistently just solutions when the power relations between disputants are relatively equal, otherwise, the powerful tend to win.[10] Yet Nader's critique of current conflict resolution scholarship is not entirely warranted insofar as she identifies a tendency to write and speak about conflict without mention of root causes. Many in the international development field make a clear distinction among conflict triggers, intermediate conflict drivers, and structural contributions to conflicts with the recognition that conflicts between groups, whether of a legal or political nature, can only be controlled by a holistic view of the three conflict layers.[11]

Local Governance/Decentralization

To the extent that local governance and decentralization serves to increase the voice of and accountability to the poor, this area may also tend to yield direct benefits for the poor. However in practice, the benefits of decentralization measures for the poor are not always evident. There are at least three important reasons for this. First, there is considerable variety among cases of decentralization with some cases of decentralization being nothing more than window dressing while others devolve some power locally but provide no resources for service provision or policy implementation. In fact, Mali has been identified as pursuing relatively meaningful decentralization policies and having a high level of political commitment to such policies.[12] The impact of a variety of institutional arrangements all being classified as decentralization is that some of these arrangements may serve to empower local communities while others may only provide centralized policymakers with some measure of political cover. Second, some decentralization policies (those in which local administrators are given power to make decisions, but not fiscal capacity to carry them out) lead to blurred lines of authority and further difficulties on the part of the poor in determining appropriate and productive advocacy targets. Third, comparatively speaking, the welfare states that have had success in eliminating mass poverty in Europe and North America did so using largely centralized power and often against the wishes of reluctant local authorities. While in some instances, e.g., when the local power holders are politically connected to the poor, we may well expect to see pro-poor policy emerge as a result of decentralization, it is not entirely clear that bringing a greater range of policy decisions and implementation closer to local leaders will consistently lead to poverty reduction strategies. In fact, some observers have argued that "national policy intentions to empower the weak through decentralization may be noble, but the traditional dynamics of political economy at the local level inevitably skew things to the benefit of the locally powerful."[13]

Decentralization should not be viewed as a silver bullet and surefire pro-poor strategy. In fact relatively little is know about the actual impact of decentralization on the poor in the developing world. Instead, the power relations between the poor and local administrators should be carefully considered in each empirical case. Instances where leaders are chosen by, and directly accountable to local people will likely yield responsive policy *when* the means for implementation are also provided for (either through local taxation, or redistribution from the center when local resources are insufficient). However, even responsive and efficient local-level policy is not guaranteed to have a positive impact on poverty unless the policies them selves are consistent with pro-poor agendas.

On balance, this result may be less likely to occur in many decentralized circumstances than at the level of a singular national government. Crooks and Manor conclude that even the most successful cases of decentralization that they studied " . . . showed little evidence of having been particularly responsive to 'vulnerable groups', the poor or the marginalised, a finding echoed more generally in the literature . . . It would seem that the strong tendency for decentralization to reinforce existing patterns of uneven development can only be counteracted by very vigorous and centrally directed financial equalization schemes such as are reported to exist in Chile, or by the determined action of a central government with an ideological mandate, as in West Bengal.[14]

While these authors stress the importance of a powerful central government, empirically speaking, powerful centralized states (particularly those in the third world) have traditionally been much more likely to be used in the interest of powerful economic interests than to be used in the service of the poor. If decentralization may have little automatic pro-poor effects, is decentralization more likely to have pro-poor outcomes than nondecentralization? If decentralization provides an institutional means for overcoming or at least instilling competition into local fiefdoms, district level/family or clan-based power relationships, and if it does not simply serve to reinforce the extant power of these local-level power holders, then decentralization may offer hope for poverty friendly policy, but it will not do so automatically.

What might be the role of a donor-funded pro-poor decentralization activity under these circumstances? To start, it should be sensitive to and aware of the basic premise that empowering decentralized government and local-level civil society, while ignoring the makeup and agenda of these institutions for their poverty credentials, is likely to result in the rearticulation of the status quo, namely the further decentralized disempowerment of the poor. Unless donors consider decentralization assistance in a critical manner and look at poverty and democracy issues explicitly, they are likely to have little impact on the actual experience that the poorest have vis-á-vis local democratic institutions. At the very least, for decentralization to systematically benefit the poor, advocacy by and on behalf of the poor must be articulated and heard at the level of the local decision makers.

Civil Society

One such mechanism for articulating pro-poor agendas is through the institutions of civil society. Civil society assistance can be an efficient means of reaching poor people and involving them in the political process as well. Much has been written about the copasetic influence of civil society on both transitional and established democracies. While there has been some worthwhile skepticism, most analysts and practitioners still believe that civil society plays an important role and serves as a valuable partner in the promotion of democracy. Civil society is expected to serve as a counterweight to the state, at times checking excessive authoritarian tendencies, it is also thought to be a sight for the development of social capital that in turn lubricates democratic participation and encourages cooperation across social, class, and ethnic cleavages. Finally, civil society provides an arena in which individuals can learn democratic skills of participation, organization, and mobilization. These can then be applied in support of advocacy positions. The question at issue for this analysis is the degree to which the poor participate in, and benefit from, the advocacy of civil society-based groups.

In some cases, civil society is clearly vertically structured with national-level groups in wealthy urban centers that have few linkage to the poor. In other circumstances, civil society organizations are well integrated with poor areas of the country (both urban and rural). It seems that any particular case of civil society's impact on the poor needs to be examined on a sector or country wide basis. This because even if a high-profile civil society organization (CSO) does not regularly consult with poor constituents, they still may advocate for and pursue policies to benefit the poor. Granted, participation by the poor generally creates ownership, sustainability, and ultimately long-term empowerment, but in some instances support for a nongovernmental organization (NGO) or CSO that has poverty related activities oriented toward policymakers could be an efficient way to attain pro-poor policies and to win wider political acceptance of such policies. Thus poverty-friendly democracy assistance, like all development assistance, needs to be designed with flexibility and capacity to respond to a variety of case-specific circumstances.

Overall though the greatest benefit, in terms of poverty reduction is likely to occur for the poor when civil society-based groups are both representing the interests of and engaged with the poor. As with assistance targeted at the decentralization issue, project implementers should be sensitive to the makeup of civil society organizations that receive support. Training and institutional support provided to civil society organizations by donors can either serve to reinforce the power of elite leadership or can promote internal democratic practice giving greater voice and power to nonelite rank-and-file members. The second eventuality seems more likely to result in pro-poor outcomes than the first.

Anticorruption

The burden of corruption is often born inordinately by the poor as they rarely benefit from illicit government contracts, and corrupt leaders tend to respond not to a broad constituency but to those who are their direct benefactors. Patterns of patronage politics and clientalism serve to further alienate the poor when they are articulated in democratic systems. The example of Jamaica is instructive here. Nearly forty years of multi-party democracy have given Jamaica a long history of democratic institutions, however the practice of patronage politics that target the poor has led many to view democratic leaders as providers of state goods during election periods. The lack of accountability to the poor is palpable and results in violent clashes between poor constituencies at election time because of a winner-take-all practice. The ruling party typically starves opposition constituencies of development funds making victory at the next election all the more important and contributing to a spiral of violence.

This example may be an extreme, but petty corruption nearly always serves to make life more difficult for the poor than for others. Bogus traffic fines, fees assessed for services that should be given free or at low cost, police protection rackets, the higher cost of doing business in corrupt environments that lead to slow or negative economic growth, and the opportunity costs of lost state revenue diverted to the pockets of corrupt politicians all make poverty seem more hopeless. Further, opportunities for corruption abound in poor societies. When people do not have adequate education to know their basic rights, unscrupulous actors have an easier time operating.

Thus anticorruption activities can be seen as pro-poor because if successful, they should increase opportunities for economic growth, provide for more efficient state services, and ease the prosaic interactions that the poor have with bureaucracies and state security forces.

Institutions of the State and Political Society

While the activity areas treated above may hold the most promise for directly reaching the poor, the institutions of the state and political society should not be ruled out as important contributors to poverty reduction and thus as vital USAID partners in democracy and governance as well. This is so for a number of linked reasons. First, there is good evidence to suggest that when political parties have strong support among poor people, that they adopt pro-poor policies when in power and fight for them when out of power.[15] Secondly, democratic public institutions are (or should be) designed to include and account for the opinions of a wide range of citizens, including those of the poor. Private organizations, like NGOs, CSOs, etc., while often public service-oriented and very responsive to the poor, do not hold state power and thus cannot make ultimate decisions on state service delivery for or on behalf of the poor. Some have argued that because CSOs and NGOs are not elected that they have no incentive to respond to public pressure or that they have no obligation to be accountable to citizens at-large.[16] In practice however, CSOs and NGOs must respond to their constituencies and their boards. In both instances, CSOs and NGOs typically champion maximum participation in order to counter claims of elitism. When CSO missions are pro-poor (and they often are) then their very sustainability rides on fidelity to their mission and internal coherency of their strategic plans. If a CSO has a mission such as promotion of human rights, even if the poor are not directly targeted by that particular CSO, their activities are likely to provide significant benefits to the poor. Finally, if political voice on the part of the poor is linked to a party, and that party competes for political power, it will only be likely to find success if the electoral process is clean and transparent. Otherwise, more powerful political constituencies (who have the capacity to manipulate the system) are likely to prevail. Thus electoral assistance that establishes and promotes honest and transparent voting in a sustainable manner will serve the goal of poverty reduction. It seems that most pro-poor actors and constituencies will not be flush with resources that would enable them to take advantage of opportunities for buying elections or otherwise purchasing access to policy decisions, thus open and transparent political processes are much more likely to benefit the poor than shady ones.

This important caveat is particularly relevant insofar as the design and implementation of electoral support, party strengthening, or institutional strengthening of the state activities account for and directly target the linkages between the poor and electoral participation as well as links between the poor and the institutions of state. Because "neutral" institutions normally have an unequal impact on the poor, accommodation and outreach to the poor are likely to be necessary to assure full institutional integration into the lives of the poor.

In fact one might argue that without the basic cornerstone of procedural democracy in place, many of the other more direct interventions designed to aid the poor would be relatively meaningless. As recognized in the introduction above, counterpoising procedural and substantive democracy has animated many debates, but the likelihood of achieving substantive democracy when there are serious procedural flaws is very low indeed. Thus it is suggested that even the most militantly pro-poor advocates should not lose sight of democratic institutions as a natural ally.

Unlikely Democracy in One of the World's Poorest Countries

The case of Malian democracy presents an anomaly of sorts. While one of the world's poorest countries, it has maintained democratic institutions for nearly a decade. Modest but consistent economic growth has accompanied the political evolution of Mali's democracy and similarly modest reductions in poverty indicators have been reported over the past ten years. Yet Mali remains extremely vulnerable both economically and politically. Eighty percent of Mali's foreign exchange comes from the export of only two raw materials, a very high quality cotton and gold. Mali has only briefly been able to feed itself over the past decade being a net food importer in all but a handful of years. A landlocked nation situated in the heart of the West African Sahel Zone, Mali is extremely sensitive to seasonal variations in rainfall. Many years of abundant rains have provided ample cereals and cotton production through much of the country while periodically drought or near-drought conditions prevail. Additionally, heavily dependent on imported oil, the fluctuations of world commodity markets can play havoc on Mali's economic prospects. When gold and cotton prices are high and the rains cooperate, Mali can achieve remarkable yearly growth figures but when petroleum prices spike and rains are few (2000/01), stagnant or negative growth is the norm. (See Table 3.1.)

Table 3.1: GNP Growth Rates

	1994	1995	1996	1997	1998	1999	2000	2001 est
GNP	2.7%	7.0%	4.3%	6.7%	5.0%	6.6%	4.%	-1.2%

Source: La Direction Nationale de la Statistique et de l'Informatique, Comptes économiques du Mali as reported in Dante et al. (2001b), 2.

Clearly the structural factors that govern Mali's economic prospects can mean very severe constraints and the impact of this type of erratic economic performance on the poor who already live on the margins of survival can be very severe. However, public policies and the play of politics have also been important components of economic development in Mali.

Mali is also in a vulnerable political situation. In spite of having completed a decade of democratic governance under the Third Republic, Mali faces significant challenges in the process of consolidating democratic rule. Most of Mali's post-independence history gave little sign of its democratic potential. Following independence from France in 1960, Mali was ruled by Modibo Keita's strongly left-leaning civilian government. In reaction to revolutionary excesses in the final years of Keita's rule, a 1968 military coup brought to power Moussa Traoré, a young lieutenant whose corrupt leadership undermined his initial popularity and quickly eroded the military's reformist reputation.

After more than two decades of military rule, pro-democracy agitation surged in the fall and winter of 1990–91. Students, labor unions, human rights organizations, members of the media, and other civil-society groups united in opposition to Traoré's regime. These disparate groups coalesced around a common agenda for reform that included an end to the single-party state dominated by the Mali People's Democratic Union (UDPM); the institutionalization of multiparty politics; respect for basic human liberties like freedom of expression, freedom of association, and freedom from repression and torture; and an end to corruption in public office. Overall there was a palpable sense that the single-party state had failed in promoting either development or good government. By March 22, when the military opened fire on unarmed protesters and killed hundreds, the People's Revolution had gained unstoppable momentum. Hundreds of thousands of Malians took to the streets to demand an end to the UDPM's unresponsive and authoritarian rule. After days of unrest and rioting, a reform-minded faction of the military arrested Traoré and brought tentative calm to the country. The military was immediately pressured by civil society to include a majority of civilians in a new transitional government of national unity which guided the country through a national conference, a constitutional referendum, and the founding elections of a newly instituted multiparty political system, known at Mali's Third Republic.

Both great hope and deep pessimism have colored Mali's first decade of democracy. Yet Mali has succeeded in preserving democratic institutions while weathering storms of social protest, political intrigue, party infighting, labor unrest, and a violent separatist movement. The surprising success of Mali's democratic experience has been credited to a combination of recent economic growth, social structures conducive to democracy,[17] a unique political culture, a favorable international environment, and effective political leadership.[18]

Local elections for newly created decentralized political entities (communes) occurred in 1998 (urban communes) and 1999 (rural communes), with nearly 10,000 local office holders elected across the country. Systematic data on the capacity and performance of decentralization has yet to be gathered, and impressionistic views differ widely. However, in general, the effectiveness of the new political and administrative organization seems to remain uneven and hampered by what have been described as decentralized "gray areas," where competencies and authorities have yet to be clearly defined or implemented. Nonetheless, decentralization in Mali seems to offer, at the very least, a promising opportunity for greater voice and empowerment to grassroots groups, marginalized populations, and the poor, than did the top-down administrative structures which it now replaces. However, the liberal opportunity is not a guarantee and the potential for localized authoritarian rule that reproduces the most oppressive components of traditional society is also extant.

Presidential elections scheduled for the late spring of 2002 were front page news for months in Bamako and many politicians as well as international donors remain hopeful that the controversies of the 1997 presidential elections as well as the relatively low voter turnout will not be repeated. The l'Alliance pour la Démocratie au Mali (ADEMA) party seems well poised to field a successful presidential choice as there is no single opposition party poised to provide a serious challenge. Some speculate, though, that in the absence of a well-known personality on the ADEMA ballot the opposition could elect a consensus candidate. From an outside perspective, there seems little likelihood that the fractious opposition could either agree on or engineer a consistent campaign in support of a single candidate.

The results of the election will be important in two regards significant to this study. First, to the extent that a new president puts his or her weight behind the poverty reduction strategy paper (PRSP) process and promotes both poverty reduction and growth, the PRSP process will be enhanced and its prospects for positive impact will improve. Second, the inclusion of a larger number of opposition parties in the National Assembly will begin the process of restoring that institution to its rightful function as a balance to the Executive and as a source of ideas and healthy debate that it has not enjoyed since 1997. This could bring greater attention to issues of poverty and the role of donor coordination, as well as to government of Mali (GOM)/donor activities in support of poverty reduction.

Democracy Promotion in Mali

Assistance to democracy in Mali on the part of the United States Agency for International Development dates to the earliest days of the Third Republic. For the purposes of this study however, the past six years of assistance under the current USAID/Mali country strategic plan (1996–2002) are examined. The democracy and governance portfolio in Mali represents approximately 10 percent of the total assistance provided by USAID/Mali during this time period. Democracy and governance activities account for 16 million dollars, or an average of 2.65 million per year.

The 1996–2002 mission strategic plan focuses on highly interrelated strategic objectives within the socio-economic and political realms. Among these is a Democratic Governance Strategic Objective (DGSO), which is identified as: *"Community organizations in target communes are effective partners in democratic governance, including development decision making and planning."* The promotion of democratic governance in which community organizations (COs)—as the base unit of civil society—participate as equal partners in sustainable national development efforts is viewed by the mission as a means to achieving USAID/Mali's broader program goal, as well as a desirable end in itself.

A central and important characteristic of the Democratic Governance Strategic Objective is its clear, single-minded focus on capacity building among the constituent organizations of civil society. This is in stark contrast to the efforts of many democracy and governance strategic objectives around the world where support and assistance to democratic institution building at both national and regional levels takes pride of place. USAID/Mali has chosen instead to target a large proportion of assistance at community-level civil society. The democracy and governance strategic objective also articulates a commitment to promoting an enabling environment for democratic governance by support for meaningful decentralization through devolution of power and not simply deconcentration of the state apparatus. In spite of this, the bulk of activities focus on community organizations and the linkages between community organizations and local government, (with the exceptions noted in Table 3.2) relatively little actual support for the decentralization process independent of community organization capacity has taken place. With a handful of additional exceptions (again noted below) policy, institutions of governance, and national-level politics are relatively de-emphasized in this portfolio.[19] The USAID/Mali democracy and governance strategic objective is clear in its focus on grassroots development which in turn has a number of important positive implications for the impact of the strategic objective on poverty reduction. However some additional attention to enabling environment, related national-level political and policy issues, and more precise and informed targeting of the poor could make this approach an even more powerful antipoverty tool.

Implementers

Democracy and governance strategic objective civil society support to date has been primarily conducted through a hierarchy of intermediary non-governmental organizations (INGOs) as follows: USAID supports the programs of three American private voluntary organizations: Save the Children-United States (SAVE), World Education (WE), and CARE, and one cooperative, the Cooperative League of the United States of America (CLUSA). These American organizations, in turn, provide program support and training to thirty different Malian INGOs. These INGOs—"modern," formal organizations—collaborate with and represent 750 community organizations at the village level. The village-level community organizations include producer associations, community development committees, urban neighborhood associations, women's groups, health committees, student-parent associations, livestock cooperatives, etc.

Intermediary NGOs are seen by the democracy and governance strategic objective as a means to reach community organizations and are also considered as a crucial aspect of civil society. The mediating and mentoring role of INGOs vis-á-vis community organizations constitutes a necessary and desirable end in itself. Ideally they should not only provide training and assistance to the community-level groups but a reciprocal relationship should also be developed whereby the INGOs can serve as an avenue for grassroots participation at the regional- and national-level. Impressionistic evidence indicates that this situation is not yet common with the INGOs seeing themselves more as service deliverers than as advocates for their constituencies. One INGO leader articulated this self-vision by describing himself as a *"functionnaire de la société civile"* (a bureaucrat of civil society).

Of the 16 million spent on democracy and governance (DG) activities since 1996, 11 million has been allocated for private and voluntary organizations and their activities while another 5 million has been spent on other short-term or periodic activities. These activities are summarized in Table 3.2.

Table 3.2: USAID/Mali DG Strategic Objective Periodic Activities

Periodic Activity	Date	DG Budget	Targeted at Enabling Environment
Election Monitoring Assistance	1997	$1,000,000 (estimated)	$1,000,000
Election Assistance	2001	$750,000 (estimated)	$750,000
Women Internship Program	2001	$700,000	$700,000
Community Organization Advocacy Training/Cooperative Law	1998–99	$500,000	
Women in Public Life/Civic Education	2000	$500,000	$500,000
Elected and Civil Society Leaders Financial Management Training	2001	$320,000	
Newly Elected Leaders Training	2000/01	$300,000	
Monitoring and Evaluation Annual Surveys	1997–2000/01	$250,000	
Best Practices Assessment and Curriculum Development	1998/99	$200,000	$200,000
Misc. Studies, Assessments, Surveys, etc.	1997–2001	$150,000	$75,000 (estimate)
Role of Traditional Leaders Study	1998	$120,000	$120,000
Cooperative Law and Education Reform Study	1998	$99,000	$99,000
INGO Financial Sustainability Workshop	Aug–Nov 2001	$70,000	
Anticorruption Conference Participants (Durban and United States)	1999 & 2000	$50,000	$50,000
Women Parliamentarian Group Information Technology Assistance	2000	$16,000	$16,000
TOTAL		**$5,025,000**	**$3,510,000**

By reducing the total of periodic activities by the amounts either targeted directly at CSOs and the minor amount allocated for monitoring and evaluation studies, we estimate that the amount of money allocated for general enabling environment work in the democracy and governance sector in Mali is 3.5 million over 6 years or a little more than .5 million per year. This represents slightly less than 22 percent of the democracy and governance portfolio resources.

Poverty Reduction and the USAID/Mali Democracy and Governance Strategic Objective

In many important regards, the USAID/Mali democracy and governance strategic objective is a model application of poverty reduction strategies integrated into a democracy and governance framework.[20] The strengths of the democracy and governance strategic objective include

- targeting most assistance to rural areas where the large majority of Malian poor live
- working in close consort with other USAID strategic objectives to integrate democracy and governance into health and education activities
- using health, education, and community development (all significant areas of concern for most poor Malians) as entrèes to promote good governance and democratic principles of transparency, rotation of power, leadership skills, accountability, financial management, and advocacy
- leveraging the skills and experience of private voluntary organizations and Malian NGOs
- sustaining a focus on the role of women politicians and the importance of women's participation in the political process to target a highly marginalized group (for the most part, the target beneficiaries have been elite and not poor women)
- creating methodologically sound and defensible indicators to provide rich information on democracy and governance strategic objective impact and to offer opportunities to examine the impact on the poor

Yet in spite of these strengths, there are also areas that could result in more sustained and positive impact on the poor. Overall the democracy and governance strategic objective does not conduct political economy analysis to inform its strategy and consequently assumes a uniform poverty in the countryside that makes targeting any community organization in rural areas a pro-poor activity *by definition.* Some specific weaknesses of the democracy and governance strategic objective in relation to poverty reduction include

- The democracy and governance strategic objective believes that their strategy targets the poor, yet there is very little articulation of a pro-poor agenda in interactions with private and voluntary organization partners or GOM and in at least one instance poverty reduction as a goal was explicitly rejected in USAID mission-level (not strategic objective-level) meetings with private and voluntary organization partners, poverty reduction is clearly seen as a product of USAID/Mali's sustainable development focus and not an area that should be focused on independent of sustainable development.

- The democracy and governance strategic objective has not paid significant attention to national political institutions and the impact of policy making and policy implementation on the poor.
- Legal constraints placed on community organizations and access to justice for the poor is not an issue that the democracy and governance strategic objective has addressed systematically.
- The targeting of funds at the grassroots has not for the most part taken account for extant local power structures and the ways in which community development efforts can serve to reinforce and sustain the power or local elites over less-favored groups at the commune and village-level. A "political economy" analysis of activities and impacts may allow a more nuanced set of guidelines for targeting as well as a more realistic understanding of how project assistance is used to both assist and in some instances further marginalize the poorest.
- The development of a cadre of professional civil society bureaucrats has tended to monopolize training resources and may have had the effect of excluding the poorest from democracy and governance assistance.
    - All USAID private and voluntary organization partners have recognized this problem and most have taken steps to reduce or eliminate the reliance on per diem through a process of decentralized training.
    - Attention to this point may be again warranted as the new democracy and governance strategy places more focus on strengthening local elected officials.

Prominence of Poverty Reduction and Targeting Issues, Vulnerability, and Empowerment

By and large, the democracy and governance strategic objective has not put an explicit emphasis on poverty reduction in the design, implementation, or evaluation of its portfolio. However, the democracy and governance strategic objective believes, as do all of the private and voluntary organization partners and most cooperating INGOs, that the rural and grassroots focus of the majority of their activities is *prima fascia* evidence of its pro-poor credentials. One Malian INGO said

> We don't really talk about poverty reduction per se but we know that our work is targeted at it. . . . Our approach is first to improve the human capacity of the

> village organizations. We have an evaluation method that looks at the organization and its capacity. We look at all aspects of the organization, their participation, their democratic practice, their management capacity, and financial sustainability. We then look at the capacity of the organization to improve and evolve and respond to training, including involving and benefiting the poorest in the community.
>
> For example, there is a small village that we may work in that does not have a maternity. There may be one 10 kilometers away however. The woman who has a husband with a moped can get there when she is going to give birth, the poor woman cannot, and her baby is more likely to die being born unattended by trained medical personnel. So the fact of working with the village health committee to get a trained mid-wife and a place for birthing will benefit both women, but will benefit the poor woman more.

These types of activities can have a direct impact on reducing the vulnerability of the poor. However, without an explicit and consistent strategy aimed at the poorest levels of society, it is possible that these benefits will not be seen systematically or that the pro-poor aspects of such a program will go unmeasured and unreported. The explicit empowerment of the poor is also not a normal subject of strategic planning or activity implementation for the democracy and governance strategic objective though again the democracy and governance strategic objective and private and voluntary organization partners see their activities as having important empowerment benefits for marginalized groups, particularly women.

One private and voluntary organization partner has begun to strategize and utilize a more nuanced political economy approach as it formulates its new strategic plan in the democracy and governance area. It is not clear if this will be embraced and funded by the democracy and governance strategic objective in the context of the new strategy; however, the private and voluntary organization is hopeful that it will have an impact on improving targeting of democracy and governance interventions so that they benefit the most disempowered and poorest groups.

Direct versus Indirect Approaches to Poverty Reduction

Much of the democracy and governance strategic objective portfolio over since 1996 has been direct aid (training, capacity building, advocacy support targeted at grassroots community groups and local officials). This assistance could arguably be reaching the poor. The indirect components of the portfolio include support for decentralization, civic education, support for reform of the cooperative law, support for fair election process, and other enabling environment issues.

A judicious balance between direct targeting of the poor and attention to the enabling environment with an eye to how it will impact on the poor is needed for maximal benefit to accrue to poor people. One particularly enthusiastic informant articulated the need to increase indirect approaches with the following example:

> We have . . . had many direct interventions . . . but take gender issues for instance (waiving booklet in the air) . . . see this, we have trained 30 women's groups for 20 years now. This is fine . . . but it is only a drop in the bucket. We can either try to continue this or we could really make a difference by looking at issues of advocacy and legal reform, things that could impact on the lives of ALL women for a long period of time.

The basic notion of increasing the scope of action on the part of donors in general and of USAID in particular is becoming more widely articulated among the international donor community in Mali. In spite of direct assistance being associated with pro-poor outcomes, the importance of a good balance between direct and indirect assistance seems intuitive if issues of sustainability and long-term impact are to remain important considerations.

Policy Coherence

By and large, the democracy and governance strategic objective has a demonstrated commitment to and in fact has played somewhat of a leadership role in assuring donor coordination and coherence in the democracy and governance sector at a national level. This is particularly evident in the activities of the democracy and governance strategic objective staff as well as some of their cooperating INGOs in the Poverty Reduction Strategy Paper (PRSP) process. "The contributions of USAID to the PRSP process have been multifaceted and very valuable . . . They have been one of the most significant contributors to the process," said the GOM coordinator of the PRSP at the Ministry of Economy and Finance.

The USAID/Mali democracy and governance strategic objective Team Leader led one subgroup of the governance technical committee and drafted the civil society section of the PRSP. It was at her insistence that a gender component was placed into the governance section of the PRSP. Further, one of the USAID-supported INGOs was described by a number of interlocutors outside of USAID as the single most active civil society group in the process. This group provided meeting space, conducted workshops, and even drafted a separate (unsolicited) report that it then gave to the GOM PRSP team. Even though the report was largely critical of both the process and the content of the PRSP, the GOM described their participation as both helpful and important.

Overall, the participation of civil society in the PRSP process was not high and by some accounts was quite perfunctory, but what participation there was can be directly attributed to active support from the democracy and governance strategic objective team both in terms of USAID staff and support to INGOs. According to knowledgeable sources involved in the drafting of the PRSP, without the input of USAID democracy and governance strategic objective, the PRSP process would have been even less participatory and less legitimate.

USAID/Mali Democracy and Governance Strategic Objective and the Ideal Type

Section III above outlined what might be considered a generic and ideal pro-poor democracy and governance assistance strategy. The actual strategy of the USAID/Mali democracy and governance strategic objective described in this article inevitably falls short. In the area of human rights and rule of law, there are no activities whatsoever. In the area of local governance and decentralization, although part of the USAID/Mali democracy and governance strategy brings focus on this, implementation of training for local government officials was delayed for a number of years as the local elections occurred many months late. Further there is a less than subtle assumption about the nearly inevitable liberating nature of decentralization that may prove disappointing in the future. Civil society assistance is the key activity for this strategic objective with no activities focused on either anticorruption and only a handful that target higher-level state institutions and broad enabling environment issues.

While there may be some legitimate criticisms that can be leveled against this single-minded commitment to community organization strengthening, it should first be noted that this was a strategic choice made by the democracy and governance strategic objective team at the time of the inauguration of the current strategy back in 1996. Based on the premise that local-level community organizations are the building blocks of Malian democracy, the democracy and governance strategic objective team has endeavored to build institutional capacity at the local-level for literally hundreds of community organizations across the fairly widely disbursed areas in which USAID partners choose to work. The result of this decision and the subsequent efforts of the democracy and governance strategic objective team and their partners has been impressive progress among many of the most capable community organizations in the universe of assisted organizations.[21] But at least one important difficulty with pursuing work in the realm of community organizations is that resources are spread across a large number of groups. To change the behavior and improve the performance of even one national institution (such as is often attempted by USAID with national election commissions, legislative committees, ministries, etc.) can be painstaking work. When one multiplies the number of institutions by hundreds, the challenges also multiply. Just because a local-level community organization has a lower profile and is less significant at the national political level than an electoral commission, the basic organizational development issues at play remain similar. Thus, efforts to strengthen the capacity of a set of local-level community organizations should be viewed with a degree of patience and commitment to long-term and incremental changes.

It has already been noted that with little more than 20 percent of an already modest assistance budget being devoted to issues of national- or regional-level politics, the general lack of visible impact on enabling environment issues (such as legal reform to protect women, strengthening of the party system to provide a viable alternative party and reduce personalistic politics, reform of restrictive laws governing CSOs and the media, or a host of others) is explicable if not ideal. But it is inevitable when one makes strategic choices that some good ideas and noble efforts will be left undone. It is hoped that proper coordination and cooperation among donors, GOM, and activity implementers can provide reasonably complete rational assistance packages.

Conclusions—Putting Poverty First

What relevant lessons for democratic theory can be drawn from the experience of democracy promotion by one donor in an extremely economically poor West African nation? At the level of the normative debate between democracy's outcomes and democratic process, the harsh realities of life in an isolated Malian village with no school, health center, or source of potable water, as well as infant mortality rates of 113/1,000, help focus on the need for democracy to deliver. The poor in Mali have been betrayed by a long series of local potentates and global ideologies that have vied for adherents but failed to deliver basic human dignity. To the degree that democratic participation can enhance dignity, establish some measure of control for poor people, and most importantly contribute to more efficient and transparent governance that in turn leads to more efficient and effective economic development, democracy will find no shortage of adherents. Democracy's goods do matter in this context, they matter greatly, but democratic process also brings value added. Because Mali has established traditions of holding leaders accountable, checks and balances on power, and reciprocity and trust across religious and ethnic backgrounds, the process of democratic participation in local decision making resonates. If democratic institutions allow local people to challenge the power of unwanted leaders rather than reinforcing these local despots by virtue of the assumption that everyone in rural areas is equally poor, then devolving power to local entities will make a positive difference.

By putting poverty first programmatically, democracy assistance can be greatly enhanced. By putting poverty first comparatively, Mali remains an anomaly 10 years on, well below all thresholds and cutpoints that would predict capacity to sustain democratic institutions. Credit a combination of political leadership, unique cultural assets, international support, and modest economic growth. By putting poverty first theoretically, the reciprocal nature of democratic outcomes and democratic process is dramatically highlighted.

Notes

1. Research on which this chapter is based was funded in part by the United States Agency for International Development (USAID). The author wishes to thank Jonathan "Jack" Sleeper of USAID, Lynn Salinger of Associates for International Resources and Development, and Jim Fremming of Management Systems International for comments on previous drafts of this chapter. The analysis and conclusions are strictly the responsibility of the author and do not represent the opinion or position of USAID or the U.S. government.

2. Ian Shapiro and Casiano Hacker-Cordon, *Democracy's Value* (New York: Cambridge University Press, 1999), 4.

3. John Iliffe, *The African Poor: A History* (New York: Cambridge University Press, 1987), 5.

4. See Zeric Kay Smith, *Democracy and civic community in Mali* (Masters Thesis. University of North Carolina at Chapel Hill, 1993) and Zeric Kay Smith, "The rhythm of everyday politics in Mali" in *This is How We Flow: Rhythm and Black Culture,* ed. Angela Nelson, (Columbia, S.C.: University of South Carolina Press, 1999) and Timothy Docking, "Mali: The roots of democracy's success" in *L'Afrique Politique: Revendications Populaires et Recompositions Politiques* (Bordeaux, France: Editions Karthala/Centre d'Etude d'Afrique Noire, 1997).

5. See Dye and Ziegler cited in Benjamin Barber, *Strong Democracy: Participatory Politics for a New Age* (Berkeley: University of California Press, 1984), 8, fn 5.

6. Shapiro, 16. See also a rich literature on issues of participation and democratic theory that advocates increasing the scope of action for *communities* so that they share power and participate in its use (rather than the minimalist notion that power must be controlled and contained to assure *individual* freedom) by authors such as Barber, Jane Mansbridge, *Beyond Adversary Democracy* (New York: Basic Books, 1980), and Carole Pateman, *Participation and Democratic Theory* (New York: Cambridge University Press, 1970).

7. Shapiro, 16.

8. Amartya Sen, *Development as Freedom* (New York: Alfred A. Knopf, 1999, 3).

9. Richard Crook, "Making law matter: Rules, rights and security in the lives of the poor. Editorial introduction." *IDS Bulletin.* 32,1(January 2001), 2.

10. Laura Nader, "The underside of conflict management in Africa and elsewhere." *IDS Bulletin* 32, No. 1(January 2001): 22.

11. Lynn Carter, Michael Lund, and Zeric Smith, "USAID REDSO/GHA Conflict Assessment Protocol: Pastoralist Conflicts," *Management Systems International* 2001.

12. Arun Agrawal and Jesse Ribot, "Accountability in decentralization: A framework with South Asian and West African cases," *The Journal of Developing Areas* 33 (Summer 1999): 473–502 and Jennifer C. Seely, "A political analysis of decentralization: Coopting the Tuareg threat in Mali," *Journal of Modern African Studies* 39, No. 3 (2001) 499–524.

13. Harry Blair as quoted in Thomas Carothers, *Aiding Democracy Abroad: The Learning Curve* (Washington, D.C.: Carnegie Endowment for International Peace, 1999), 194.

14. Richard C. Crook and J. Manor, *Democracy and Decentralisation in South Asia and West Africa: Participation, Accountablity and Performance* (Cambridge, U.K.: Cambridge University Press, 1998), 301–2.

15. See Dietrich Rueschemeyer, Evelyne Huber Stephens, and John D. Stephens, *Capitalist Development and Democracy* (Chicago: University of Chicago Press, 1992).

16. Mick Moore and James Putzel, "Politics and poverty: A background paper for the World Development Report 2000/1." www.worldbank.org/poverty/wdrpoverty/dfid/synthes.pdf (7 August 2002), 10.

17. While there are many aspects of traditional Malian social organization that support democracy (social reciprocity, habits of community care, religious and ethnic tolerance, checks and balances on traditional power holders, etc.) there are also counterveiling and antidemocratic forces (caste system, slavery/limbry traditions, marginalization of women, and the handicapped, etc.) that often prevent many subgroups from full participation in local-level decision making.

18. See Smith 2001.

19. Data from Table 3.2 indicates that the democracy and governance strategic objective activities spend roughly 22 percent on activities that have an arguable impact on the enabling environment with 78 percent of resources being targeted at CSOs and their local-level partners.

20. The poverty reduction paradigm is articulated in Lynn Salinger and Dirk Stryker, "Comparing and evaluating poverty reduction approaches: USAID and the evolving poverty reduction paradigm. Assessment prepared for USAID/PPC/CDIE/POA." Associates for International Resources and Development (AIRD) and Management Systems International (MSI) (28 July 2001).

21. See Smith 2001.

Chapter Four

Citizenship and Difference in Latin American Indigenous Politics: Democratic Theory and Comparative Politics[1]

John Peeler

The ideal of democracy assumes that all citizens will have an equal voice in public deliberation and decision making. This ideal was stated most forthrightly by Rousseau, in *The Social Contract:* that all of the people should simultaneously rule and be ruled by all of the people. Twentieth-century pluralist theory has dealt with the obvious practical difficulty of that ideal in a large-scale polity by accepting as practically democratic any polity characterized honest and competitive elections of public officials and respect for such political liberties as the freedom of speech. Such polities are acknowledged to be short of the ideal, but are usually accepted as "liberal democracies" or polyarchies.[2]

This chapter addresses the question of how the most powerless and excluded of citizens, the indigenous populations who form a majority or near-majority in Bolivia, Ecuador, Guatemala, and Peru, are attempting to make their citizenship effective in the newest and most precarious of Latin American democracies. Iris Marion Young[3] has recently argued that *inclusion* should be a basic principle of democracy: Those affected by a decision should be included in the decision making processes and have an opportunity to influence the outcomes. That criterion has patently not been met historically for the indigenous populations of the four countries studied here. Young further argues that both civil society and the state itself must be part of the inclusive solution. Indigenous people in these countries will be shown to have pursued a variety of strategies to organize themselves in civil society and in political movements, not little has so far been accomplished in terms of a response from the respective states.

Benhabib defends the idea of deliberative democracy in a context of pluralism. A deliberative and proceduralist model of democracy privileges

> a *plurality of modes of association* in which all affected can have the right to articulate their point of view. These can range from political parties, to citizens' inititiatives, to social movements, to voluntary associations, to consciousness-raising groups, and the like. *It is through the interlocking net of these multiple forms of associations, networks, and organizations that an anonymous "public conversation" results. It is central to the model of deliberative democracy that it privileges such a public sphere of mutually interlocking and overlapping networks and associations of deliberation, contestation, and argumentation.*[4]

These large indigenous populations have entered the political stage in unprecedented ways and with unexpected weight. They have gained political power and cultural rights within these fragile new democracies, either by emphasizing class and economic issues or by stressing cultural identity. The former emphasis constitutes a demand for equality among citizens, while the latter constitutes a demand for recognition of difference. What prospects either strategy offers for effective inclusion will be subject to further analysis in the conclusion of the chapter.

The Political Context of Indigenous Mobilization

The indigenous responses to the colonial regime after the Spanish conquest entailed a repertoire from submission (with a variety of insubordinate subterfuges), to flight, to armed rebellion. Most of the time, most people do not appear to have thought that flight or resistance were likely to be fruitful. The local *jefes* usually had good reason to collaborate with the authorities because they would get a share of the proceeds from exploiting their own people. Others may have felt that by going along, they could at least survive, while flight or resistance would raise the probability of destruction. Nevertheless, flight to remote areas like the Guatemalan Petén and the eastern fringes of the Andes did regularly occur, and there were numerous serious indigenous rebellions, most notably those of Tupac Amaru (Peru) and Tupac Katari (Bolivia) in the 1780s.

After independence, policy throughout the region shifted increasingly toward economic liberalism (and its ideological auxiliaries, social Darwinism and positivism), which in promoting capitalist private property facilitated the dispossession of the indigenous peoples and their reduction to wage laborers. Many communities, with a weakened material base in the land, were hard-pressed to survive. Political liberalism showed no concern for community integrity, but considered indigenous individuals, in principle, as citizens. However, the exercise of citizenship was usually limited to those with either property or literacy, so the vast majority of the indigenous were politically marginalized. To the extent that there was indigenous political participation, it usually took the form of *gamonalismo*, or local clientelism, whereby a local *jefe* (perhaps indigenous, perhaps mestizo) would buy and sell votes in return for favors.

By about 1930, all four countries displayed a remarkably similar pattern: an indigenous majority politically marginalized, socially and culturally besieged, and economically exploited. The indigenous were not part of the nation, but they were part of the economy. The politically marginalized indigenous populations were frequently seen as a drag on national development, a block to national integration. Indigenismo, a movement among white or mestizo intellectuals, sought to address this political subjection by affirming the indigenous heritage of Latin America while advocating the integration of the indigenous into the mestizo nation. Indigenismo became the dominant approach to indigenous affairs in most Latin American countries in the rest of the twentieth century.[5]

Pursuant to this ideology, there were numerous attempts after 1930 to mobilize indigenous peoples in each of the four countries for political action in support of their own interests, both from top-down and bottom-up. Frequently, leftist and populist movements saw the peasantry (indigenous and mestizo) as potential allies and thus supported the organization of peasant *sindicatos*. A similar pattern occurred in Chiapas, where the Cárdenas government itself promoted land redistribution and peasant organization under the emerging clientelistic structure of the official party. Up to the 1960s, in short, indigenous political activity was frequent, but in a context of class conflict more than ethnic conflict.[6]

After the Cuban Revolution and the rash of attempted insurgencies throughout Latin America in the 1960s and 1970s, the response of the authorities took two forms, reformist and repressive. The Peruvian military regime of Velasco Alvarado that took power in 1968 and ruled until 1975 is the prototype of the reformist type. Similar regimes held power for shorter periods in Bolivia (1966–70) and Ecuador (1972–76), but military reformism had only a faint echo in Guatemala during the weak civilian presidency of Méndez Montegnegro (1966–70). Although the intent of the military reformers was to prevent revolution, their redistributive strategy usually provoked resistance from both national economic elites and from multinational corporations.[7]

The result was a more repressive response to the revolutionary threat, a series of conservative to reactionary military regimes during the 1970s that repressed popular movements, imposed rigorous controls on indigenous communities, and promoted the concentration of income and property at the expense of the poor and indigenous. Guatemala was distinguished both by the presence of a nationally significant insurgency during the 1970s, and by a much higher level of repression. The insurgency, both stimulus and response to the repression, showed increasing ability to appeal to the Maya population. By contrast, the three Andean countries had only localized insurgencies and less repression. This is not to say that they were politically quiescent, only that mass political action was not channeled into insurgency in the Andean cases, and was the case in Guatemala.[8]

Although as noted the United States emphasized counterinsurgency and promoted authoritarian regimes in the 1970s, by the mid-1980s it also pushed for respect for human rights and transitions to democracy, as another means of preventing revolution. This emphasis was particularly evident in the early years of President Carter (1977–1979), but re-emerged in the later years of President Reagan (1985–1989). The military rulers in all four countries would have had to swim against a strong current to avoid a transition to formal democracy. Even in Guatemala, where repression was strongest and the insurgency the most threatening, movement toward a transition began to emerge with the Ríos Montt coup of 1982, and was completed in 1985 with the inauguration of President Cerezo. However fragile and even fictitious these new democratic regimes were, they did provide more political space for citizens—including indigenous citizens—to organize and express themselves. The widespread economic crisis of the 1980s provided them with additional grievances about which to express themselves.[9]

The prolonged economic crisis mobilized indigenous political movements, pushing people into the political arena to demand attention to their needs as well and to work together in order to maximize influence. The establishment of democratic regimes gave them space to act politically with much less fear of repression. The emergence of important indigenous movements in all four countries since the early 1980s is thus directly related to these global changes.

Indigenous Political Action

Majorities systematically excluded, exploited, and repressed for half a millennium have found ways, in the last quarter century, to demand equality, to demand respect, to demand, in short, meaningful citizenship. How they did so depended on varying circumstances in the four countries and varied along the dimensions of equality and difference.

Bolivia

Following the breakdown of the clientelistic Military-Peasant Pact in the mid-1970s, the energy of Bolivian peasants was increasingly directed toward autonomous organization, in the hope of breaking definitively with the paternalism and clientelism that had characterized peasant organizations since the Revolution of 1952. A perennial and basic cleavage among peasant organizations had to do with relative emphasis on class or culture. Leftists in general emphasized the class status of peasants and viewed ethnic appeals as divisive. This had been the thrust of most opposition efforts to organize the peasantry since the Revolution. However, as early as the 1960s, parties and movements were founded that emphasized indigenous (especially Aymara) culture and tradition. The symbolic inspiration for most of these movements was the figure of Tupak Katari, indigenous rebel of 1781 in what was then the colonial province of Upper Peru.

Katarismo was less a movement than a banner, in that it was prone from its inception to fragmentation based on competing leadership ambitions and ideological perspectives. Nevertheless, Katarismo was notably more successful than class-based movements in gaining adherents from among indigenous peasants of the altiplano. By the 1990s, there were at least six Katarista political parties active on the national scene. The most prominent was the Tupak Katari Revolutionary Movement for Liberation (MRTKL), led by Víctor Hugo Cárdenas, who became Vice President of the Republic from 1993–97 as a result of a pact with the candidate of the Nationalist Revolutionary Movement (MNR), Gonzalo Sánchez de Losada. The pact undoubtedly helped Sánchez win election in 1993, but it is not so clear what benefit indigenous peoples received from having a vice president in a government that systematically pursued neoliberal economic reforms at the expense of the poor.

Paradoxically, while Katarismo helped to place indigenous issues on the national agenda, none of the Katarista parties ever captured a large vote. Recently, two new parties have been founded intending to appeal to the indigenous population, the Movimiento Indígena Pachakuti (led by Felipe Quispe Huanca), and the Movimiento al Socialismo (led by Evo Morales Ayma). By the 1990s most of the major parties and candidates were appealing to indigenous voters on the basis of themes originally raised by the Kataristas.

Katarismo wielded more power as a principal current in the organization of peasant unions (both Quispe and Morales are union leaders). Here, too, the conflict between a class orientation and a cultural orientation has been generally present, posing a challenge to unity. However, since 1983, the Confederación Sindical Única de Trabajadores Campesinos de Bolivia (CSUTCB) has held together in spite of this strain. Its founding document reaffirmed class struggle, but it also condemned ethnic discrimination and called for a plurinational state.[10]

By the late 1980s, as pressures for development of their regions intensified, the diverse indigenous peoples from the tropical lands to the north, east, and southeast of the Andes began to organize regional organizations to defend their rights and interests. They emerged into the consciousness of the altiplano peoples in 1991, when hundreds of persons from the northern lowlands (Beni) marched for 35 days over high passes to La Paz at 14,000 feet, demanding recognition of their right to "Territory and Dignity." The lowland peoples have organized Confederación Indígena del Oriente, Chaco y Amazonía de Bolivia (CIDOB). However, there is not yet (in contrast to Ecuador; see below) an organization that links indigenous peoples of highland and lowland. There are both cultural divergencies and conflicts of interest based on the fact that many lowland settlers, infringing on local indigenous territories, are Quechua and Aymara from the highlands.

Bolivia has a long tradition of class-oriented organization of its peasants, who are predominantly indigenous (Quechua and Aymara). Without losing that tradition, the emphasis has shifted in the last fifteen to twenty years to organization on the basis of indigenous cultural interests. The two orientations are not totally incompatible in a society where the vast majority of peasants are indigenous and the vast majority of indigenous are peasants—and virtually all are poor. For example, coca growers from the eastern fringe of the Andes, confronting government efforts (under U.S. pressure) to eradicate their crop and to push them into cultivating other crops, have formed militant organizations and staged major demonstrations and marches. Evo Morales Aymas's Movimiento al Socialismo (MAS) has a strong base among *cocaleros*. They define themselves by economic interest, not by indigenous identity, but their lingua franca is Quechua. But it is not clear as yet whether the increasing consciousness and organization of Bolivia's indigenous peoples will yield more than symbolic gains.[11]

Ecuador

Indigenous political organization in Ecuador has, as in Bolivia, two distinct histories, one in the Sierra, and another in Amazonia. As distinct from Bolivia, however, in Ecuador movements from the distinct regions have overcome their distinct origins and social bases to build a durable and powerful national movement.

Ecuador is also like Bolivia in that its indigenous movements have consistently had to address the conflict between a class-oriented analysis and strategy and one built on ethnicity. The earliest modern indigenous organization in Ecuador, the Federación Ecuatoriana de Indígenas (FEI), was founded in 1944 under the aegis of the Ecuadoran Communist Party, and sought to organize indigenous people as workers and peasants. The Catholic Church responded to the challenge of FEI by promoting indigenous *sindicatos* independent of the FEI and its class analysis. It was the Church that sponsored the national meeting in 1972 that produced the leading indigenous federation of the Sierra, Ecuador Runacunapac Riccharimui (ECUARUNARI). However, by 1980, the Church had lost much of its influence on ECUARUNARI, which increasingly shifted toward a more leftist, class-oriented stance, but without abandoning its indigenous identity.[12]

Indigenous organization in both the Sierra and Amazonia was given strong impetus by the agrarian reform of 1964. In the Sierra, many indigenous communities sought to gain advantage in their fight for land by gaining state recognition as formally organized *comunas*, to enable them to fight their battles in the courts. In Amazonia, agarian reform paradoxically promoted indigenous organization by encouraging colonization by Andean peasants in lieu of large-scale land redistribution in the Sierra. The result, as in Bolivia, was to set up a basic conflict between the original indigenous inhabitants and the newly arriving indigenous colonists from the Sierra. Several Amazonian nationalities organized in response, with the Salesian religious order providing crucial help to the largest group, the Shuar, in the 1960s. Quichua colonists also organized OPIP (Organización de Pueblos Indígenas de Pastaza) in the 1970s. In 1980, CONFENIAE (Confederación de Nacionalidades Indígenas de la Amazonía del Ecuador) was founded to integrate all indigenous organizations from the Oriente, or Amazonia.

In 1986, the separate indigenous communities in Ecuador formed the Confederación de Nacionalidades del Ecuador (CONIAE), a national indigenous confederation that merged ECUARUNARI, from the Sierra, and CONFENIAE. CONAIE, moreover, has become much more than a passive umbrella organization. It has provided the principal organizational force behind the succession of indigenous demonstrations and strikes that have marked Ecuadoran politics since 1990.[13]

In 1990, members of CONAIE occupied the Cathedral of Santo Domingo in Quito, while thousands of others closed roads and shut down commerce and transportation for over a week. The principal demand was for action by the government to expedite land claims in the Sierra and territorial claims of indigenous peoples in the Oriente. The government agreed to negotiate, but little that was concrete was accomplished. An intangible result, however, was overwhelmingly important: A unified, coherent coalition of indigenous peoples had forced their way onto the national stage, demanding attention to their needs, as defined by them. Nothing like it had been seen in Ecuador, or indeed in the Americas.

In 1992, OPIP (Organización de Pueblos Indígenas de Pastaza) organized a march from the lowland province of Pastaza to Quito, to demand the settlement of indigenous land claims in Pastaza. In 1994, CONAIE (with two other organizations, the Federación Nacional de Organizaciones Campesinas-Indígenas—FENOC-I—and the Evangelical Federation of Indigenous Ecuadorians—EFIE) organized another mobilization that shut down the country for two weeks. In 2000, an indigenous uprising in league with military reformers forced President Jamil Mahuad from power after he attempted to implement neoliberal economic reforms. However, the military high command, responding to U.S. pressure, prevented the consolidation of a reformist government.

Through these massive demonstrations, and through countless local and regional acts of political assertion, CONAIE in particular and indigenous organizations in general have definitively placed indigenous concerns and perspectives on the Ecuadoran agenda. As early as 1993, CONAIE had decided to found a separate political party, Pachacutic/Nuevo País, to compete in the 1996 national elections. They are very far from controlling the state, but they have achieved recognition as a legitimate voice to be heard in making national policy. CONIAE continues to play a prominent role in popular opposition to the neoliberal economic policies of successive governments; the party did win seats in Congress and in local government, and came close to electing the vice president.[14]

Selverston (1994: 131) argues that the leaders of the indigenous movement have created this political space by couching their demands in "cultural" terms. However, in spite of the tendency to organize along ethnic lines, basic economic issues have always been a central part of the agenda of indigenous organizations. Class is a meaningful organizational principle, but it apparently needs to be mediated by ethnicity to reach indigenous people. There is an economic agenda, but it is not framed in revolutionary terms, but rather as piecemeal, very focused reforms.[15]

Peru

Indigenous communities have had legal recognition in Peru since the Leguía government of the 1920s. This change had two major effects in shaping the character of indigenous politics in Peru. First, communities could resort to the courts to regain lands taken from them in previous decades. Second, and perhaps paradoxically, it cemented an equation between indigenous status and peasant class that still characterizes Peruvian society today. Thus, the indigenous/peasant communities of the Andes characteristically make demands that focus on economic or class-based objectives, rather than cultural objectives.[16]

The Amazonian indigenous peoples of Peru have had a distinct experience that, as in Bolivia, has set them apart from their Andean compatriots. Remy argues that until the 1980s the state did not have a strong presence in Amazonia, that it left administration of the region largely to Catholic missions and other private actors. The indigenous inhabitants were not seen as being effective citizens with rights until they became "civilized." Finally in the 1950s the state organized the first reserves for Amazonian peoples.[17]

By the 1950s, the Peruvian Andes witnessed a mix of peasant communities, and haciendas with quasi-feudal laborers attached to the hacienda rather than to a community. In general, the departments of the Southern Sierra were predominantly populated by Quechua- and Aymara-speaking peasants whom we would classify as clearly indigenous; the Central and Northern Sierra tended to be populated by Spanish-speaking peasants who nevertheless often showed strong indigenous cultural features in their customs, including the strength of community organization. Both peasant/indigenous sectors (communities and haciendas) were increasingly organized in *sindicatos* organized into regional confederations such as the Federación Provincial de Campesinos de La Convención y Lares, in the Department of Cuzco. Strikes and land invasions became increasingly common tactics. Peasant unrest escalated in the La Convención Valley northwest of Cuzco in the early 1960s, as a small guerrilla insurgency gave the United States an early opportunity to test its counterinsurgency doctrine in the context of social reforms supported by the Alliance for Progress.[18]

After the 1968 military coup, the military government of Velasco Alvarado sponsored the most sweeping agrarian reform in Peruvian history, as well as local and national peasant organizations. Both initiatives were part of an authoritarian and nationalistic "revolution" that sought to benefit and mobilize the poorest sectors of society in order to prevent a more radical and uncontrolled revolution. The reform destroyed the haciendas of the sierra and constituted peasant cooperatives to replace them (other types of cooperatives were set up in the commercial plantations of the coast). The reform was an economic failure in that production did not increase and most cooperatives could not sustain themselves, but it did irreversibly change the rural class structure in favor of the indigenous peasantry. Moreover, although the government failed in its attempt to control all peasant organizations, it did have a durable effect, notably with the survival to the present day of the Confederación Nacional Agraria, an organization originally sponsored by the military government and today one of the major national peasant organizations. On the other hand, several autonomous peasant organizations have survived as well, including the leftist Confederación Campesina del Perú, and weaker centrist organizations linked to Acción Popular (Belaúnde) and Apra. The result is a highly organized but fragmented peasantry, tied to various parties but not under state control, and defining its demands more in terms of class than ethnicity.[19]

The military coup of 1968 opened new opportunities for Amazonian peoples. The new government recognized native communities, which would have a status quite distinct from that of peasant communities in the Andes. Whereas the main concern of the latter would be access to agricultural land, infrastructure, and Spanish education (practical economic concerns), the native communities of the Amazon tended to be concerned with retaining or regaining territory, and with demanding bilingual education in order to maintain their cultures. These preoccupations certainly have an economic dimension, but they are principally aimed at preserving cultural integrity and autonomy in the face of economic and political pressures from outside.

A major development of the 1980s in the Peruvian Sierra was the emergence of the Sendero Luminoso insurgency. The Sendero insurrection that began in 1980 sought to mobilize the peasantry for revolutionary struggle. Although they had some early success in the southern highlands, and the army overreacted to the threat by attacking peasant villages on the mere suspicion of complicity, by the mid-1980s indigenous peasant communities throughout the highlands and in much of Amazonia had organized local self-defense squads (*rondas campesinas*) that kept the guerrillas from dominating many communities. These squads were at first resisted by the Army, but later encouraged as part of its counterinsurgency strategy. Indigenous peasant communities, with a long-standing tradition of autonomous organization and defense of their interests, increasingly resisted Sendero's hegemony, and even collaborated with the Army (compare

Guatemala, below). It may be that their willingness to do so is a fruit of the Army's agrarian reform and its promotion of peasant organizations after 1968. One result, argues Remy, is that the indigenous peasantry has gained increased acceptance in urban circles as a legitimate and respected interlocutor in Peruvian national affairs. Paradoxically, this brutal revolutionary insurgency may have finally cemented a bond between the indigenous peasants and the mestizo nation.[20]

As in Ecuador and Bolivia, the Amazonian indigenous peoples have had a markedly distinct experience, and as in Bolivia, that distinct experience continues to set them apart from their Andean compatriots. Remy argues that until quite recently the state has not had a strong presence in Amazonia, that it left administration of the region largely to Catholic missions and other private actors. The indigenous inhabitants of the region were seen as savages who were to be drawn into civilized life, but who were not seen as being effective citizens with rights until they became "civilized." Finally in the 1950s the state organized the first reserves for Amazonian peoples.[21]

As early as 1965, some Amazonian peoples (specifically, the Asháninka) became involved in one of the episodes of guerrilla warfare that shook Peru during the period. Brown and Fernández argue that the receptiveness of the Asháninka was attributable to a belief that the leader of the guerrilla column had the same spiritual authority as an eighteenth-century rebel called Juan Santos Atahualpa. As in La Convención (see above), government repression was not long in coming. The Asháninka mounted an active self-defense in the 1980s and 1990s.[22]

The reforms of the military government from 1968–75 opened new opportunities for the organization of Amazonian peoples. The Amazonian native community was granted a status quite distinct from that of peasant communities in the Andes. Whereas the main concern of the latter would be access to land, infrastructure, and Spanish education (practical economic concerns), the native communities of the Amazon were concerned with retaining or regaining territory, and with demanding bilingual education in order to maintain their cultures. These preoccupations certainly have an economic dimension, but they are principally aimed at preserving cultural integrity and autonomy in the face of economic and political pressures from outside.

Since the 1970s, Amazonian indigenous populations have increasingly built organizational alliances among themselves capable of engaging the state and the national society of Peru. Both ethnic and zonal federations have emerged.[23] Amazonian peoples received strong backing from a variety of outside interests that have their own reasons for supporting indigenous organizing in the region.[24] But these peoples are certainly not simply instruments of outside manipulation, as some opponents allege (e.g., pro-development Peruvians and multinational corporations that want access to Amazonian lands). Rather, they seem to be learning from these outside groups how better to define and defend their societies and cultures.

Amazonian peoples have been deeply affected by the confluence of insurgency, counterinsurgency, illegal drugs, and drug control. There has been a rapid expansion of coca and cocaine production by settlers from the Andes in territories of Amazonian peoples, which has led to the displacement and exploitation of the latter. Further, insurgents have financed themselves by protecting the cocaine producers, which means they have needed to exercise control over the Amazonian peoples in the area. Finally, the state (under strong pressure and with aid from the United States) has engaged in repeated sweeps and scorched-earth tactics that are extremely destructive of the environment within which the Amazonian peoples must subsist. These conflicting forces have led to intense battles in the Amazonian region, with Amazonian peoples often fighting each other, as well as the drug traffickers, the insurgents, and the army.[25]

Indigenous peoples from the Sierra and the Amazon have yet to make common cause. The massive Quechua and Aymara population of the highlands, along with their close relatives who live in the nation's slums, have become indisputably the mass base of Peruvian politics, speaking through their own organizations as peasants and workers, more so than as indigenous people.[26] It is still largely the case in Peruvian consciousness that to be a peasant is to be indigenous, and to be indigenous is to be a peasant. The minority Amazonian populations, in contrast, still see themselves principally as distinctive peoples who want to preserve their identity and autonomy even while demanding their rights as Peruvians.

Guatemala

The relations between Guatemala's indigenous Maya population and the state have been more conflictual than in any of the Andean countries. The Guatemalan insurgencies were more durable, affected a larger portion of the territory and population, and may have posed as serious a challenge to the state as did the Peruvian Sendero Luminoso of the 1980s. The Guatemalan guerrilla movements persisted into the mid-1990s; from the 1970s, they were able to recruit substantially from the Maya population. In the 1980s, the Unión Revolucionaria Nacional de Guatemala (URNG) posed a very serious challenge to the Guatemalan state and elicited an army response that was unprecedented in the savagery visited upon the Maya.

Prior to the 1970s, the Guatemalan approach to indigenous peoples was roughly parallel to those of the Andean countries, at least at the level of rhetoric: There was some commitment, in constitution, law, and policy, to protecting indigenous communities. But Guatemalan governments did even less than their Andean counterparts to actually carry out these policies. As a result, when the insurgency began to gain indigenous support in the 1970s, the military response was predictably repressive. The Guatemalan military had not produced anything like the reformist Peruvian junta of 1968–75. The closest analogue would be the reformist civil-military coalition of 1944–54, and all military elements sympathetic to that regime were systematically purged after the CIA coup of 1954.[27] The reactionary army dominated Guatemalan politics from 1954 to 1985 and continued thereafter to control the counterinsurgency effort, notwithstanding the election of civilian presidents after 1984.[28]

Over the long course of Guatemalan history, the Maya peoples have contrived to survive in a repressive environment by avoiding direct assertions of their rights or direct challenges to authority. But the escalating repression of the

1970s and 1980s forced them to forge new, more assertive organizations. These new associations included (1) community-level or grassroots movements; (2) popular organizations; and (3) Maya institutions.[29]

The community, of course, is the foundation of Maya life, so it was predictable that the army would attack indigenous communities as a basic aspect of counterinsurgency. Maya communities throughout the country responded to these attacks by organization for flight into exile or into the forests of northern Guatemala, or by remaining in place and organizing to resist. In the first case they remained organized as communities in Mexican refugee camps, demanding that the state create the conditions for their safe return. Communities that fled into internal exile also remained organized, demanding that the state recognize them as refugees rather than combatants. Finally, communities that stayed were subjected to a variety of counterinsurgency tactics too. Virtually all villages were required to set up Patrullas de Autodefensa Civil (Civil Self-Defense Patrols, PACs). Whereas in Peru many indigenous communities supported such patrols (rondas campesinas) and collaborated with the Army to block the guerrillas, in Guatemala the patrols were seen exclusively as an imposition by the army on a population that saw itself as "between two armies."[30] By the late 1980s, many communities had succeeded in dismantling their PACs. In 1990, the community of Santiago Atitlán went further: Outraged by the murder of community members at the hands of an army patrol, the community successfully demanded that the army withdraw entirely from the village.[31] Another counterinsurgency tactic was to force suspect villages into fortified settlements euphemized as "development poles," (strategic hamlets along the lines of U.S. practice in Vietnam). Once under army control, there was not much people could do except protest their confinement. In this they were supported by popular movements on the national scale, and by international solidarity groups.[32]

Organization at the community level naturally led to national popular organizations with a strong indigenous thrust. As Adams puts it, these are "associations that have arisen to deal with Guatemalan social problems to which the Maya have proven to be especially vulnerable."[33] Among the most notable of these predominantly indigenous popular organizations was the Committee of Campesino Unity (CUC), organized in 1978 to unify indigenous and ladino peasants in struggles for land and labor rights. Its predominantly class-based orientation, and its open alignment with the left, led to the later formation of the National Coordinating Committee of Indigenous People and Campesinos (CONIC), which took a more explicitly ethnic stance. The two principal human rights organizations, the Mutual Support Group (GAM), and the National Committee of Guatemalan Widows (CONAVIGUA), both had majority indigenous memberships, and the latter had indigenous leadership. The resistance to self-defense patrols (PACs) took on a national dimension with the organization of the Council of Ethnic Communities "Runujal Junam" (CERJ) in the late 1980s. The Guatemalan contribution to the debate on the significance of the Columbian Quincentenary in 1992 was led by the Maya Coordination of the New Awakening, usually called Majawil Q'ij. In 1994, over 150 Maya organizations joined to form the Coalition of Organizations of the Maya People (COPMAGUA), which made a proposal on behalf of the Maya peoples to the peace talks between the government and the URNG.

The third form of Maya organizations, major Maya cultural institutions, include the Academy of Maya Languages of Guatemala, which was chartered by the Guatemalan Congress in 1990 and charged with standardizing the Maya alphabet and setting up schools for each of the twenty-one Maya languages. The Maya Educational and Cultural Center (Mayab' Nimajay "Cholsomaj") was established in 1988 to promote all aspects of Maya culture. The Council of Maya Organizations of Guatemala (COMG) was established in 1990, linking fifteen Maya institutions.[34]

Maya popular organizations were active in the formation, in 1995, of the New Guatemala Democratic Front (FDNG), which elected six candidates to Congress (including two Maya women), and has become the principal force on the Guatemalan left, in spite of continuing repression. In the same campaign, other Maya groups supported the successful presidential candidacy of the conservative Alvaro Arzú of the National Advancement Party.[35] Arzú, during 1996, would finally bring to a conclusion years of peace negotiations between the government and the URNG, begun in 1991 under the terms of the 1987 Esquipulas II Central American peace accord. Guatemala thus became the last of the Central American countries to achieve a peace settlement—if it holds. Part of the settlement involved revisions to the constitution to recognize the special status of indigenous peoples and to define Guatemala as a plurinational state, but these proposals were rejected in a national referendum in 1999 characterized by extremely low turnout.

Since the 1996 settlement, Guatemalan Maya organizations have been active participants in the difficult process of implementation. This has frequently involved responding to echoes of past repression, as in the assassination of Bishop Juan Gerardi in 1998, shortly after he had released a report on human rights violations during Guatemala's long civil war. Increasingly, however, the transition to peace has set up conflicts among Mayas, especially over land, as returning refugees seek to reclaim land now occupied by others (often with Army support). The government has done little to solve these disputes and has been pressed by various Maya and peasant organizations, such as the Coordinadora Nacional de Pueblos Indígenas y Campesinos (CONIC).

In the last thirty years, Guatemala's Maya have made major advances in their organization and their ability to defend their interests in the political arena, in the context of durable and widespread insurgency, and brutal counterinsurgency. During this period legal politics was completely devoid of a left wing, and labor and peasant unions were repressed. Some Maya organizations, such as the CUC, have been allied with the URNG, and Nobel Peace Prize winner Rigoberta Menchú has never made a secret of her sympathy for the guerrillas' cause.[36] Other Maya groups have adopted a much more conservative political stance. Other organizations avoid open partisan commitments, emphasizing cultural interests such as Maya languages and community autonomy. Economic and political demands tend to be placed within the context of cultural concerns. Maya concerns have achieved an unprecedented prominence in the political discourse of ladinos, among whom one may note a certain nervousness about the future.

Conclusions

It is not surprising to find considerable parallels in the political roles of indigenous peoples in these four countries. Authoritarian regimes during the 1970s reached a point of exhaustion and yielded to a transition to constitutional democracy. Under democratic regimes, the energies and pressures produced by years of insurgency and counterinsurgency and economic crisis could be more openly expressed. Yashar argues that indigenous organizations in all countries had strong incentives to organize as a result of the dismantling of state programs in rural areas in the 1980s and 1990s. Hence we have observed a blossoming of indigenous political action. Yet the four cases represent four distinct approaches to the issues of equality and difference in democratic citizenship. How can we explain these differences?[37] The last quarter century presents a set of international circumstances that have made it possible for indigenous peoples to assert themselves, in the context of democratization. But these new opportunities come within the historically shaped political arenas of each country.

In Peru, we find not only Andean but also Amazonian populations that are objectively indigenous, in terms of language and culture, and who see themselves as such. Yet their intervention in the political process is largely cast in terms of demands for economic advancement, especially through land tenure in the Sierra, and collective territorial rights in Amazonia. Peru represents a commitment of indigenous people to a strategy of incorporation into the larger society, and of struggle for advancement as citizens within it. The cultural rights being demanded by the Maya are largely recognized in Peru. Peru's Quechua and Aymara are relatively secure in their cultural integrity. Government repression is aimed squarely at class-based revolutionary activity (e.g., Sendero Luminoso), and not at all at the relatively unimportant cultural organizations. Economic issues come to the fore in a context of chronic poverty, inequality, and economic uncertainty. The open path in Peru is that of ad hoc struggles of local communities for immediate economic interests.

Guatemala represents the opposite case. Class-oriented peasant organizations exist, but what is striking is that explicitly Maya organizations have come to the fore. Such organizations use traditional, liberal citizenship rights the better to make demands for cultural autonomy and acceptance of the principle of the plurinational state. Such demands are not being seriously articulated at all in Peru. In Guatemala, it is urban Maya who have taken the lead in forming diverse Maya cultural and political organizations, in defense of difference. These organizations have some similarity to those in Ecuador and Bolivia, but the latter are more active in forging alliances for economic objectives than their Guatemalan counterparts. Guatemala displayed the most repressive political environment, especially toward revolutionary class-based movements. Maya cultural organizations could appear less threatening as long as they avoided direct identification with a revolutionary insurgency like the URNG. National Maya cultural organizations (e.g., COPMAGUA) were thus able to pose a significant challenge to the established political order precisely by divorcing themselves from the more threatening URNG.

Ecuador and Bolivia are intermediate cases. Bolivia and Ecuador had less consistent repression since 1980 (in the absence of both major insurgencies and strong states), well-established indigenous peasant participation in economically oriented *sindicatos*, and the persistence of indigenous identity among peasants. Thus both the paths of economic demands and of cultural reaffirmation are open in Bolivia and Ecuador, and both have been taken.

The tradition of class struggle is very strong in Bolivia and has a strong organizational base. In the Revolution, indigenous peasants defined themselves as campesinos, not Indians. Yet, the last generation the Katarista movement has brought indigenous Aymara consciousness to the center of Bolivian politics, even as minority peoples from the eastern lowlands have begun to assert themselves. The Bolivian pattern is thus mixed, but probably closer to the Peruvian pattern than to the Guatemalan. When *indios* became campesinos after the Revolution, they did not forswear their Aymara and Quechua languages and cultures. The various Katarista movements and parties took advantage of the space afforded by the emergence of democracy in the 1980s and rode waves of popular protest against neoliberal economic policies that predominated after 1985. At the same time, the overtly class-oriented protests of the Central de Obreros Bolivianos (COB) met decisive repression as the tin mines were closed and the miners' union destroyed. Nevertheless, class-based, economically oriented protest continues to be a staple of Bolivian politics—but the rallies may be conducted in Aymara or Quechua.

In Ecuador, explicitly indigenous organizations moved beyond a stage of exuberant proliferation, to achieve substantial national unity. CONAIE, with its demands for ethnic autonomy and for the acceptance of Ecuador as a plurinational state, is now a major player in national politics. Yet Ecuador also retains a significant element of class-oriented organizations making economic demands. CONAIE and other indigenous organizations continue to be major protagonists in protests against neoliberal policies. Ecuador is thus also a blend, but perhaps closer to Guatemala than to Peru in its pattern. The Ecuadoran Quichua know that they are both *indio* and campesino. Long organized into peasant *sindicatos,* the Quichua took advantage of the democratic opening and the weakness of the Ecuadoran state to make common cause with Amazonian peoples in defense of cultural rights beginning in the 1980s. The series of indigenous uprisings beginning in 1990 were the result.

Have the indigenous populations in these four countries made substantial progress toward effective inclusion in their respective polities? In terms of the diverse grassroots organizations that Benhabib found essential to democracy and difference, the answer would seem to be yes. But if we consider how political authorities have responded, the picture is much less clear. Rueschemeyer, Stephens, and Stephens found that meaningful democratizing reforms such as suffrage expansion have historically depended on the existence of strong popular organizations demanding such reforms. Top-down reform without popular pressure does not suffice.[38]

Popular pressure without government willingness to reform is also ineffective. In Guatemala, the continued dominance of hard-liners in government has meant a repressive response to popular demands. In Bolivia and Ecuador, the weakness of the state has rendered impossible any coherent response to popular pressure. In Peru, popular pressure itself has been either repressed by counterinsurgency or coopted by clientelism. In none of the four cases do we find a match between an effective indigenous popular movement and a government ready and able to respond inclusively. Without such a match, it is difficult to see how indigenous movements will advance very far in enhancing democratization.

Notes

1. Earlier versions of this paper were presented to the Northeastern Political Science Association, 13–15 November 1997, Philadelphia; to the Escuela Andina de Postgrado, Centro Bartolomé de las Casas, Cusco, 10 June 1998; and to the Latin American Studies Association, 24–26 September 1998, Chicago; Southern Political Science Association, 4–6 November 1999, Savannah. I acknowledge the helpful comments of Brian Selmeski and Deborah Yashar.

2. John Peeler, *Building Democracy in Latin America* (Boulder, Colo.: Lynne Rienner, 1998); Robert Dahl, *Polyarchy: Participation and Opposition* (New Haven, Conn.: Yale University Press, 1971).

3. Iris Marion Young, *Inclusion and Democracy* (New York: Oxford University Press, 2000), 5–6.

4. Seyla Benhabib, "Toward a Deliberative Model of Democratic Legitimacy," in *Democracy and Difference: Contesting the Boundaries of the Political*, ed. Seyla Benhabib (Princeton, N.J.: Princeton University Press, 1996), 73–4. Italics Benhabib's.

5. *Indigenous Peoples and Democracy in Latin America,* ed. Donna Lee Van Cott (New York: St. Martin's, 1994), 4–6.

6. On the Bolivian Revolution and the peasantry, see James Malloy. *Bolivia: The Uncompleted Revolution* (Pittsburgh, Pa.: University of Pittsburgh Press, 1970); James Dunkerley, *Rebellion in the Veins: Political Struggle in Bolivia, 1952–1982* (London: Verso, 1984). On the Maya role in the Guatemalan reform governments of 1944–54, see Jim Handy, "'A Sea of Indians': Ethnic Conflict and the Guatemalan Revolution, 1944–1952," *The Americas* 46, no. 2 (October 1989): 189–204. On peasant organization in Peru, see María Isabel Remy, "The Indigenous Population and the Construction of Democracy in Peru," in *Indigenous Peoples and Democracy in Latin America*, ed. Donna Lee Van Cott (New York: St. Martin's, 1994), 107–30; Howard Handelman, *Struggle in the Andes: Peasant Political Mobilization in Peru* (Austin, Tex.: University of Texas Press, 1975). On peasant organization in Ecuador, see Alicia Ibarra, *Los Indígenas y el Estado en el Ecuador* (Quito: Abya-Yala, 1992); Melina Selverston, "The Politics of Culture: Indigenous Peoples and the State in Ecuador," in *Indigenous Peoples and Democracy in Latin America*, ed. Donna Lee Van Cott (New York: St. Martin's, 1994), 131–152.

7. This conservative resistance was generally supported by the United States, which had responded to the Cuban Revolution by promoting the reformist Alliance for Progress in the early 1960s, but after 1965 increasingly emphasized counterinsurgency and a very broad view of national security that encouraged Latin American military establishments to see their national defense role in terms of combating internal subversion. See Schoultz (1981)

8. On the relationship between repression and insurgency, see Timothy Wickham-Crowley, *Guerrillas and Revolution in Latin America: A Comparative Study of Insurgents and Regimes since 1956* (Princeton, N.J.: Princeton University Press, 1992); Cynthia McClintock, *Revolutionary Movements in Latin America: El Salvador's FMLN and Peru's Shining Path* (Washington D.C.: United States Institute of Peace Press, 1998); Susanne Jonas, *The Battle for Guatemala: Rebels, Death Squads, and U.S. Power* (Boulder, Colo.: Westview, 1991); James Malloy, *Revolution and Reaction: Bolivia,*

1964–1985) (New Brunswick, N.J.: Transaction, 1988); John D. Martz, *Politics and Petroleum in Ecuador* (New Brunswick, N.J.: Transaction, 1987). An important influence on the indigenous response to repression and counterinsurgency was the progressive sector of the Roman Catholic Church. Doctrinal changes emerging from the Second Vatican Council, as interpreted by the 1968 and 1979 Latin American bishops' conferences, reemphasized the scriptural basis of the Church's concern for social justice. Within this tradition, clergy and religions motivated by a prophetic demand for social justice developed liberation theology as a systematic rationale for the Church's special concern for the poor and for social justice. In the parishes, both indigenous and nonindigenous, these religious leaders promoted *concientización*, that is, a consciousness of being oppressed, of solidarity with other oppressed people, and a disposition to demand justice. Important elements of the Church, in short, not only affirmed its traditional, paternalistic commitment to social justice, but actively promoted the empowerment of the poor (including indigenous people) to act for themselves. The progressive Church also made itself felt among the more isolated populations of the Amazonian region and the Guatemalan Petén, where the conservative developmentalism of the 1970s opened the way in all four countries for rapid penetration by petroleum companies, loggers, ranchers, and developers, who were usually well-connected to the military authorities. The Church was not simply acting paternalistically to defend the weak and exploited. Rather, it was helping them empower themselves. See Phillip Berryman, *Liberation Theology* (New York: Pantheon, 1987).

9. Lars Schoultz, *Beneath the United States: A History of U.S. Policy toward Latin America* (Cambridge, Mass.: Harvard University Press, 1998), 362–66. See also Schoultz, *Human Rights and United States Policy toward Latin America* (Princeton, N.J.: Princeton University Press, 1981); Schoultz, *National Security and United States Policy toward Latin America* (Princeton, N.J.: Princeton University Press, 1987); Peeler, *Building Democracy,* Ch. 3; Stephan Haggard and Robert Kaufman, *The Political Economy of Democratic Transitions* (Princeton, N.J.: Princeton University Press, 1995).

10. Xavier Albó, "And from Kataristas to MNRistas? The Surprising and Bold Alliance between Aymaras and Neoliberals in Bolivia," in *Indigenous Peoples and Democracy in Latin America*, ed. Donna Lee Van Cott (New York: St. Martin's, 1994), 61. See also Albó, "Bolivia: Making the Leap from Local Mobilization to National Politics," *NACLA Report on the Americas* 29, No. 5: 1996; José Antonio Aruquipa, "Indigenous Groups Enter Politics" *Latinamerica Press* (April 23, 2001): 4–5; Mike Ceaser, "Expression of the Indigenous Majority," *Latinamerica Press* (April 23, 2001): 4–5;Carlos Iván Degregori, "Ethnicity and Democratic Governability in Latin America: Reflections from Two Central American Countries," in *Fault Lines of Democracy in Post-Transition Latin America,* eds. Felipe Agüero and Jeffrey Stark (Miami, Fla.: North-South Center, 1998), 203–36.

11. On recent indigenous politics in Bolivia, see Albó, "Bolivia: Making the Leap;" Dwight Hahn, *The Divided World of the Bolivian Andes: A Structural View of Domination and Resistance* (New York: Crane Russak 1992); Juliana Ströbele-Gregor, "Culture and Political Practice of the Aymara and Quechua in Bolivia," *Latin American Perspectives* 23, no. 2 (1996): 72–90; Silvia Rivera Cusicanqui, "Aymara Past, Aymara Future," *NACLA Report on the Americas* 25, no. 3 (1991): 18–23.

12. Selverston, "The Politics of Culture," 138.

13. Selverston, "The Politics of Culture," 135; Brian Selmeski, *Transformational Politics: The Development and Effect of Indigenous Organizations in Ecuador* (Lewisburg, Pa.: Bucknell University Program in Latin American Studies Honors Thesis, 1992), 94–97; Nina Pacari, "Ecuador: Taking on the Neoliberal Agenda," *NACLA Report on the Americas* 29, no. 5 (1996): 24.

14. Francisco Sánchez and Flavia Freidenberg, "El Proceso de Incorporación Política de los Sectores Indígenas en el Ecuador: Pachakutik, un Caso de Estudio," *América Latina, Hoy* 19 (July 1998): 65–80; Melina Selverston, "Pachacutik: Indigenous People and Democracy in Ecuador," *Native Americas* (Summer 1998): 12–21.

15. Selverston, "The Politics of Culture," 131.

16. Indeed, Remy reports that communities typically have demanded education in Spanish, not in indigenous languages, even though their everyday language is likely to be Quechua or Aymara. The point is that Spanish is the language of economic and political power. María Isabel Remy, "The Indigenous Population and the Construction of Democracy in Peru," in *Indigenous Peoples and Democracy in Latin America,* ed. Donna Lee Van Cott (New York: St. Martin's, 1994), 111–3.

17. Remy, "The Indigenous Population," 117; Michael Brown and Eduardo Fernández, *War of the Shadows: The Struggle for Utopia in the Peruvian Amazon* (Berkeley: University of California Press, 1991).

18. Remy, "The Indigenous Population," 114–5; Handelman, *Struggle in the Andes,* 70–83.

19. Alfred Stepan, *State and Society: Peru in Comparative Perspective* (Princeton, N.J.: Princeton University Press, 1978); Cynthia McClintock, *Peasant Cooperatives and Political Change in Peru* (Princeton, N.J.: Princeton University Press, 1981); *The Peruvian Experiment Reconsidered,* eds. Cynthia McClintock and Abraham Lowenthal (Princeton, N.J.: Princeton University Press, 1983).

20. Remy, "The Indigenous Population," 127. On the Sendero Luminoso, see *Shining Path of Peru,* ed. David Scott Palmer (New York: St. Martin's, 1992); Carlos Iván Degregori, "After the Fall of Abimael Guzmán: The Limits of Sendero Luminoso," in *The Peruvian Labyrinth: Polity, Society, and Economy,* ed., Maxwell Cameron and Philip Mauceri (University Park, Pa.: Penn State University Press, 1997), 179–91; McClintock, *Revolutionary Movements.* On the Peruvian *rondas campesinas*, see Carlos Iván Degregori, et al., *Las Rondas Campesinas y la Derrota de Sendero Luminoso* (Lima, Peru: Instituto de Estudios Peruanos, 1996), especially chapters by Degregori, del Pino, and Starn.

21. Remy, The Indigenous Population," 117.

22. Brown and Fernández, *War of the Shadows.*

23. In 1980 there was a "Primer Congreso de Nacionalidades Quechuas, Aymaras, y Nativas de la Selva," but this attempt to unite Andean and Amazonian peoples was apparently never repeated. "Primer Congreso de Nacionalidades Quechua, Aymara, y Nativos de la Selva, (Cuzco, Peru: Centro Bartolomé de las Casas, 1980).

24. In addition to the long-standing Catholic missions, a variety of nongovernmental organizations such as Cultural Survival, environmentalists and anthropologists working in the region. Protestant groups include the Summer Institute of Linguistics, a missionary-linked conservative Protestant organization active throughout Latin America that has faced charges of collaboration with the CIA. All these groups in their various ways seek to support (and guide) the organization of Amazonian peoples.

25. Remy, "The Indigenous Population," 126–7.

26. Urban *cholos* played a key role in the popular protests that led to the self-exile of President Fujimori in 2000, only months after a disputed election had given him another term in office.

27. Indeed, the first insurgency of the 1960s was led by one such ex-officer, Yon Sosa.

28. George Black, "Garrison Guatemala," *NACLA Report on the Americas* 27, no. 1 (1983): 2–35.

29. Santiago Bastos and Manuela Camus, *Quebrando el Silencio: Organizaciones del Pueblo Maya y Sus Demandas (1986–1992)* (Guatemala: FLACSO, 1993), cited in

Richard N. Adams, "A Report on the Political Status of the Guatemalan Maya," in *Indigenous Peoples and Democracy in Latin America,* ed. Donna Lee Van Cott (New York: St. Martin's, 1994), 162.

30. David Stoll, *Between Two Armies in the Ixil Towns of Guatemala* (New York: Columbia University Press, 1993).

31. Adams, "A Report," 167.

32. Other sources on the Maya responses to counterinsurgency include: Rigoberta Menchú, *I, Rigoberta Menchú* (London: Verso, 1984; Víctor Montejo, *Testimony: Death of a Guatemalan Village* (Willimantic, Conn.: Curbstone Press, 1987); Víctor Perera, *Unfinished Conquest: the Guatemalan Tragedy* (Berkeley: University of California Press); Richard Wilson, *Maya Resurgence in Guatemala: Q'eqchí Experiences* (Norman, Okla.: University of Oklahoma Press, 1995).

33. Adams, "A Report," 162.

34. Adams, "A Report," 165–6.

35. Antonio Otzoy, "Guatemala: The Struggle for Maya Unity," *NACLA Report on the Americas* 29, no. 5 (1996): 35.

36. See David Stoll, *Rigoberta Menchú and the Story of All Poor Guatemalans* (Boulder, Colo.: Westview, 1999), for a provocative and controversial analysis of the uses of Menchú in North American scholarship on Guatemala. See also an interview with Menchú by Jo-Marie Burt and Fred Rosen, and with Stoll by Steven Dudley, *NACLA Report on the Americas* 32, no. 5 (1999): 6–10.

37. Deborah Yashar, "Contesting Citizenship: Indigenous Movements and Democracy in Latin America," *Comparative Politics* 31, no. 1 (1998): 31–32, argues that the countries she studied varied in the scope of political liberalization experienced in the 1980s, from relatively full openings in Ecuador and Bolivia, to partial opening in Mexico and uneven opening in Guatemala, to growing restrictions and authoritarianism in Peru (notwithstanding its formal transition to democracy after 1980). However, although the Peruvian regime did become more restrictive after 1980, it started out in 1980 much less repressive than the Guatemalan regime, and is certainly no more repressive than Guatemala in the late 1990s. And if we take a longer view, back to the 1950s, there is no doubt that the Guatemalan military has been more consistently repressive than those in the other countries, and much less involved in promoting ameliorative reforms for the indigenous population.

38. Dietrich Rueschemeyer, Evelyne Huber Stephens, and John Stephens, *Capitalist Development and Democracy* (Chicago: University of Chicago Press, 1992).

Chapter Five

Plan Colombia,[1] Violence, and Citizen Support in Colombia

Jennifer S. Holmes

What are the effects of Plan Colombia and the war on drugs on democratic stability in Colombia? Will the Plan Colombia exacerbate or alleviate Colombia's challenges? The answers are complicated by the four types of violence: state violence, guerrilla violence, paramilitary violence, and drug-related violence. In order to examine the consequences of violence in Colombia and the likely effectiveness of the Plan Colombia, an innovative concept of citizen support, derived from an Aristotelian approach, will be used.

The Aristotelian Framework

Certain Aristotelian concepts and categories are applicable to the study of violence.[2] They are useful since the existing concepts of legitimacy do not provide guidelines of what citizens expect the state to do, since they are based on a concept of the state that does not include any ends, only means. An Aristotelian approach focuses on the purposes of the state, allowing an assessment of citizen support based on how well the state meets its purposes.

Most definitions of the state and democracy are procedurally or means based. The majority of scholars operate within the general framework outlined by Max Weber or by Robert Dahl. Within this tradition, the state is defined by process or means, instead of ends or purposes. Max Weber provided a general definition of the state that has continued to influence contemporary scholars.

> Sociologically, the state cannot be defined in terms of its ends. . . . Ultimately, one can define the modern state sociologically only in terms of the specific means peculiar to it, . . . we have to say that a state is a human community that claims the monopoly of the legitimate use of physical force.[3]

Other prominent scholars follow in the same approach. An example of a contemporary scholar of democratic stability following this tradition is Juan Linz, who defines the state in the following manner: "A chief characteristic of the modern state is the monopoly of legitimate force in the hands of police and the military under the direction of political authorities."[4] Similarly, democracy is defined in terms of processes. For example, Robert Dahl focuses on whether or not open and competitive elections are held, freedom of speech and organization is protected, social pluralism exists, and if a system of institutional checks and balances is employed.[5]

According to Weber, there are three basic legitimations of domination: traditional, which would include habit and "ancient recognition;" charisma; and virtue of legality, which includes a "belief in the validity of legal statute and functional 'competence' based on rationally created rules."[6] Today, the three main contemporary concepts of legitimacy and socialization, procedural and evaluative, fit within the bounds espoused by Weber.

Within the contemporary concepts of legitimacy, exactly what the state is supposed to be doing is not part of the theory. The concept of legitimacy involves a state without ends. The socialization-based concepts do allow analysis involving citizen evaluation of the state. The efficiency-based concepts are silent on what functions the state is expected to fulfill. The concept of legitimacy is void of the standards of evaluation necessary to understand the consequences of violence. Evaluation becomes a critical foundation for democratic support when history provides a choice of regime type and when habit-based legitimacy is not strong. The concept of purposes of the state provides a purpose or end-based concept that is essential to understanding the consequences of terrorist and state violence.

There are limitations inherent in this type of conventional analysis. Neither the process-based approach nor the concept of legitimacy allows a focus on a purpose or end of a state.[7] Aristotle's standard of judging whether or not a form of constitution was good was absolute justice, "those constitutions which consider the common interest are right constitutions, judged by the standard of absolute justice. Those constitutions which consider only the personal interest of the rulers are all wrong constitutions, or perversions of the right forms."[8] What this simply means for this analysis is that procedural democracy, in itself, is not enough.

To begin such a study, an assessment of the regime is necessary. Aristotle provides two indicators for a well-ordered state: general approval and stability. Stability is identifiable, but what about general approval? Understanding public opinion by using the purposes of the state as guidelines allows a better understanding of violence and its consequences.

The Purposes of the State

Instead of legitimacy, this approach invokes a notion of purposes of the state. The effects of violence can be understood given Aristotle's account of what a polis or state ought to do. What does this mean for a contemporary analysis? Instead of utilizing a concept of legitimacy, the analysis proceeds based upon a two-level notion of the purposes of the state.

In the first level, some rudimentary conditions must be guaranteed before more ultimate purposes are even proposed. Stephen Salkever states "before it is possible to live well, it is necessary for us to live and to live together."[9] To achieve this, stability and integration are necessary. "Survival and internal tranquility . . . are only necessary conditions of virtue, but they are very necessary."[10] The first level of purpose involves the achievement of the proximate goals of security and integration. As Leo Strauss says, "the most urgent and primary task is self-preservation." The second level entails achieving the goal of developing flourishing and virtuous citizens, or self-improvement.[11] For an Aristotelian, the second threshold needs to be achieved, or at least attempted.[12] However, Aristotle acknowledges that fulfilling even just the first threshold is important: "for perhaps there is some simple element of the good in just living, so long as the evils of existence do not preponderate too heavily."[13] In his emphasis on the second threshold, he does not minimize the importance of the first.

How well a state is achieving its purposes provides a basis for understanding and appraisal, rather than to what extent the state had achieved legitimacy as currently understood in most of social science. The two levels of purposes of the state give insight into how the different types of violence harm the security and integration of the political community. Destruction of the first level makes progress towards the second level of achieving living well or the good impossible.

Security

In Aristotelian terms, state, guerrilla, paramilitary, and drug-related violence can create further instability. Violence creates fear and a desire for safety. If the state does not successfully respond to violence, fear and a lack of safety undermine democracy, at the rudimentary level of state purposes. Fear of becoming a victim and contempt of those in power for their inability to deal with the problem provide potential support for sedition. If a significant portion of the community believe themselves to be victims of injustice, then additional support for change could develop within the affected group. This can be seen with the emergence of violent groups on the right, in response to the groups on the left. Attitudes of superiority and concern for safety or honor can result in contempt for those in power, and ultimately support for change by the affected group.

Integration

Violence also undermines the second rudimentary purpose of the state, integration. Violence encourages mutual suspicion and enmity and discourages people from attempting to achieve common goals, from deliberating in common affairs, and from actively engaging in politics. In healthy communities, in the Aristotelian sense, peers deliberate, participate, and act to further both individual and common goals. In sum, violence encourages fear, creates intolerance, and becomes a hindrance to participation in the political community.

The treatment of justice is extremely complex in Aristotle's work. However, in exchange-based societies, (societies that Aristotle defines as societies that are not bound by a common pursuit of the good) reciprocal justice is used. Reciprocal justice is based on the idea of a proportionate return, roughly analogous to the idea of "tit for tat." Violence undermines political stability by creating situations of unequal exchange.[14] The victims and those who fear being victimized want to restore balance to this exchange. But, in a situation where it is not always known who is responsible, it is not easy to restore the reciprocity. As Aristotle states, "the well-being of every polis depends on each of its elements rendering to the others an amount equivalent to what it received from them."[15] Random acts of violence, such as the detonation of bombs in crowded civilian areas or widespread kidnapping begin to unravel the social ties. State repression isolates people, making mutual distrust common. Participating in politics becomes dangerous. Indiscriminate repression and violence are essential to capture the concept of an uneven exchange. This way of understanding repression illuminates how it can undermine democratic stability. The effects of violence then spread. "An offense against the laws destroys those possible relationships which make common pursuit of the good possible; defective character, while it may also render someone more liable to commit offenses, makes one unable to contribute to the achievement of that good without which the community's common life has no point."[16] Violence, an uneven exchange in terms of reciprocal justice, can undermine the political association at the very first level of stability and integration. Targeted force, such as in legal prosecution and punishment, renders an equivalent response. This would not be acting against reciprocal justice.

Violence erodes citizen confidence. If the state unsuccessfully deals with the initial violence, other factions within society may begin to believe that they could handle the situation better. In many cases, the other faction is the military. Moreover, if the military is handed this role and succeeds, then there is the risk that this will change the composition of the state, and open up the possibility that some may act against the state. Aristotle warns, "constitutions may also be changed . . . as a result of the growth in reputation or power of one of the magistracies, or of some other part of the state."[17] This problem becomes especially salient during times of an internal conflict, in which the military may be called in to suppress a violent insurrection. Success of the military and growth of their prestige increase the possibility of the emergence of some military men to seize power. The potential appeal to people in these cases is not whether or not the military will act democratically but whether or not the military will act effectively to fulfill the purposes of the state. Of course, the hopes of the people can be betrayed. The new regime might turn out to be worse than an ineffectual, enfeebled democracy.

In addition, three contextual factors must be addressed. First, in most countries, a certain level of violence is expected and almost impossible to eliminate within normal means. Throughout history, some countries have been afflicted more than others and some times are more turbulent than others. The Colombian case is unique. During the civil war, known as *la violencia*, hundreds of thousands lost their lives. This extended period of violence raises concern for instability and fear of change. It also provides an example of the need to examine acceptable levels of violence that exist in each country. Second, potentially acceptable forms of authority need to be determined to distinguish what other models of authority and governance are available. If the current regime cannot fulfill its purposes, people are likely to search for options to replace it with some form of government that is more capable. The available choices depend on each country's history and circumstance. Third, the military must be studied, since most attacks against democracy involve indirect or direct military support and action.

Historical Overview

Since the 1960s, Colombia has faced a rebel insurgency, which has generated many active paramilitary groups in response. Beginning in the 1970s, Colombia has been struggling with the illegal drug industry that has created expansive networks that have penetrated Colombian politics, society, and economy. The guerrilla groups, drug-related violence, and the paramilitaries have made Colombia one of the most violent nations in the world. Approximately two million Colombians have fled the country since 1985. This is a significant number in a country of population of fewer than 42 million. Due to the rebel conflict and the drug war, hundreds of bombs have been set off in Colombian cities; the Unión Patriótica, a left-wing political party of former guerrillas, had over 3,500 members murdered or "disappeared" by paramilitaries; four presidential candidates, half of the Supreme Court justices, over 1,200 police officers, 200 journalists and judges, and more than 300,000 average Colombians have been murdered since 1985.[18] Colombia is also a dangerous place for union organizers,[19] journalists,[20] and human rights activists. In 2000, for example, 153 leaders of trade unions were assassinated. Since 1986, in total, 3,800 trade unionists have been killed.[21] The challenges of violence are severe and hydra-like.

Economic Crisis

It has been estimated that the economic cost of the guerrilla conflict between 1990 and 1994 was 4 percent of GDP.[22] Other estimates are as high as 9 percent. The conflict, combined with other economic factors, led Colombia to have the highest unemployment in the hemisphere in the year 2000. For a country that had avoided the problems typical of the "lost decade" of the 1980s, the economic crisis is severe.

Table 5.1

	Growth Rate	Unemployment
1991	2.4	9.8
1992	3.8	9.2
1993	5.3	7.9
1994	5.3	7.6
1995	5.4	8.7
1996	2.0	11.9
1997	3.2	12.1
1998	0.6	15.7
1999	-4.8	19.5
2000	3.0	20.8

Source: Departamento Administrativo Nacional de Estadistica

As seen in Table 5.1, the late 1990s were particularly severe for Colombia. Although growth returned in 2000, unemployment continued to grow.

Colombian Guerrilla Groups

In Colombia, four major guerrilla groups have been active. The largest and best equipped is the FARC, the Armed Forces of the Colombian Revolution. Numbering approximately 17,000 members, the FARC wants a revolution to establish a Marxist/Leninist state. The group finances its organization through extorting part of the profits from businesses in areas under its control, including drug traffickers.[23] The FARC is the "dominant force in over 50 percent of the country's municipalities"[24]

The second largest group used to be the M-19 (19th of April Movement). In November 1985, the M-19 seized the Palace of Justice in Bogotá and took the Supreme Court hostage. After a brief attempt to negotiate, the military stormed the building, killing most of the M-19 leaders and half of the justices. In 1989, the remaining M-19 leaders signed an agreement with the Barco administration to turn over their arms in return for reincorporation into civilian life. Now as a legal political party, the M-19 has become the Democratic Alliance/M-19.[25]

The third group is the EPL, the Popular Army of Liberation. This relatively small, but highly disciplined, group consists of 300 to 500 members. The EPL has criticized the ties of the FARC to drugs. The EPL finances itself through kidnappings and violence against the landed elite.[26] Earlier, in the early 1990s, a majority of the EPL entered a peace agreement with the government to end their rebellion. The remaining EPL is a splinter group that did not accept the peace agreement.[27]

Finally, the ELN, the Army of National Liberation, is a group of about 4,000 to 5,000 guerrillas. It gained notoriety by bombing the pipeline that carried most of Colombia's export oil from the eastern plains to the Caribbean.[28]

Drug Traffickers

The drug trade in Colombia began with some small-scale cultivation of marijuana in the 1960s. By the 1970s, some Colombians in the drug trade began to process and export cocaine. Cocaine paste was imported from Peru and Bolivia and the necessary chemical supplies were brought in from Europe. The final product was smuggled into the United States. By 1982 the business had grown to the point where the drug trade accounted for 10 to 25 percent of the country's exports. At first, the growing drug trade did not appear to be a threat to the Colombian democracy.[29]

Table 5.2 Coca Cultivation in Colombia (thousands of hectares)

1995	1996	1997	1998	1999	2000	2001
40.9	67.2	79.5	101.8	122.5	136.2	169.8

Source: Office of National Drug Control Policy (ONDCP)

Table 5.2 demonstrates that despite efforts to eradicate coca production in the 1990s, more and more land was cultivated.

In the beginning, a few main groups controlled the drug trade in Colombia. One major group was the Medellín cartel, headed by Pablo Escobar and Jorge and Fabio Ochoa. This cartel was arguably at its height in the mid to late 1980s. When Escobar was killed in a shootout with Colombian police on December 2, 1993, the Cali cartel took over most of the production. Less violent than the Medellín cartel, it operated differently. It focused its attention on legalizing parts of the operations and moving into legitimate businesses. Colombian President Samper received six million dollars from Cali legal businesses during his presidential campaign. Despite this, President Samper pursued an anti-drug strategy and the main "cartel kingpins" were jailed by 1996 with relatively light sentences.[30]

Despite these two well-known cartels, there are many more independent organizations that produce, refine, and smuggle drugs. Sometimes these smaller groups cooperate and coordinate their actions with the larger groups.[31] Since the targeting by law enforcement of the Cali and Medellín groups, others have quickly filled the void to meet the demand for drugs.

President Samper's attempts to combat drug production were evident in 1996, a year with a large number of cocaine labs destroyed and an increase in the eradication of opium. However, this success was short-lived. By 1999, the potential acres of coca harvest had almost quadrupled from 1993.[32]

The business of drugs is more complicated than just another illegal activity. It has profoundly affected preexisting social conflict. Prior to the emergence of drug trafficking, there was a conflict between the traditional landowners and popular groups. There were struggles over unused latifundios (large estates or ranches), demands by peasants for property titles, and disagreements caused by state support of rural modernization programs. Until the 1970s, large landowners usually won this struggle. However, the drug trade changed this by introducing competition from the narcos to the traditional landowning elites. By the 1980s, armed protection of the haciendas was reinforced "so that in the middle of that decade almost all of the struggle for land had been eliminated through a combination of military harassment and paramilitary terrorism."[33] The peasants who had earlier demanded land had clearly lost. The spread of the drug trade eliminated the "troublesome" obstacles to it, including judges, police, etc. The result was a growth in criminal groups and a change in the dynamics of the traditional conflict.

Relationship between the Drug Traffickers and the Guerrillas

Drug traffickers and guerrillas have a complex relationship. Bloody conflicts between the narco-traffickers and the guerrillas have been common in areas of drug cultivation and processing. Moreover, when the drug traffickers have taken over land, they have created death squads/paramilitary groups to deal with the guerrillas, to terrorize the local population, and to remove the effectiveness of the government. In short, they reorganized society by eliminating the previous social organization and by creating their own social base. In areas where the guerrillas cannot be defeated, a pragmatic relationship has developed. In these cases, the producers and traffickers pay tribute to the guerrilla groups.[34]

Some have tried to label the guerrilla groups as nothing more than another drug cartel. For example, General Barry McCaffrey, director of the Office of National Drug Control Policy, has called the FARC the "principle organizing entity of cocaine production in the world."[35] According to Marc Chernick, Director of the Andean and Amazonian Studies Program at Georgetown University,

> Some have tried to obfuscate this issue by collapsing the two issues into one, saying that the guerrillas work with the drug traffickers and are therefore effectively "narco-guerrillas." However, this is a gross distortion of the situation in Colombia. The guerrillas do not constitute another "cartel." Their role in the drug trade is in extorting a percentage of the commercial transaction of coca and coca paste, just as they do with many other commercial products in the areas in which they operate, be it cattle, petroleum, or coffee.[36]

The relationship between the guerrillas and the narco-traffickers is complex. However, certainly the drug violence makes the guerrilla problem harder to solve and vice versa.

The Paramilitaries

Civil defense groups formed in response to the guerrilla conflict back in the 1960s and 1970s. Decree 3398 in 1965 and Law 48 of 1968 allowed civil defense units to support the army in counterinsurgency efforts. Their activities greatly increased after 1980. However, as violence increased and corruption invaded these groups, they were declared illegal in 1989. In general, paramilitary groups are supported by landowners, drug traffickers, and some parts of the military. The paramilitaries also finance themselves by taxing the drug trade.[37] A type of paramilitary group, the *convivir* units, originated in the Antioqua department in the early 1990s to avoid the appearance of the outlawed paramilitary groups. They were limited to holding only small sidearms. Later, in the mid-1990s, these too were declared illegal as many of them armed themselves and acted in excess of what was allowed by law.[38] However, instead of disbanding, many have continued to operate clandestinely.

The largest paramilitary group was the AUC, or the United Self Defense Groups of Colombia. Led by Carlos Castaño until May 2001, this group of approximately 15,000 active paramilitaries is funded by landowners, businessmen, and drug dealers.[39] These groups claim to be an alternative to the guerrillas and purport to assume the traditional counterinsurgency role of the military. Castaño does not deny that the AUC kills. He believes that the AUC is winning the war against the guerrillas by killing "guerrillas dressed as peasants."[40] In recent years, the paramilitaries have been responsible for over 80 percent of the human rights violations in Colombia. In addition, responsibility for the infamous massacres at Mapiripán in July 1997, Barrancabermeja in May 1998, and La Gabarra-Tibú in August 1999 have been attributed to them. In addition, he promised that in response to criticism for massacres, the AUC would no longer execute more than three people at a time.[41] In addition, he claims that the AUC would need to be a part of any peace process, since the AUC is performing roles that the state has not been able to fulfill. The AUC has become actively involved in promoting candidates in the 2002 elections. Castaño resigned control of the AUC because he said he could no longer control hardliners. He retained the role of political commander until July 2002 when he stated that the AUC was out of control and too involved in drug trafficking. He remains in control of a paramilitary group, affiliated with the AUC, active in the Cordoba and Uraba regions.[42] Formally, the AUC disbanded in July 18, 2002 because of the difficulty in controlling the group. Castaño and Mancuso promise to attempt to build a new national antirebel force.[43]

The lines among the violent are not always clear: In Barrancabermeja, the AUC bought off former guerrillas with offers of $250 per month, a cell phone, and a pistol. The ELN and FARC have joined forces to repel AUC advances and there are documented ties between the paramilitaries and the Colombian government.[44]

The State

The Colombian state has been charged with committing human rights violations and contributing to the violence. This is a concern of many governments, NGOs, and international leaders. Part of the controversy involved whether military groups had ties to paramilitary groups, which have been responsible for approximately 75 percent of all political killings. In its *World Report 2000*, Human Rights Watch documented the ties between the Colombian Army's Fourth Brigade and Carlos Castaño's paramilitary group. Reportedly, Castaño's men were able to exchange civilian corpses for weapons from the Fourth Brigade. The army would then dress the corpses as guerrillas and claim that they had been killed in combat. Even the State Department, in its *1999 Country Reports on Human Rights,* said "security forces actively collaborated with members of paramilitary groups by passing them through roadblocks, sharing intelligence, and providing them with ammunition."[45] Many groups contended that the most recent aid package did not do enough to prevent these ties and to prosecute those who are responsible for collaborating with the paramilitary groups.

Institutions have been put into place to improve the situation. In November 1998, the Procurator Delegate for Human Rights disclosed that in the previous fifteen months, there were fifty dismissals and other disciplinary sanctions against 126 military officers and police personnel for violations of human rights. The Procurator Delegate opened 600 cases against the security forces to investigate 1,338 victims of torture, massacres, and disappearances.[46] In 1999, four generals were removed by President Pastrana for links to the paramilitaries. One was even put on trial. Also in 1999, the infamous Brigada XX, closely connected to the paramilitaries, was shut down. With the assistance of U.S. aid, military intelligence units began to be reorganized and modernized. In 2000, President Pastrana, by decree, delegated the authority to the armed forces command to dismiss offending personnel. Due to this law, 89 officers and 299 others were dismissed. However, charges were not filed against any of them. As Amnesty International points out, many senior officials in the military and in the justice system are implicated in human rights violations and remain in their jobs.[47] In July 2000, Act No. 589 was enacted, formally criminalizing the forced disappearance of persons. Also in that year, the Ministry of the Interior initiated programs to protect journalists and human rights activists, such as the Program for the Protection of Journalists and People in the Media. However, one bill was introduced to allow law enforcement to put people into protective custody without a court order.[48]

U.S. Policy Toward Colombia

In 1989, U.S. military presence in and aid to Colombia were minor. However, after the assassination of leading Colombian presidential candidate, Luis Carlos Galán, U.S. policy responded to strengthen the Colombian military and to jump-start the war on drugs. Within one day, President Bush announced the release of $65 million worth of stockpiled Defense Department weapons and supplies to Colombia. The U.S. Congress quickly approved a U.S. Export–Import bank $200 million credit line to the Colombian military. Three weeks later, President Bush announced that $261 million more in aid would be given to the Andean nations of Colombia, Peru, and Bolivia. By 1992, efforts had began to concentrate more on attacking the drug traffickers and cartels directly, by focusing on the cartel “kingpins” instead of on crop eradication efforts. As the U.S. aid started to direct more military and police aid to combat the drug traffickers, many people became concerned that the United States was being drawn into counterinsurgency operations against the long-standing conflict with the Colombian rebels. In fact, the GAO audited the drug war expenses in Colombia in 1992 and 1993, raising concern that counternarcotics funds were being illegally used for counterinsurgency operations.

According to the State Department’s Bureau for International Narcotics and

Law Enforcement Affairs, there are three main goals for U.S. drug policy in Colombia. The first goal is to eliminate the cultivation of illegal drugs in Colombia, including opium poppy, coca leaf, and marijuana. The second goal is to strengthen Colombia's own capabilities to disrupt and dismantle major drug trafficking organizations and prevent their resurgence. Finally, the aim is to destroy the cocaine and heroin processing industries.[49]

Colombian Efforts to Control the Drug and Guerrilla Problems

The last two decades have been characterized by Colombian attempts to craft both political and military solutions. However, to date, few of the efforts have enjoyed long-lasting success. President Turbay (1978–1982) relied on the military and paramilitary units to try to control the violence. President Betancur (1982–1986) initiated peace talks that resulted in the formation of a legal political party (the Unión Patriótica) by the FARC. However, paramilitary groups killed over six thousand Unión Patriótica members, and the cease-fire agreement failed. Both rural and urban violence escalated under President Barco (1986–1990). President Gaviria (1990–1994) attempted to restart peace talks, with extensive negotiations in 1991–1992, but these talks did not produce a peace.

The response to the drug trade also varied. An extradition treaty with the United States was signed by President Turbay in 1979. However, no extraditions were requested until the administration of President Betancur. These extraditions created cycles of drug violence followed by state retaliation followed by more violence. The bloody offenses by drug traffickers finally got so bad that President Gaviria stopped extraditions to the United States. In 1991, Gaviria tried a policy of voluntary submission to justice, in which drug traffickers were able to exit from crime and legalize their assets if they would plead guilty to a few offenses and receive light sentences. President Samper's administration (1994–1998) was hampered by allegations that he received millions of dollars in drug money for his campaign. However, during his term, the Colombian Congress passed an asset forfeiture law and resumed extradition of drug traffickers to the United States. Nonetheless, Colombia's relationship with the United States was severely strained by the allegations of his accepting drug-tainted campaign money.[50]

In 1998, newly elected President Pastrana began attempts to solve both the drug problem and the guerrilla conflict. He started peace talks with the FARC and the ELN for the first time in eight years. Both were offered safe havens as a precondition to the negotiations. The FARC received a block of land in the center of Colombia approximately 42,000 square kilometers in size (about the size of Switzerland), and the ELN spent most of the year negotiating the location. A twelve-point agenda, called the *Common Agenda for Change* was announced for peace talks with the FARC. Included to be addressed were a negotiated political settlement, an interim agrarian reform, efforts against drug trafficking and corruption, political reform, the restructuring of the legal system, and the application of international human rights law.[51]

However, by 2000, these efforts did not produce a peace, so Pastrana proposed Plan Colombia. There seemed to be a broad consensus in Colombian society that "a negotiated settlement to the internal conflict is essential if the fundamental problems besetting the nation are to be addressed"[52] The Colombian government abolished the FARC's safe haven in 2002 because of the breakdown of peace talks. As of 2002, the FARC holds approximately 750 people hostage, including presidential candidate Ingrid Betancourt, four members of Congress, and one senator.[53]

Initially, talks with the smaller group, the ELN, seemed promising. The state was demanding a promise to end kidnapping, release their current prisoners, and the cessation of attacks against the state and general sabotage. The rebels demanded supplemental state financing to replace lost ransom income.[54] By the end of Pastrana's term, peace talks with both the FARC and the ELN had failed.

This failure cost President Pastrana's political party as it appeared to bear the brunt of disappointment with the peace process. The Conservative Party candidate, Juan Camilo Restrepo, withdrew. In addition, the party president, Carlos Hoguin, resigned because the party lost 10 percent of its congressional seats in the March 2002 congressional elections.[55] The winner of the 2002 elections was Álvaro Uribe of the Colombia First multiparty movement. Uribe was inaugurated on August 7, 2002. While governor of Antioquia in the early 1990s, he encouraged the growth of self-defense groups.[56] His running mate was Francisco Santos Calderón, founder of Pais Libre, a group dedicated to the plight of the kidnapped. Uribe did request UN mediation of future peace talks.[57]

The Effects of the Violence on the Purposes of the State, Citizen Confidence, and Democratic Stability

Whatever plan is determined to combat the multifaceted violence in Colombia, it also needs to address the tepid confidence in the state. The concept of the purposes of the state helps to identify challenges and constraints that need to be addressed in the process of achieving peace.

Purpose of the State Security

The security of Colombians is threatened. The violence from the narcos, paramilitaries, and guerrillas has also created a situation where everyday crime is exacerbated. The conflict has affected the ability of authorities to function. For example, the percentage of homicides investigated declined from 80 percent in 1985 to less than 30 percent in 1995. An increase in homicides, coupled with the violence and intimidation of the judicial system, contributed to this decrease in effectiveness.[58] For example, Colombia has the highest rate of homicide in the world. Even after millions of dollars of aid, in 1999, approximately 98 percent of crimes were unpunished, 74 percent were unreported, and almost 100 percent of the human rights violations went unpunished.[59]

Figures 5.1 and 5.2 demonstrate the extent of the violence. Since the late 1980s thousands of people have been killed each year.

Figure 5.1
Political Homicides and Extrajudicial Executions

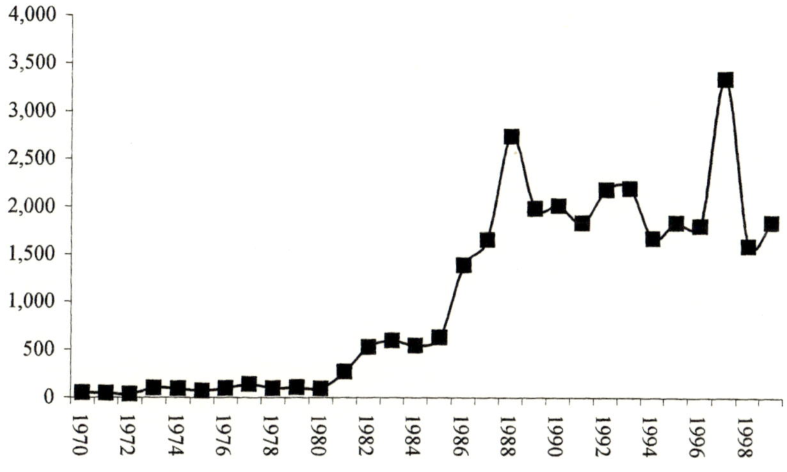

Sources: 1970 through Sept. 1996 CINEP. (1996 data only includes through September and it reported as 1,200. We estimated the total of the year to be 1,800.) 1998–1999 Office of the People's Advocate.

The Organization of American States estimates an increase in the political violence. In 1988, an average of ten people were killed a day. From 1988 to September 1999, an average of twelve were killed daily. From October 1999 to March 2000, the number rose to fourteen and between April and September 2000, the average rose to nineteen a day. The average daily rate of disappearances has also increased from one to two. In 1999, 238 people were confirmed as disappeared. In 2000, that number had increased to 664. It is estimated that the state and paramilitary forces are responsible for 79.5 percent of the violations and 20.5 percent to the guerrillas.[60] In addition, thousands of Colombians were kidnapped. Recently, anyone with one million dollars in total assets, such as a home, etc., is considered at risk for kidnapping. Kidnapping is one of the major sources of income for the guerrilla groups.

Figure 5.2:
Kidnappings 1997-June 2002

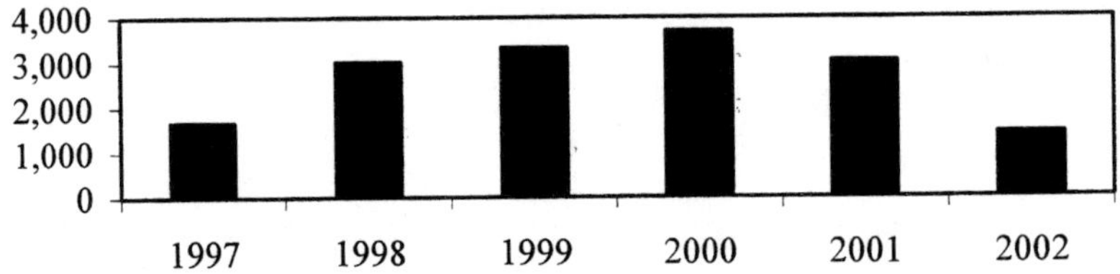

Source: Pais Libre. Please note that 2002 data includes only through June.

According to Gonzalo Sánchez, between 1987 and 1998, there were 15,181 kidnappings.[61]

Whereas the guerrilla and paramilitary violence continues to increase, state violence has decreased. Human rights complaints against Colombian security forces have declined from more than 3,000 complaints in 1996 to 586 in 1999. Moreover, the government has become more aggressive in investigating and removing military officers involved in human rights violations and/or paramilitary groups.[62]

One response to the risk of violence or kidnapping is to leave. As seen in Figure 5.3, in the last fifteen years, 2,088,000 Colombians were displaced within the country. Consultoría para el Desplazamiento Forzado y los Derechos Humanos (CODHES) estimates that paramilitaries were responsible for 54 percent of the displaced, guerrillas 29 percent, police and military 6 percent. Eleven percent were displaced by unknown actors. Another option is to leave the country. Indeed, many have permanently left the country, causing a "brain drain" effect. From January to March 2002, an additional 90,179 people were displaced.

Figure 5.3
Colombians Internally Displaced 1985-2001

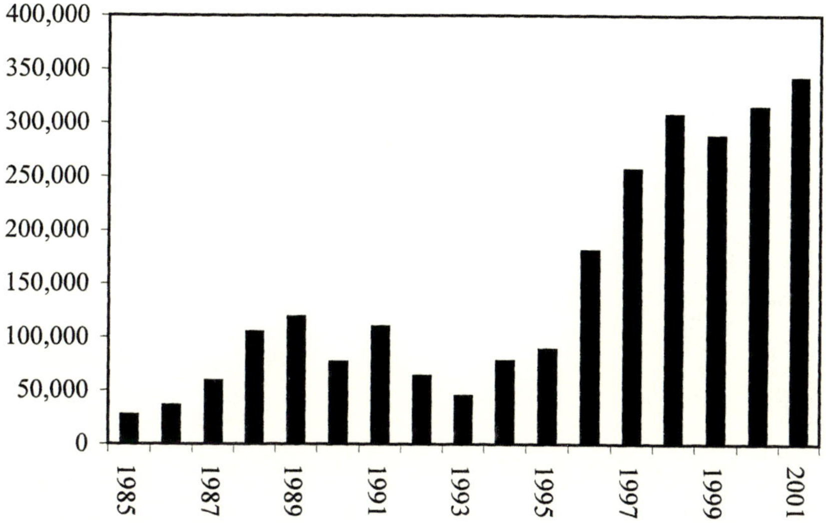

Source: CODHES (Consultoría para el Desplazamiento Forzado y los Derechos Humanos) "Desplazamiento y Violencia en una Nación Fragmentada" and Boletin 35 "Hasta Cuando"

There are some public opinion data available about the violence. Unfortunately, time series data are unavailable. However, a snapshot of attitudes of the public's beliefs about the violence is available. Despite the extent of the violence, a majority of Colombians reject the use of violence for political means. When asked in 1997, How strongly do you agree or disagree with this statement: "Using violence to pursue political goals is never justified," 67 percent agreed and 32 percent disagreed.[63] It is noteworthy however, that one third thought that violence could be justified.

Colombians realize the extent of drug trafficking in their nation and the harmful effects. Table 5.3 provides the response to the following question: When asked, "From the list of issues that I am going to read out to you do you think they have increased a lot, increased a little or have decreased a lot or decreased a little," many Colombians perceive that drug trafficking has increased.

Table 5.3

Drug trafficking has increased or decreased from the previous year.

Year	"Increased a lot"
1996	28%
1997	54%
1998	43%

Source: Latinobarómetro 1996–1998. Here only increased a lot.

In addition, as seen in Table 5.4, four out of five Colombians believe that the drug problem is very serious.

Table 5.4

"Thinking about the drug problem in Colombia today, would you say that the problem is very serious, not very serious, or not at all serious?"

Year	"Very serious"
1997	80%
1998	82%

Source: Latinobarómetro 1996–1998.

Clearly, Colombians view the drug problem as serious and as increasing in severity.

This past year, when asked what the principle problem facing Colombia was, the complexity of the situation was evident. In a nation beleaguered by violence and the most severe unemployment in Latin America, delinquency and crime followed unemployment and corruption. Table 5.5 provides the responses.

Table 5.5 Principal Problem Facing the Nation December 2000–January 2001

Unemployment	33%
Corruption	30%
Delinquency/Crime	23%
Education	10%

Source: Barometro Iberoamericano Informe de Opinión de Latinoamerica y de la Peninsula Ibérica Enero 2001 Consorcio Iberoamericano de Empresas de Investigación de Mercados y Asesoramiento

When asked who is to blame for the violence, a majority of the Colombians blame the guerrillas. In 1997, Colombians were surveyed the following question: "I'd like to ask you about some groups that some people feel are threatening to the social and political order in this society. Would you please select from the following list the one group or organization that you like least?"

Table 5.6

Least-liked Group	
Paramilitaries	21%
Guerrillas	52%
Narcos	3%
Homosexuals	1%

Source: World Values Survey, 1997.

Table 5.6 demonstrates that although one out of five Colombians blamed the paramilitaries, over half viewed the guerrillas as more responsible for threatening order. Another study conducted by Yankelovich, Acevedo, and Associates conducted in October 1999 asked which group is the greatest enemy to Colombia's welfare. Thirty-nine percent chose the guerrillas, 9 percent chose common criminals, and 8 percent chose the paramilitaries. Twenty-three percent chose others, 19 percent chose all of the above, and 1 percent the armed forces.[64] Colombia faces several serious problems. In order to successfully control the violence, these other problems also need to be addressed.

Purpose of the State Integration

Forty years of conflict has taken a toll on the integration to the Colombian political community. Intolerance is high and the elections have been hampered.

An example of intolerance for the least-liked group (the guerrillas, paramilitaries, narcos, or homosexuals) is high, as shown in Table 5.7.

Table 5.7

"Do you think that [the least liked group just identified] should be allowed to"

Least liked	Yes	No
Hold office	15%	82%
Teach	11%	86%
Demonstrate	13%	84%

Source: World Values Survey, 1997.

Over 80 percent of those polled do not want members of the least-liked groups to teach, hold office, or to demonstrate. This indicates grave polarization in the political community. An earlier, May 1992 poll by Yankelovich Colombia found that 61 percent of Colombians believed that the armed forces should "take the initiative and utilize all methods to combat the guerrillas."[65] Among Colombians, there appears to be strong support for an unyielding position against the rebels.

In addition to attitudes demonstrating a lack of integration, it can be seen that the everyday functioning of democracy has been disrupted by the violence.

According to CIDEC (Centro do Información sobre Desarrollo de la Democracia en Colombia), before the 1997 regional elections which the guerrillas attempted to block, 200 candidates were targeted for assassination by guerrillas and paramilitaries, 22 municipalities had no candidates, 359 mayoral candidates withdrew, 244 were kidnapped, and 110 candidates were murdered.[66]

Citizen Confidence

Public opinion provides a gauge of how little confidence the majority of Colombians have in their institutions and government. The intransigence of the country's problems translates into extremely low approval ratings for those in power. For example, when asked, "How satisfied are you with the way the people now in national office are handling the country's affairs? Would you say you are very satisfied, fairly satisfied, fairly dissatisfied, or very dissatisfied?" Only 27 percent answered very or fairly satisfied, whereas 70 percent answered very or fairly dissatisfied.[67] President Pastrana's attempts to negotiate a political end to the conflict have not found favor with many Colombians. When asked in 2000, "The manner in which the president has handled security has been very good, good, neither good nor bad, bad or very bad," only 19 percent said good or very good.[68]

The extent of the problem is detailed by the following assessment of different institutions, shown in Table 5.8.

Table 5.8

Institution	**Confidence**	**Lack of Confidence**	**Confidence**
	1997	**1997**	**2001**
Church	82%	18%	78%
Armed Forces	60%	38%	49%
Legal System	47%	51%	
Press	45%	54%	51%
Police	49%	50%	
National Government	35%	62%	
Political Parties	17%	81%	
Congreso Nacional	24%	73%	14%
Civil Service	37%	66%	
Companies	57%	41%	

Source: World Values Survey, 1997. 2001 Latinobarometro. Responses of confident include the percentage of valid responses who answered the following: great deal of confidence and quite a lot of confidence. Responses of lack of includes not very much confidence or none at all.

When asked, "I am going to name a number of organizations. For each one, could you tell me how much confidence you have in them: Is it a great deal of confidence, quite a lot of confidence, not very much confidence, or none at all?" Only the Catholic Church, the armed forces, and companies enjoy the confidence of more than half of respondents. The legal system, the police, the national government, political parties, parliament, and civil service suffer great levels of a lack of confidence among Colombians.

Democratic Stability

Colombian democratic stability, in terms of citizen support, appears strong. However, other forms of rule also enjoy some support.

In Table 5.9, the responses to the following question are provided. "I'm going to describe various types of political systems and ask what you think about each as a way of governing this country. For each one, would you say it is a very good, fairly good, fairly bad, or very bad way of governing this country?"

Table 5.9

	Acceptable	Unacceptable
Strong Leader	51%	44%
Experts	68%	28%
Army Rule	32%	63%
Democratic System	82%	14%

Source: World Values Survey, 1997. Responses of acceptable include the percentage of valid responses answering very good or fairly good. Responses of unacceptable include the percentage of valid responses answering very bad or fairly bad.

Interestingly, the only option that was viewed as unacceptable by more than half of the respondents was army rule. However, strong leader and expert rule were viewed as acceptable by more than half of the respondents. In an earlier survey, democracy is viewed as preferable. Respondents were asked, "Which of the following do you agree with most: 'Democracy is preferable to any other kind of government' or 'In certain situations, an authoritarian government can be preferable to a democratic government' or 'To people like me, it doesn't matter whether we have a democratic government or a nondemocratic government.'"

Table 5.10

	Democracy is preferable	Authoritarian government	It's the same
1996	60%	20%	18%
1997	69%		
1998	55%		
2000	50%		
2001	46%		

Source: Latinobarómetro 1996, 2001.

Table 5.10 shows that democracy is still preferred by a majority of respondents. However, for Latin America's oldest democracy, the size of the majority is modest. Although democracy is preferred, Colombians in general are not satisfied with the way democracy works. When asked, "In general, would you say that you are very satisfied, fairly satisfied, or not at all satisfied with the way democracy works in Colombia?" fewer than half of Colombians report satisfaction.

Table 5.11

Satisfaction with how democracy works in Colombia

1996	1997	1998	2000	2001
16%	40%	24%	27%	14%

Source: Latinobarómetro 1996, 2001.

Only 16 percent were satisfied in 1996. With a new president in 1997, that number rose to forty percent, still shy of a majority. By the end of Pastrana's term, that optimism had evaporated, leaving only 14 percent satisfied with democracy as practiced in Colombia.

Prospects for Plan Colombia[69]

President Pastrana's Plan Colombia, introduced in Fall 1999, is aimed to combat drug trafficking and reduce drug cultivation by 50 percent, strengthen Colombian political and judicial institutions, sponsor alternative development in coca growing areas, and regain the initiative in the conflict with the guerrillas. The estimated cost of these programs is $7.5 billion dollars. Colombia requested aid from the international community, the European Union, and the United States. Colombia itself has committed 4 billion dollars to the effort.[70] The United States has already committed 1.3 billion to the plan, whereas the European Union has resisted giving its full share of aid due to concerns about the nature of the plan.

U.S. Aid

The majority of U.S. aid to Colombia under the 2000–2001 plan goes to either the police or the military. The idea is that a stronger Colombian military will force the drug-financed rebels to seriously negotiate peace. A total of $589.2 million dollars is for military aid and $363.1 million for police aid. The remaining $238 million dollars in the aid package is distributed among alternative development, aid to the displaced, human rights, judicial reform, law enforcement, and peace efforts. The final aid package of $1.319 billion contained a human rights certification aspect, in which the government of Colombia was required to meet six conditions or receive a national security waiver in order to receive the aid. The conditions are

1. The president of Colombia must issue a written order demanding that all military personnel facing credible allegations of human rights violations be tried in civilian courts.
2. The commander general of the Colombian armed forces must promptly suspend those facing credible allegations of human rights violations or of participating in paramilitary groups.
3. The Colombian armed forces must fully cooperate with the investigations of civilian authorities in the investigation of those accused of human rights violations.
4. The Colombian government must actively prosecute paramilitary leaders and members, and any military personnel who assist them, in civilian courts.
5. The Colombian government must craft a plan to get rid of all coca and poppy production by the year 2005.
6. The Colombian armed forces are supposed to develop and deploy a Judge Advocate General Corps in field units to investigate military personnel misconduct.[71]

In the end, Colombia only met one of the requirements, but it received a waiver from President Clinton. He justified his action by praising President Pastrana's commitment to human rights and by expressing confidence that the Colombian government would eventually comply with all of the restrictions. He stated, "I don't think anyone seriously believes that either the guerrillas or the narco-traffickers will be more careful with human rights than this president."[72]

Criticism of the U.S. aid package focused on two concerns. Many were concerned that U.S. aid was really being used for counterinsurgency purposes. Others wanted to make sure that U.S. aid would not be used to benefit groups implicated in human rights violations. Some critics have asked why the Plan Colombia focused on actions in southern Colombia, a traditional rebel stronghold, instead of the northern regions where the paramilitaries were active in the drug trade. Critics thus suspected that the real purpose of this U.S. aid was to assist Colombia in its internal conflict, in addition to reducing the drug trade.

Previously in 1994, Amnesty International had charged the Pentagon with allowing counternarcotics aid to be used for counterinsurgency purposes. Others have criticized the U.S. aid as not being supportive of the peace process.

The government of Colombia is sensitive to criticisms of the U.S. aid package being predominately military in nature. However, it notes that in terms of overall planned spending for Plan Colombia, counternarcotics, security, and judicial reform account for 58 percent of the package, the peace process 1 percent, economic policy 14 percent, and democratization and social development 27 percent.[73]

President George W. Bush has proposed additional funding under the Andean Regional Initiative. Sensitive to criticisms that the earlier aid package was too focused on military aid, the new package is divided almost equally among law enforcement/security assistance and social development, economic development, and institutional reform. The total package of $882 million is divided among the Andean nations; however, Colombia is slated to receive 45 percent of the total funding, totaling $399 million. However, $253 million of the aid to Colombia is military or security in nature.[74] The rest, $146 million, would go to development and reform programs such as USAID programs dealing with reforming the judiciary, improving local governments, crop substitution, and alternative development.[75]

Since the tragic events of September 11, 2001, in the United States, U.S. policy toward Colombia has become more focused on the guerrilla problem, as opposed to limiting its aid only to counternarcotics efforts.[76] Consequently, the Bush administration wants to end the counterinsurgency versus counternarcotics distinction in the law. Currently, Congress is considering new counternarcotic and counterinsurgency aid for Colombia.

The Response of the European Union

In May 2001, the European Union (EU) announced plans to give $330 million in funding to Colombia. However, EU officials have been consistent in denouncing the military emphasis of the U.S. aid program. Instead, EU aid is focused on strengthening democracy and helping individual farmers to switch to legal crops. According to EU External Relations Commissioner Chris Patten, "We are supporting the peace process in Colombia. We are not supporting any military plans or activities whatsoever." Instead, the EU is interested in a "comprehensive and balanced approach" that would include manual coca crop eradication as opposed to aerial crop spraying. Patton stressed that any counterdrug policy "needs to be backed up by long term alternative income-generating plans [and meet] the social needs of the population."[77] The EU opposes aerial spraying because it does not provide a long-term solution for the farmers in the area. In addition, the main herbicide used, glyphosate, is banned in several U.S. states, including Florida, because of its potential environmental effects. In January 2001, a delegation from the UN High Commission for Refugees (UNHCR) visited an area in Colombia where glyphosate was used. They reported the area as "desolate" with "indiscriminate destruction of the jungle, legal crops, medicinal plants and fish ponds. There is clear evidence that wildlife has fled, rivers are contaminated and production in the region has fallen." In human terms, many health problems have been reported and the spaying contributes to the internal displacement in Colombia.[78] In February 2002, the EU said it would provide $30 million dollars to encourage development in the region of Magdalena Medio. This money is the first part of the EU aid approved the year before to support reform.[79]

Conclusion

An effective plan will have to not only address security concerns, but also concerns of integration and reform of institutions to regain citizen confidence in institutions. Does the Plan Colombia aim to achieve all of this? To answer this, two problems need to be addressed. First, the heavily military focus of the U.S. aid plan will undeniably intensify the conflict, leading to greater casualties and a decrease in security for Colombians. The intensification of the conflict will also lead to more internal displacement and will not promote greater integration or tolerance within the political community. Furthermore, an emphasis on aerial eradication undermines the economic stability of the country, exacerbates internal displacement, and creates resentment of the citizens toward the state, undermining citizen confidence. Moreover, the reluctance of the United States to enforce the human rights components of its aid package does not promote compliance with international human rights protocol. Finally, more attention should be focused on the paramilitaries who are responsible for a majority of the violence and who are involved in the drug trade. Since the Barco government in Colombia, the government has defended a theory of "cause and effect, according to which the paramilitary groups were a result of the guerrilla groups."[80] However, the paramilitaries need to be dealt with as a powerful source of violence and the drug trade. A successful plan would work to strengthen security, integration, and citizen confidence and it would support the peace process. The purpose-based Aristotelian approach is particularly well suited to the Colombian case, which procedurally appears to be very stable given the decades of democratic elections, but where the reality is of a state that has never had effective control over its territory or been able to achieve its rudimentary purposes.

Notes

1. Under the administration of George W. Bush, this plan is now called the Andean Regional Initiative.

2. Some scholars in the philosophy of science have argued for an Aristotelian approach to politics. See the works of Stephen Salkever, Martha Nussbaum, Leo Strauss, Bernard Yack, and Alasdair MacIntyre. For an application of this approach to a comparative study of violence, see Jennifer S. Holmes, *Terrorism and Democratic Stability* (Manchester, U.K.: Manchester University Press, 2001).

3. Max Weber, "Politics as a Vocation," in *From Max Weber: Essays in Sociology* Edited by H. H. Gerth and C. Wright Mills. (New York: Oxford University Press, 1946), 77–8.

4. Linz, 1978, 58.

5. Robert Dahl, *A Preface to Democratic Theory* (Chicago: University of Chicago Press, 1956)

6. Weber, "Politics as a Vocation," 79.

7. According to Aristotle, the most practicable form of constitution is not always a form of rule by the many. Aristotle believed that there were good forms of rule by one and rule by few. This idea is rejected by many contemporary scholars who believe that only democracy is preferred. It is not uncommon to find normative references such as Guillermo O'Donnell and Philippe Schmitter's statement that "political democracy constitutes per se a desirable goal." in *Transitions from Authoritarian Rule: Tentative Conclusions about Uncertain Democracies* Baltimore, Md.: Johns Hopkins University Press, 1986, 3.

8. Aristotle, *Politics.* Translated by Earnest Barker. London: Oxford University Press, 1958, 11, 112.

9. Stephen Salkever, "Aristotle's Social Science" *Political Theory* 9 No. 4, (November 1981), 492.

10. Salkever, 1981, 492

11. Leo Strauss, *Natural Right and History* (Chicago: University of Chicago Press, 1965), 6.

12. The component of attempting to achieve the good is inseparable from the Aristotelian approach. It would be inconsistent to call an approach Aristotelian that denied the value component. However, this does not mean that the approach needs to be disregarded by those who disagree with the incorporation of empirically unverifiable aspects. The orientation of the study is directed by the quest for the good, however, an empirical component remains, one that still may be examined according to those who may disagree with the approach in general.

13. Aristotle, 1958, 111.

14. Aristotle, *Nicomachean Ethics* Translated by David Ross. (Oxford, England: Oxford University Press, 1980), 110–6. (NE1130a15–1132b20).

15. Aristotle, 1958, 41.

16. Alasdair MacIntyre, *After Virtue* (Notre Dame, Ind.: University of Notre Dame Press, 1984), 152.

17. Aristotle, 1958, 213.

18. Rafael Pardo, "Colombia's Two Front War," *Foreign Affairs,* (July/August 2000), 65.

19. Colombia shattered the world record for the number of trade unionists killed in 2000. In fact, more trade unionists were killed in Colombia than in the entire world the year before. *Colombia: Annual Survey of Violations of Trade Union Rights (2001)* International Confederation of Free Trade Unions.

20. International Press Institute, *2001 World Press Freedom Review*. Available online at www.freemedia.at/wpfr/world.html.

21. David Bacon, "The Coca Cola Killings," *American Prospect* (28 January 2002), 14

22. Granada and Rojas "Violence in Colombia: Building a Sustainable Peace and Social Capital" World Bank: Washington D.C., 2000 Table 2.

23. Michael Shifter, "Colombia on the Brink," *Foreign Affairs* (July/August 1999), 15.

24. James Petras, "The FARC Faces the Empire" *Latin American Perspectives,* Issue 114, Vol. 27, No. 5 (September 2000), 134.

25. Jonathan Hartlyn, "Colombia: The Politics of Violence and Accommodation" in *Democracy in Developing Countries,* Volume 4, ed., Juan Linz, Larry Diamond and Jonathan Hartlyn (Baltimore, Md.: Johns Hopkins University Press, 1993), 318–9.

26. Harvey Kline, *State Building and Conflict Resolution in Colombia* (Tuscaloosa, Ala.: University of Alabama Press, 1999), 18, 198.

27. Bruce Bagley, "Drug Trafficking, Political Violence and U.S. Policy in Colombia in the 1990s" *Mama Coca* 2001 (Accessed 15 December 2002) www.mamacoca.org/bagley_drugs_and_violence_en.htm.

28. Bagley, 2001.

29. Francisco Thoumi, Why the Illegal Psychodelic Drug Use Industry Grew in Colombia" in *Drug Trafficking in the Americas,* eds., B. M. Bagley and W. O. Walker (Coral Gables, Fla.: North-South Center, University of Miami Press, 1995).

30. Alejandro Reyes, "Drug Trafficking and the Guerrilla Movement in Colombia" in *Drug Trafficking in the Americas,* eds. B. M. Bagley and W. O. Walker (Coral Gables, Fla.: North-South Center, University of Miami Press, 1995).

31. Fabio Castillo, *Los nuevos jinetes de la cocaína* (Bogotá, Colombia: Oveja Negra, 1996).

32. U.S. Government, International Narcotics Strategy Report, 1999.

33. Reyes, 125.

34. Reyes, 122. See also Roberto Steiner "Hooked on Drugs: Colombian-U.S. Relations" in *The United States and Latin America: The New Agenda,* ed. Victor Bulmer-Thomas and James Dunkerley (London: Institute of Latin American Studies, University of London, 1999), 171.

35. "U.S. Drug Chief Tries to Boost Colombian Resolve," *Washington Post,* November 21, 2000, A22.

36. House of Representatives Committee on International Relations. *U.S. Narcotics Policy Toward Colombia.* 104th Cong. 2d. sess., 47.

37. Bruce Bagley, "Drug Trafficking, Political Violence and U.S. Policy in Colombia in the 1990s," *Mama Coca,* 2001 (Accessed 15 December 2002) www.mamacoca.org/bagley_drugs_and_violence_en.htm.

38. Fernando Cubides, "The Paramilitaries" *Violence in Colombia 1990–2000 Waging War and Negotiating Peace,* eds. Charles Bergquist, Ricardo Peñaranda, and Gonzalo Sánchez. (Wilmington, Del.: SR Books), 2001.

39. Bruce Bagley, "Drug Trafficking, Political Violence and U.S. Policy in Colombia in the 1990s," *Mama Coca,* 2001 (Accessed 15 December 2002)

www.mamacoca.org/bagley_drugs_and_violence_en.htm.

40. Bagley, 2001.

41. Margarita Martinez, "Colombia Paramilitary Boss Speaks Out," Associated Press, February 12, 2002.

42. Jason Webb, "Colombia Warlord to Free Venezuelan, Quit AUC Role," Reuters, 12 July 2002.

43. "Colombian Right-Wing Fighters Disband," *Reuters*, 19 July 2002.

44. Scott Wilson, "Colombia's Rights cleaning Campaign," *Washington Post,* 17 April 2001, 1.

45. Bureau of Democracy, Human Rights and Labor, U.S. Department of State, February 25, 2000. (Accessed 15 December 2002) www.state.gov/www/global/human_rights/1999_hrp_report/colombia.html.

46. *Annual Report Colombia,* Amnesty International, 1998.

47. *Annual Report Colombia,* Amnesty International, 2001.

48. Organization of American States, "OAS Inter-American Human Rights Commission 2000 Report: Colombia."

49. Fact Sheet provided by the Bureau for International Narcotics and Law Enforcement Affairs, April 23, 1999.

50. For an in-depth overview of the responses to the guerrilla and drug conflict, see Alejandro Reyes, "Drug Trafficking and the Guerrilla Movement in Colombia" *Drug Trafficking in the Americas,* eds. Bruce Bagley and William Walker. (Miami, Fla: North-South Center Press, 1995) and Roberto Steiner "Hooked on Drugs: Colombian-U.S. Relations" in *The United States and Latin America: The New Agenda* ed. Victor Bulmer—Thomas and James Dunkerley (London: Institute of Latin American Studies, University of London, 1999).

51. GAD (Support Group for Displaced People Organizations). "Report of Forced Displacement in Colombia 1999."

52. "Building Peace in the Midst of War: Civil Society Initiatives in Colombia: Introduction." Seminar hosted by Washington Office on Latin America at George Washington University in Washington D.C. on 3 May 2000.

53. Charles Gepp, "Colombia's Kidnapped Candidate," *Christian Science Monitor,* 12 March 2002.

54. "Cease-fire Possible in Colombia, President Says" *Associated Press*, 20 March 2002, and "Colombia's ELN rebels propose 6-month truce," *Reuters,* March 20, 2002.

55. "Get Tough Presidential Candidate Gains Momentum in Colombia Congressional Election," *Associated Press,* 11 March 2002

56. Geov Parrish, "Call This a Plan?" WorkingForChange.com, February 11, 2002.

57. "U.N. Considers Proposal to Mediate Colombian War," *Reuters*, 28 May 2002.

58. Mauricio Ruben, "La violencia en Colombia: dimesionamiento y políticas de control" Serie de documentos de trabajo R 345, Interamerican Development Bank, Washington, D.C., October 1998, 42–9.

59. Javier Giraldo, "Corrupted Justice and the Schizophrenic State in Colombia" *Social Justice,* 26 no. 4 (1999).

60. Organization of American States, "OAS Inter-American Human Rights Commission 2000 Report: Colombia."

61. Yadira Ferrer, "Gov't Takes FARC Terrorism Charges to UN," *Inter Press Service,* 10 April 2002.

62. Republic of Colombia. "Plan Colombia and U.S. Support for Democracy, Peace and Economic Prosperity in Colombia," June 2001.

63. World Values Survey, 1997. Responses of "agree" include the percentage of valid responses answering strongly agree or agree. Responses of "disagree" include the percentage of valid responses answering strongly disagree or disagree.

64. *La fuerza pública y los derechos humanos en Colombia,* 29

65. "Guerra para rato" *Semana* 2 June 1992, 30–35

66. "La democracia en peligro: Los alcaldes como objectivo military," CIDEC, (August 2000).

67. World Values Survey, 1997. Responses of "satisfied" include the percentage of valid responses answering very satisfied or fairly satisfied. Responses of "unacceptable" include the percentage of valid responses answering very dissatisfied or fairly dissatisfied.

68. Barometro Iberoamericano. *Informe de Opinión de Latinoamerica y de la Peninsula Ibérica Enero 2001* Consorcio Iberoamericano de Empresas de Investigación de Mercados y Asesoramiento, Dec. 2000–Jan. 2001.

69. Under President George W. Bush, the Plan Colombia is now referred to as the Andean Counter-drug Initiative.

70. A copy of the Plan Colombia is available online at www.usip.org/library/pa/colombia/adddoc/plan_colombia_101999.html.

71. (Section 3201, PL 106–246)

72. Miles Pomper, "Leaders Push Trade Aid for Colombia," *CQ Weekly,* 2 September 2000, 2037.

73. Republic of Colombia. "Plan Colombia and U.S. Support for Democracy, Peace and Economic Prosperity in Colombia" June 2001.

74. U.S. Department of State, "On the Record Briefing: Andean Regional Initiative" 18 May 2001.

75. Christopher Marquis, "New Drug Plan Shifts Focus in Latin America," *New York Times,* May 17, 2001.

76. This division in law has always been difficult to implement on the ground. See Otto Reich, "Crucial Battle for Colombia," *Washington Times,* 19 July 2002.

77. David Adams and Paul de la Garza, "EU Backs Colombian Peace," *St. Petersburg Times,* 3 May 2001.

78. Nelson Fredy Padilla Castro, "Toxic Rain Kills More than the Coca," *UNESCO Courier,* (May 2001), 10–1.

79. "Settling Nationalism Aside," *Associated Press*, 7 February 2002.

80. Harvey Kline, *State Building and Conflict Resolution in Colombia, 1986–1994* (Tuscaloosa, Ala.: University of Alabama Press, 1999), 76–77.

Chapter Six

The Kantian Peace through a Radical Theoretic Lens

Kirk Bowman and Seán Patrick Eudaily

The belief in the proposition that democratic states do not go to war with one another is both widespread among and intuitively pleasing to a large number of political scientists.[1] A leading advocate of the democratic peace proposal, James Lee Ray, attributes this popularity to the "stunning simplicity of the democratic peace proposition, and the equally impressive simple evidence that supports it."[2] However, not everyone is convinced. The democratic peace proposition has been challenged from a number of angles—there are exceptions to the rule, democratic states are not pacific in their dealings with nondemocracies, the small number of democracies and interstate wars make the statistical correlation potentially spurious, and no satisfactory theory has yet emerged to explain the empirical result.[3] Defenders such as Ray have attempted to engage such critiques with varying degrees of success.[4] However, a new (or rather a rediscovered) argument has emerged recently from within scholars of the democratic peace. Advocates such as John Oneal and Bruce Russett have led a "return to Kant" in arguing that democracy is only one part of a larger liberal peace that also involves international trade and the institutionalization of nonanarchic relations between liberal states.[5] This paper seeks not so much to interject itself into those earlier debates as to open a new line of argument and analysis over the dominant liberal readings of the Kantian peace based upon the perspective of radical political theory.

The major benefit that a radical approach brings to a discussion of the liberal peace proposition is to provide a critical, alternative lens through which to view the three "definitive articles" of Kant's program for perpetual peace. The first article, that states should have a republican form, has received the majority of the attention of "democratic" peace research. Although Kant distinguished a republican constitution from *democratic* politics, the modern liberal-democratic states that are the subject of most empirical research are certainly more liberal than democratic.[6] However, the mainstream reading of liberal regimes as internally free and pacific is challenged by a radical view based upon Michel Foucault's concept of "governmentality."[7] The second article of perpetual peace, the cessation of anarchic relations between liberal states, has been written as an intermediate point between "realist ad hoc alliances" and "full-fledged collective security," and has been operationalized as interdependence via international organizations.[8] Richard Ashley's vision of the constitution of anarchy and the "heroic practice" of states reorients our attention to how interdependence among like states also entails the marginalization and abuse of others.[9] Kant's final article of perpetual peace involves the creation of minimal cosmopolitan laws (primarily hospitality to foreigners) necessary for free trade. Recent scholarship has focused on the role of international trade as the third major leg of the liberal peace.[10] Yet, there is a long tradition of radical theory that addresses the relationship between international trade (with the uneven development it brings) and conflict. By reengaging the traditional Marxian debate over imperialism one is able to further a critique of this "third leg" of the Kantian system.[11]

In this paper we seek to advance a framework for analysis which links the democratic peace proposition, derived in international relations theory, to a more developed schema for viewing the internal constitution of states. This approach attempts to problematize the assumptions, critically evaluate the conclusions, and explore the potentialities of alternative lines of inquiry into the connection between democratic states and peace. In addition to the theoretical critique, we establish the empirical observation that two groups of countries constitute the vast majority of contiguous democratic dyads where the greatest possibility of democratic wars would exist—the advanced industrial nations and Latin America. We propose two alternative explanations for the absence of interstate war within these subsets of countries. The advanced capitalist countries do not wage war against each other as they act as an oligopoly and Latin American countries rarely wage wars against each other whether they are democratic or not, while frequently waging war against their own populations. Until a more satisfying theoretical foundation for these discrete causal linkages between democracy and peace is presented, the liberal reading of the democratic peace will remain unconvincing. Thus, our approach seeks to reorient our view of the Kantian system to the perspective of the periphery of both the discipline of political science (radical political theory) and the international system itself (Latin America).

Framework for an Alternative Explanation of the Democratic Peace

In our construction of an alternative approach for analyzing the Kantian peace we will be drawing on voices from the margins of both the fields of international relations and comparative politics. This framework seeks to locate some of the major exceptions and difficulties that plague traditional theories of the Kantian peace within a perspective that treats these events as symptoms of the practice of liberal peace rather than as anomalies. Thus we seek a vantage point from which one can see the "peaks and valleys" of the democratic peace. Unlike conventional approaches to the democratic peace proposition, our account makes explicit the exclusionary nature of *liberal* democracy in the world system. Much of this new framework draws upon Michel Foucault's studies of "governmentality," Richard K. Ashley's concept of "heroic practice," and the debate over the question of imperialism that emerges from the Marxian tradition—V. I. Lenin's critique of Karl Kautsky's theory of "ultra-imperialism," Kwame Nkrumah's concept of "neocolonialism," and Michael Hardt and Antonio

Negri's recent arguments about an emerging "Empire."

Foucault and the Liberal Governmentality of Modern States

How is it that liberalism comes to be the ideal form of internal state constitution? To answer that question, we now turn to Foucault's discussion of the evolution of modern liberal governmentality—variously referred to as governmentality, government rationality, or the analytics of government.

The core of this approach is the treatment of government as "*la conduite de la conduite*," or "the conduct of conduct."[12] The conduct in question is both that of rulers and of the ruled. This is an early indication of the plural character of governmentality. The analysis of governmentality is focused on both the practices and "explicit *programmes*" of government.[13] Thus, a more detailed definition of governmentality would be as follows:

> Government[ality] is any more or less calculated and rational activity, undertaken by a multiplicity of authorities and agencies, employing a variety of techniques and forms of knowledge, that seeks to shape conduct by working through our desires, aspirations, interests, and beliefs, for definite but shifting ends and with a diverse set of relatively unpredictable consequences, effects, and outcomes.[14]

Any study of governmentality will then have to consider three axes of political practice—*techne*, or the techniques of government; *episteme*, or the practices of knowledge and truth; and *ethos*, or the modes of political subjectivity.[15] Taken as a whole, the investigation of these objects and themes constitutes governmentality as an independent research agenda focusing on "the contingent trajectories by which the state assumes its present and changing form."[16]

There are three concepts that are of central importance to governmentality. The first is the connection of a Foucauldian "microphysics" to the study of macropolitical practices, in the form of the modern state.[17] However, it is crucial to note that this analysis of state practices does not equate to a totalizing theory of the state, from which one should abstain such "as one might abstain from a indigestible meal."[18] A second aspect in this study will be the analysis of the *problematization* of government—in the form of critiquing the liberalism at the root of the Kantian peace. Mitchell Dean identifies such problematizations as a "key starting point in an analytics of government."[19] The final aspect of governmentality that will animate this work is, in direct opposition to "value-free" social science, the author's intent to fashion these analyses as a form of criticism.

> By making explicit the forms of rationality and thought that inhere in regimes of practices, by demonstrating the fragility of the ways in which we know ourselves and are asked to know ourselves, and the tissue of connections between how we know ourselves and how we govern and are governed, an analytics of government can remove the taken-for-granted character of these practices.[20]

Foucault distinguishes the modern, liberal form of government from its premodern predecessor "sovereignty." Therefore, like Krasner's recent argument, this study is based upon the evaluation that "the characteristics associated with sovereignty . . . do not provide an accurate description" of current state practice.[21] The governmentality approach, too, sees this as a long-standing fact. However, in the fifteenth and sixteenth centuries, sovereignty was the practice of both international and domestic affairs. The sovereign was concerned with his hierarchical position vis-à-vis others within and without a given territory. The only test of his rule was the fact of rule. "However rudimentary that apparatus might be it was sufficiently credible to sustain the ruler both domestically and internationally and, if it was not, he and possibly his realm might be replaced by another."[22]

This was the age of Machiavelli's Prince; states only came into being because of princes securing their sovereignty. Sovereignty was a system built on an organic conception of society (including its constituent classes) and oriented toward order and self-maintenance. "In every case, what characterizes the end of sovereignty, this common and general good, is in sum nothing other than submission to sovereignty. This means the end of sovereignty is circular: the end of sovereignty is the exercise of sovereignty."[23] The transformation from a sovereignty diagram to a governmental one was grounded in the development of new technologies of power and the resultant change in state capacity.

Power had only a weak capacity for "resolution," as one might say in photographic terms; it was incapable of an individualizing, exhaustive analysis of the social body. But the economic changes of the eighteenth century made it necessary to ensure the circulation of effects of power through progressively finer channels, gaining access to individuals themselves, to their bodies, their gestures, and all their daily actions.[24] Thus, in order to suppress resistance, the early modern state used great shows of sovereign power through the military and elaborate, public punishment, while the modern state uses surveillance, nongovernmental practices such as clinical medicine and psychiatry, and the discipline of the prison.

The dualism of a multiplicity of "individuals" and the unity of the sovereign state become the hallmark problematique of modernity. Liberalism describes the historical framing of that dilemma of governance. "Liberalism begins," Foucault says, "with the recognition of the incompatibility of the principles regulating the non-totalizing multiplicity of economic subjects of interest and those operating in the totalizing unity of legal-political sovereignty."[25]

Sovereignty does not simply fade away in the modern state. Rather it becomes one of a number of forms of power employed toward ends beyond its own perpetuation. Sovereignty's dominance is displaced from governing as a whole to the international sphere.

For the modern state "the finality of government resides in the pursuit of the perfection and intensification of the processes that it directs."[26] Liberal governmentality was a result of the confluence of three diagrams: the sovereignty model of its premodern counterpart, the pastoral diagram of the medieval

Church (as a shepherd caring for her flock), and the disciplinary model perfected by the "sciences of Man." This amalgamation resolved itself into two informal functions of liberal governmentality: the governance of bodies (*anatomo-politics*), such as the state interest in controlling drug use, and of the population (*bio-politics*) as expressed by the state interest in unemployment or poverty rates and risk factors. However, Foucault never followed this analysis of governmentality on the international level other than the comment that the "diplomatic-military technique, perfected on a European scale with the Treaty of Westphalia," was an essential element of liberal governmentality.[27] For a more detailed analysis of governmentality in world politics, we must turn to an account of the "heroic practice" of liberal states under/through international anarchy.

Ashley and the "Heroic Practice" of Modern States

Ashley sees the dominant discourse of international relations being obsessed with the "anarchy problematique." He sees both modern practice and discourse being founded upon "a dichotomy of sovereignty vs. anarchy, where the former term is privileged as a higher reality, a regulative ideal, and the latter term is understood in only a derivative and negative way, as a failure to live up to this ideal and as something that endangers this ideal."[28]

States thus assume that their internal constitution is ordered while their external relations are anarchic. Ashley sees this as a major pathology of modern thought, for states are rarely content to confront anarchy and rather most seek to order what is unordered. Ashley calls this inclination to impose order "heroic practice."[29] To impose order upon international relations, sovereignty must be superceded by some higher system of order. Therefore, the Kantian peace can be read as a result of "liberal democracy" serving as this higher order. Liberal states thus respect the integrity of other such states while still perceiving nondemocratic states as security challenges in an anarchic world. Treating the Kantian peace as a form of "heroic practice" is both consistent with Cederman's analysis of liberalism as a method of "tagging" like states as pacific and the subsequent formation of ideological alliances based upon such similitude, and also does so in a way that allows the connected violence (targeted at nonsimilar states and persons) of the Kantian system to be exposed.[30] This focus on the contradictions of the liberal peace leads us back to the constituent engine of such differentiation—the capitalist world system.

Ultra-Imperialism, Neo-Colonialism, and Empire as the "Arts of Government" for Advanced Capitalist States

In Kautsky's theory of "ultra-imperialism," Ashley's higher order and Foucault's capitalist state—whose concern is the pursuit of the perfection and intensification of the processes that it directs—are unambiguously defined as the effort on behalf of the advanced capitalist states to develop and maintain a capitalist oligopoly.[31] In this regard, Kautsky differed dramatically with Lenin, who insisted that capitalism would result in the core countries carving up the world into colonies in search of super-profits. According to Lenin, once potential colonies were depleted, declining profits would lead to a cannibalization of capitalism, where the advanced capitalist states would turn on each other in violent acts of war.[32] Kautsky instead argued that the advanced capitalist countries would eventually settle their differences, choosing collective exploitation of the periphery to internecine conflict. Kautsky thus predicted a lasting peace amongst the core capitalist countries—not because they were democracies but rather as a mechanism for protecting the oligopoly from which they all benefit. By the use of Foucault's notion of governmentality, we can link the question of the liberal internal constitution of states with a Marxian focus on liberal capitalism.

Many have taken the world wars as evidence that Lenin's arguments about imperialism were more sound than Kautsky's. However, it is important to remember that Kautsky believed that imperialism was not necessary to late capitalism, but rather a policy preferred by finance capital. Therefore, that conflict would emerge between core capitalist states that continued to practice imperialism as a policy is perfectly consistent with Kautsky's view. Something resembling "ultra-imperialism" does not appear until after World War II.

Ironically, it is the presence of the socialist states that galvanizes the liberal core to band together and abandon imperialist for ultra-imperialist policy. African theorist, and former president of Ghana, Kwame Nkrumah documents how the postwar changes in the periphery represent not an end, but rather the "last stage" of imperialism. He terms the new policy "neocolonialism" and identifies it with the simultaneous recognition of the political independence of former colonial possession and their continued economic domination by the core states.[33] Nkrumah writes, "Neocolonialism is the worst form of imperialism. For those who practice it, it means power without responsibility and for those who suffer from it, it means exploitation without redress."[34] Like Foucault's account, Nkrumah links this shift in international policy to the emergence of welfare liberalism in the core.[35] Neocolonialism is Kautsky's ultra-imperialism seen from the bottom up. In order to profit from Nkrumah's formulation, we must be attentive to not only conflict between liberal states in the periphery (particularly in Latin America), but more importantly, peripheral conflicts *funded* by the core.[36]

Michael Hardt and Antonio Negri have recently made a major contribution to this tradition by suggesting that we now stand on the cusp of a new era—beyond imperialism and into a global Empire. While their argument substantially follows ours on the evolution from imperialism to neocolonialism, one of their prime insights is that this emerging "imperial administration" separates political ends from bureaucratic means, acts as a differentiating rather than integrative mechanism, is legitimated through heterogeneous and indirect means, and is exercised first and foremost at local sites.[37] All of this must lead us towards approaching the Kantian peace, not as a system, but in its local and differentiated effects.

Foucault's micropolitical analysis, Ashley's account of anarchy, Kautsky's ultra-imperialism, Nkrumah's focus on the periphery, and Hardt and Negri's argument for the local character of imperial governmentality all point our inquiry to the margins and the specific articulations of the Kantian peace. For these reasons we will devote the remainder of this essay to the politics of Latin America. This has the added benefit of allowing us to further problematize two areas where the liberal peace has been the weakest in practice—interventions and civil wars.[38]

Linking the Concepts: The Dark Underside of the Kantian Peace

Ashley, Foucault, and the scholars of imperialism lead us to take a critical approach to the liberal peace, particularly for the peaceful behavior between advanced capitalist states. From Ashley we can take the idea that states seek to impose a higher ideal of order (i.e., liberal democracy) upon the supposed anarchy of international relations. Foucault presents us with an account of how and why liberal governments seek to promote/protect liberalism and capitalism within their own populations. Both writers outline the justification for a perfecting/heroic practice as being based upon the Western, modern states' reification of democracy as a higher order/object of governance. Kautsky predicted that advanced capitalist states would eventually discern that an oligopoly of core capitalist states would provide more utility than competition and conflict among the core countries, and both Nkrumah and Hardt and Negri have shown us how such a peace imposes violence at the periphery.

A reassessment of the Kantian peace derived from these sources contains four main assertions:

- Democracy becomes both the object and end of liberal, Western states—thus other democratic states are acknowledged and respected and treated as agents to be interacted with as opposed to nonentities to be acted upon (with force).
- Nonliberal states are seen as threats to the order/process of the Kantian system and thus are legitimate objects/targets for violent intervention.
- Individuals within states are legitimate/possible objects of "governing" and are thus held to the same ideals of liberalism as are other states, with the same potential consequences for those found to be anarchic/imperfect.
- Core capitalist states will prefer an oligopoly to competition and will have incentives to keep the peace among them.

This framework provides an alternative explanation for "peace" among the advanced capitalist democracies and simultaneously accounts for their willingness to regularly use force against periphery states—even against democracies such as Guatemala in 1954 and Chile in 1973. Given that the vast majority of geographically contiguous democratic states have been advanced capitalist countries, such as Canada and the United States, then an alternative explanation for the absence of war between such countries at least raises the possibility that the Kantian peace argument is spurious at best, and exploitive at worst.

The Democratic Peace and Latin America

It has been regularly noted that the total number of country-years of democracy is much lower than the number of nondemocratic country-years and undermines the task of reaching conclusions about the democratic peace. Not only is the total number of country-years of democracy low, but they are not evenly distributed throughout the countries of the world. A large number of country-years of democracy are concentrated in the advanced-capitalist countries. The previous section offers an alternative explanation for a lack of war amongst this subsample. Yet, democracy has emerged outside the core countries. This section presents evidence that the bulk of periphery country-years of democracy in contiguous states have been in Latin America. It is true that Latin American democracies rarely wage war with other Latin American democracies. Is this not evidence in support of the democratic peace? We argue that it is not—Latin American countries rarely wage wars with other Latin American countries whether they are democracies or not.

Contiguous Democratic Dyads in the Periphery

Since periphery countries are most likely to engage in interstate violent conflict with neighbors, we first determine the total number of contiguous democratic dyad years in Latin America and the rest of the periphery.[39] Through 1992, the total number of contiguous democratic dyad years in Latin America is 382. Given that there are a total of 2,485 country-years and many possible contiguous dyads per country, there are many more years of nondemocratic dyads than democratic dyads. Still, we have a sample of 382 possibilities for breakout of war between democracies.

In the rest of the periphery, that is the countries of Asia, the Middle East, and Africa, there are a total of 3,867 country years through 1992—fifty percent more country years than in Latin America. The number of years of contiguous democratic dyads in Asia, the Middle East, and Africa is much lower, however, totaling only ninety-eight years. Given the relative scarcity of interstate war, the chance of war between two democracies in Asia, the Middle East, and Africa is exceedingly small. It is difficult if not impossible to generate any meaningful support for or against the democratic peace from these seventy-six countries.

Table 6.1: Country-Years and Democracy in the Periphery

	Latin America	Asia, Middle East, Africa
Total Country Years through 1992[40]	2,485	3,867
Total Years of Contiguous Democratic Dyads	382	98

What type of support for the democratic peace can be generated from the Latin American experience? Is not an absence of war in the region—despite 382 years of contiguous democratic dyads—strong evidence for the democratic peace? We believe that it is not strong evidence, based on the long-held proposition that interstate wars between Latin American countries are scarce regardless of regime type.

Interstate Wars in Latin America

The observation of an absence of interstate wars between Latin American countries is not new. In Andreski's 1954 (1968) classic on military organization and development, Latin America is singled out as a region with a very particular military mission: "The military function has become introverted in Latin American republics; with few opportunities to fight for their countries, the soldiers remained preoccupied with internal politics and the search for personal and collective advantage."[41] Andreski goes on to note that in Latin America there are too many soldiers for a proper police function and too few for waging interstate wars. "A very important factor here (in Latin America) was the absence of the need for united effort in a common struggle against foreigners."[42] Others, including Bowman, LaFeber, and Janowitz, have noted the uniqueness of the Latin American military and the largely internal nature of their mission.[43] Erich Weede singles out the Latin America as a region that "seems to have suffered from parasitic praetorians more specialized in bossing, exploiting, killing, and torturing civilians than in fighting other nations' armed forces."

Is there evidence to support the proposition that Latin American countries rarely fight each other but are often plagued with internal warfare? The 1996 Correlates of War (COW) dataset yields the following evidence. Between 1816 and 1992 there were 11,158 total country-years in the world; 24.4 percent of those country-years are in Latin America and the Caribbean (22.3 percent in Latin America). There were seventy-five interstate wars with 1,000 or more battlefield deaths. Of those seventy-five, only nine were wars between Latin American countries—or twelve percent. Of these nine wars, only three had greater than 2,000 deaths and four barely met the COW standards, with the minimum number of 1,000 deaths. Since 1932, there has been only one war fought between Latin American countries, the 1969 Soccer War between Honduras and El Salvador.

In addition to a relative paucity of wars, especially since 1932, interstate Latin American wars are much less deadly than those in other parts of the world. The median number of battlefield deaths in the nine Latin American wars is 1,300 and the mean is 51,244. In contrast, the median for the other sixty-six wars in the COW dataset is 11,550 and the mean is 1,657,672.

The suggestion that Latin American countries are more likely than other countries to experience civil war is also supported by the COW dataset. Singer and Small identify 151 civil wars. While Latin America accounts for 22.3 percent of all country-years, it experiences 32 percent of all civil wars (48/151).

The scarcity of war and the relatively large number of years of contiguous democratic dyads in Latin America bias the empirical findings that support the democratic peace proposal. Latin America is the region of the periphery that has the most experience with democracy and Latin American countries rarely (and almost never after 1932 when democracy becomes slightly more widespread) fight each other, whether they are democratic regimes or not.

Conclusion

The empirical findings that show Latin American democracies as unlikely to fight each other, yet *more likely* to have civil conflicts in which the military is used to "govern" the domestic population, are striking. These results are either underexplained or unpredicted by the traditional discourse of the democratic peace proposition. In contrast, the critical framework developed in this paper suggests the likelihood of just such a result. The importance of having taken a comparativist, historicist approach in the production of this novel reading of Latin American practice should not be underestimated. Neither the critical framework nor the reading of events would have been possible without abjuring the universalistic perspective on both democracy and conflict that characterizes much of the democratic peace literature. Thus we hope that our study will decenter the discourse of the democratic peace proposal by highlighting the importance of historical and regional contexts; the nature of the capitalist world system; and the intertext of internal militarization, democracy, and peace.

Notes

1. For recent reviews of this literature see Steve Chan, "In Search of Democratic Peace: Problems and Promise," *International Studies Quarterly,* Vol. 41, Issue 1, 59–91, (May 1997); James Lee Ray, "Does Democracy Cause Peace?" *Annual Review of Political Science* 1 (1997); and Bruce Russett and Harvey Starr, "From Democratic Peace to Kantian Peace: Democracy and Conflict in the International System," in Manus Midlarsky, ed., *Handbook of War Studies*, 2nd ed. (Ann Arbor, Mich.: University of Michigan Press, forthcoming).

2. Ray, James Lee. "The Democratic Path to Peace." *Journal of Democracy* 8, no. 2. (1997), 50.

3. For critiques of the democratic peace proposition see Steve Chan, "Mirror, Mirror on the Wall . . . Are Freer Countries More Pacific?" *Journal of Conflict Resolution* 28 (December, 1984); Henry S. Farber and Joanne Gowa, "Common Interests or Common Polities? Reinterpreting the Democratic Peace." *Journal of Politics* Vol. 59, Issue 2, 393–417, May 1997; Gowa, *Ballots and Bullets: The Elusive Democratic Peace* (Princeton, N.J.: Princeton, 1999), and Jack Snyder, *From Voting to Violence: Democratization and Nationalist Conflict* (New York: W. W. Norton and Co., 2000).

4. Ray, "The Democratic Path to Peace," 58–59.

5. See Oneal and Russett, "The Kantian Peace: The Pacific Benefits of Democracy, Interdependence, and International Organizations, 1885–1992," *World Politics* 52, no. 1 (1999); and Lars-Erik Cederman, "Modeling the Democratic Peace as a Kantian Selection Process," *Journal of Conflict Resolution* 45, no. 4 (2001).

6. It is stunning to note how Kant's distinction between a republican constitution and a democratic government has been ignored by "democratic peace" scholars. Kant writes: "*democracy*, in the proper sense of the term, is necessarily a *despotism* . . . The democratic system makes [a republican constitution] impossible, for everyone wants to rule. One can therefore say, the smaller the number of persons who exercise the power of the nation (the number of rulers), the more they represent and the closer the political constitution approximates the possibility of republicanism." Immanuel Kant, "To Perpetual Peace: A Philosophical Sketch," in *Perpetual Peace and Other Essays*, Ted Humphry, ed. (Indianapolis, Ind.: Hackett Publishing, 1983[1795]).

7. Michel Foucault, "Governmentality." In *The Foucault Effect: studies in governmentality*. Graham Burchell, Colin Gordon, and Peter Miller, eds. (Chicago: University of Chicago Press, 1991).

8. For the former see Cederman, "Modeling the Democratic Peace as a Kantian Selection Process," 476; and for the latter see Oneal and Russett, "The Classical Liberals were Right: Democracy, Interdependence, and Conflict, 1950–85," *International Studies Quarterly* 40, no. 2 (1997); Russett, Oneal, and David R. Davis, "The Third Leg of the Kantian Tripod: International Organizations and Militarized Disputes, 1950–85," *International Organization* 52, no. 3 (1998); and Oneal and Russett, "The Kantian Peace," (1999).

9. Richard K. Ashley, "Untying the Sovereign State: A Double Reading of the Anarchy Problematique." *Millenium: Journal of International Studies* 17, no. 2 (1988).

10. See for example Harry Bliss and Bruce Russett, "Democratic Trading Partners: The Liberal Connection." *Journal of Politics* 58, no. 4 (1998); James Morrow, Randolph Siverson, and Tessa Tabares, "The Political Determinants of International Trade: The Major Powers, 1907–90." *American Political Science Review* 92, no. 3 (1998); Soo Yeon Kim, "Ties That Bind: The Role of Trade in International Conflict Processes" Ph.D. diss., Yale University, 1998; and Michael Mousseau, "Market Prosperity, Democratic Consolidation, and Democratic Peace." *Journal of Conflict Resolution* 44, no. 4 (2000).

11. See in particular V. I. Lenin, *Imperialism: The Highest Stage of Capitalism*. (New York: International Publishers, 1979[1917]); Kwame Nkrumah, *Neo-Colonialism: The Last Stage of Imperialism*. (New York: International Publishers, 1969[1965]); and Michael Hardt and Antonio Negri, *Empire*. (Cambridge, Mass.: Harvard UP, 2000).

12. Mitchell Dean, *Critical and Effective Histories: Foucault's Methods and Historical Sociology*, (London: Routledge Press, 1994), 176.

13. Michel Foucault, "Questions of Method," in Graham Burchell, Colin Gordon, and Peter Miller (eds.), *The Foucault Effect: Studies in Governmentality* (Chicago: University of Chicago Press, 1991), 80.

14. Dean, *Governmentality: Power and Rule in Modern Society* (London: Sage Publications, 1999), 11.

15. Dean, *Governmentality*, 18.

16. Dean, *Critical and Effective Histories*, 181.

17. Dean, *Critical and Effective Histories*, 175–9.

18. Dean, *Critical and Effective Histories*, 177.

19. Dean, *Governmentality*, 27.

20. Dean, *Governmentality*, 36.

21. Stephen D. Krasner, *Sovereignty: Organized Hypocrisy* (Princeton, N.J.: Princeton University Press, 1999), 237.

22. Robert H. Jackson, *Quasi-states: Sovereignty, International Relations, and the Third World* (Cambridge, U.K.: Cambridge University Press, 1990), 53.

23. Foucault, "Governmentality," 95.

24. Michel Foucault, "The Eye of Power," in Colin Gordon (ed.), *Power/Knowledge: selected interviews and other writings, 1972–1977* (New York: Pantheon Books, 1980), 151–2.

25. Foucault, "Eye of Power," 137.

26. Foucault, "Governmentality," 95.

27. Foucault, "Governmentality," 104.

28. Ashley, "Untying the Sovereign State," 230.

29. Ashley, "Untying the Sovereign State," 232–3.

30. Cederman, "Modeling the Democratic Peace," 475–7.

31. "Kautsky writes: 'from the purely economic point of view it is not impossible that capitalism will yet go through a new phase, that the end of the extension of the policy of the cartels to foreign policy, the phase of ultra-imperialism,' . . . a phase of 'the joint exploitation of the world by internationally combined finance capital.'" Quoted in Lenin, *Imperialism*, 94.

32. Lenin, *Imperialism*, 98.

33. Nkrumah, *Neo-Colonialism*, ix.

34. Nkrumah, *Neo-Colonialism*, xi.

35. Nkrumah, *Neo-Colonialism*, 255.

36. Nkrumah, *Neo-Colonialism*, 239 and xvi, respectively.

37. Hardt and Negri, *Empire*, 339–42.

38. For a good summary of the conventional debate surrounding the former see John A. Tures, "Democracies and Intervening States: A Critique of Kegley and Hermann," and "Addressing Concerns about Applying the Democratic Peace Arguments to Interventions." *Journal of Peace Research* 38, no. 2 (2001); and Margaret G. Hermann and Charles W. Kegley, Jr., "Democracies and Intervention: Is There a Danger Zone in the Democratic Peace?" *Journal of Peace Research* 38, no. 2 (2001). For a recent contribution to a discussion of the latter see Havard Hegre, Tanja Ellignsen, Scott Gates, and Nils Petter Gleditsch, "Towards a Democratic Civil Peace? Democracy, Political Change, and Civil War, 1816–1992." *American Political Science Review* 95, no. 1 (2001).

39. We employ the Political Regime Dataset scoring countries with more than six months of "Democracies" or "Semi-Democracies" as democratic for a given year. See Gasiorowski, Mark J. 1996. "An Overview of the Political Regime Change Dataset." *Comparative Political Studies* 29(4):469–83.

40. Total country years and all data on wars derived from Singer, J. David, and Melvin Small. Correlates of war project: International and civil war data, 1816-1992. J. David Singer and Melvin Small, 1993. Ann Arbor, Mich.: Inter-University Consortium for Political and Social Research, 1994.

41. Stanislav Andreski. *Military Organization and Society* (Stanford, Calif.: Stanford University Press. 1954(1968). 211.

42. Andreski, *Military Organization,* 211.

43. Kirk S. Bowman. *Militarization, Democracy, and Development: The Perils of Praetorianism in Latin America* (University Park, Pa.: The Pennsylvania State University Press. 2002); Morris Janowitz. *The Military in the Political Development of New Nations* (Chicago: University of Chicago Press. 1964); and Walter LaFeber. *Inevitable Revolutions: The United States in Central America* (New York: Norton. 1984).

Chapter Seven

Imagining Legal Fairness: A Comparative Perspective

Robert A. Kahn[1]

The right to a fair trial is a bedrock of the rule of law as the term is understood in liberal democracies. But what, precisely, do we mean when we say a defendant deserves a fair trial? An American might answer that the accused deserves a trial before a jury of his or her peers. At this trial, the person accused must be able to present evidence and question the prosecution's evidence. Lawyers and Court-TV addicts will add to this a number of technical rules such as the prohibition against hearsay. When a court fails to follow these rules, the trial will be seen as fundamentally unfair. In serious cases, this will result in reversal on appeal and people will speak of a travesty of justice. In Germany, by contrast, the judge gathers the evidence, decides who shall testify, and questions the witnesses; the prosecution and defense are limited to making short speeches at the end of trial. The judge and jury then retire together to consider the verdict.[2] While an American might find this outrageous, Germans take the rights of the accused every bit as seriously as Americans.

If liberal democracies share a commitment to the accused, each has its own image of legal fairness. These images shape how citizens in liberal democracies think about the criminal justice system and evaluate the fairness of particular trials. Just as Americans judge the O. J. Simpson case against the background of the ideal American criminal trial, Germans set the proceedings against Holocaust deniers against a specifically German image of a fair criminal trial. To operationalize these competing images of legal fairness—in essence competing political theories of the law—I develop the idea of the legal imaginary, by which I mean the set of values, experiences, and laws that guide how lawyers, judges, and citizens talk about legal fairness. Each legal system has its own legal imaginary. To demonstrate differences in legal imaginaries and their practical significance, I examine how four different legal systems (Germany, France, Canada, and the United States) responded to a shared legal problem (whether—and how—to prosecute Holocaust deniers under group libel and hate speech laws).

I.

While the various ways liberal democracies imagine legal fairness should be fertile ground for students of comparative law and politics, most writing on foreign legal systems falls into two narrow categories. Students of comparative law address doctrinal variations in legal systems. As most of this writing concerns fine points of particular legal doctrines—such as the law of contracts, torts, or criminal procedure—it is of little help in exploring how different legal systems imagine legal fairness. On a more general level, however, comparative law has an important contribution to make to the comparative study of legal fairness. This is the cleavage between inquisitorial and adversarial legal systems.[3] The key difference relates to the role of the judge. In inquisitorial or civil law countries, which include all of Continental Europe, the judge presents the evidence, questions witnesses, and plays a major role in reaching the ultimate verdict. In adversarial or common law countries, which include the United States, Great Britain, and most ex-British colonies, the judge's role is parceled out among other players in the courtroom: The prosecution and defense present the evidence while the jury renders the verdict. The judge's task is to see that each player carries out his or her role.

Inquisitorial and adversarial legal systems have distinctive conceptions of legal fairness. In inquisitorial systems the impartial judge develops the facts, and in a further show of rationality, provides the parties with a reasoned explanation for the verdict. Reassurance as to the judge's impartiality derives from the judge's status as a civil servant. The inquisitorial judge is the embodiment of the Continental European *Rechtsstaat*. By contrast, fairness in an adversarial system is modeled after a sporting competition. The adversarial judge is a referee who must treat both sides fairly. Whether fairness means treating each side in the same manner is a complex, often vexing question.[4] These complexities are foreign to the inquisitorial judge who seeks the "right" resolution to the case, regardless of whether this creates a surface impression of fairness. In addition, the adversarial system is distinguished by the citizen jury which resolves the prosecution with a simple verdict of "guilty" or "not guilty." The common law jury brings with it a distinctive form of legitimation. Unlike the inquisitorial judge, whose decision is respected because he or she is a state official, the validity of the citizen jury turns on its role as a check on state power.

The coexistence of competing adversarial and inquisitorial norms of legal fairness has created a dialogue among lawyers. The dialogue takes two forms. First, there is a debate—mostly among legal comparativists who see their task as creating universal norms of justice—as to whether the two procedural norms are compatible and whether, over time, they are converging. The tendency is to answer yes on both accounts.[5] Second, there is dialogue about the specific merits of each system: truth on the one side, fairness on the other. Hence the old saw about the criminal defendant who would rather be tried in an inquisitorial system if innocent but in an adversarial system if guilty. In other words, proponents of inquisitorialism (many of whom reside in adversarial countries) characterize it as a search for truth, in contrast to adversarialism which, in the name of fairness, distorts it.[6] Conversely, proponents of adversarialism warn against concentrating too much power in the hands of state officials. The danger is not simply the abuse of power, a fear symbolized by the routine use of judicial torture in medieval inquisitorial systems.[7] An equally serious concern is that the judge, backed by a monopoly of power, will not search for the truth. By contrast, adversarialism leaves evidence gathering in the hands of the parties, a circumstance more likely to uncover hidden facts.

Less common than debates over the merits of inquisitorial and adversarial justice are analyses over the type of societies these legal systems create. Aside from some passing comments by Max Weber, the most notable example of this work is Mirijan Damaska's *The Faces of Justice and State Authority* (1986).[8] According to Damaska, inquisitorial and adversarial systems can be differentiated based on their attitudes towards the state. In inquisitorial systems, where judges are civil servants, state intervention in the economy (and the rest of society) is more acceptable. By contrast, adversarial systems are more prone to take a laissez-faire attitude toward government involvement. While his work is extremely valuable, Damaska focuses on macrolevel issues such as the recruitment, promotion, and regulation of judges. There is less discussion of criminal procedure, and almost no discussion of particular trials. As a result, Damaska's work is of limited value in assessing how societies value legal fairness in the concrete context of the criminal trial.

What about the political scientists? In the early twentieth century the study of law dominated political science. The study of comparative politics was, more often than not, the study of comparative public law.[9] The problem with this approach to political science was that it was static. Once one determined that America, France, and England took differing approaches to a given legal problem, the work was over. As a result, when the behavioral movement swept over the discipline in the 1950s and 1960s comparative public law was pushed to one side. The few who still studied the law focused their attention on comparative judicial behavior.[10] This led to a gap in our knowledge of other societies.[11] Over the last decade political scientists made a renewed effort to close this gap. The collapse of communism in Eastern Europe and the global resurgence of democracy has led to reemergence of comparative constitutionalism.[12] This has been a good development. As the workings of European Constitutional Courts become better known, the U.S. Supreme Court can be put into comparative perspective. Even better, the development of the European Union has given us new occasion to study federalism and constitution making.

At the same time, this work remains constrained by the reluctance of many of its practitioners to delve deeper into the countries they study. Take freedom of speech, for example. The American proclivity towards free speech "absolutism" is high lighted by the European context, where hate speech is criminalized and routinely prosecuted. This difference is well-known but rarely do political scientists ask why it exists.[13] And, if they do ask, they will almost certainly emphasize political variables, such as Europe's experiences with fascism or, from a broader perspective, its aristocratic past.[14] Absent is any connection between European attitudes towards hate speech laws and the legal systems that enforce them. If, as I shall suggest, there is such a connection, it is to be found by looking at specific examples of hate speech litigation. If the new constitutionalism is to avoid the static nature of the old constitutionalism, it must descend from constitutional platitudes into the trenches.

This means studying legal doctrines. Too often political scientists who study comparative constitutionalism shy away from the law itself. This is unfortunate. Judges and lawyers who interpret constitutional provisions get their understanding of these terms from the prevailing legal norms of a culture. To understand constitutional law we must see the law as they do. There are many ways of doing this: interviewing, content analysis, critical cases studies, etc. Whatever the approach, the end result will be better if the researcher takes the plunge and learns about the law. As one does this, the various ways in which human societies have viewed the law, the trial, and legal fairness emerge in all their splendor.

The benefits of studying the guiding legal values of another culture are immense. Perhaps the greatest is the increased ability to communicate legal ideas across national boundaries. If an American expert on comparative electoral politics should be able to explain the 2000 election to a roomful of political scientists from other countries, an expert on comparative legal politics should be able to explain the O. J. Simpson or Louise Woodward case to the same audience.[15] And, vice versa, an American trained in French or German legal thought should be able to follow high-profile trials in those countries. To do so, one must understand how the law operates in routine cases. Those who make the effort will gain a deeper understanding of other cultures and an antidote to the presumption that the legal systems of the world parrot the United States. Studying the values of a foreign legal system opens a window on the social and political life of the country in question. We learn why a cause célèbre is a cause célèbre. Just as the study of a foreign language offers insight into the entire culture, so does law. The possibilities for learning are endless.

II.

Hopefully, I have sold you on the value of conceptualizing, comparatively, how societies assess legal fairness. To better approach this task I have relied on the concept of the legal imaginary. As I see it, a legal imaginary is a storehouse of ideas, legal rules, and experiences that animate a legal system's concept of fairness. These ideas, rules, and experiences derive from the cultural and political history of the underlying society; from its legal history; and from certain pragmatic realities created by the interplay of procedural rules. They direct the attention of prosecutors, judges, and legal commentators to the legal practices that define "what process is due." As such, they guide the legal discourse within a given system and set it apart from other legal systems.[16]

Let me illustrate with an example. A criminal defendant in the United States is entitled to a jury trial.[17] The Sixth Amendment requires this, but so does the national vision of what trial fairness requires. It is also well established that criminal defendants have the right to question prospective jurors about potential biases. This, too, forms part of the American legal imaginary. Canada uses juries to try criminal defendants, but takes a different attitude toward the questioning of jurors. Normally such questioning is forbidden; the sole exception is when the accused can make a showing of adverse pretrial publicity. Viewed from the United States, where well-heeled criminal defendants routinely use jury consultants help them select juries, the absence of questioning looks like a betrayal of the adversarial heritage both countries share. From a Canadian perspective, however, the restrictions on questioning form part of a larger set of rules that protect the anonymity (and thus the impartiality) of the trial process by preventing the media from covering pretrial hearings, forbidding the media from commenting on (as opposed to reporting) the evidence presented at trial, and prohibiting jurors from giving post-trial interviews.[18] Taken together, these rules constitute a specifically Canadian imaginary of trial fairness.

That Canada and the United States have distinct ideas of legal fairness even though they are both adversarial countries raises a key point—legal imaginaries are unique to a given legal system. To be sure, the division of the legal world into adversarial and inquisitorial legal systems plays a major role in shaping the values of a given legal community. But important variations exist within each general type. One further note on legal systems: Normally legal imaginaries operate on a national level, but this need not be the case. More than one legal imaginary can exist in a given country either because two or more legal systems exist within the country, as in the states of the European Union, or because the legal norms that apply in one doctrinal area do not apply to another. For example, the jury trial and its procedural sequelae that make American criminal trial so distinctively adversarial are largely absent in administrative proceedings, even though the person accused may face a serious penalty.

Legal imaginaries are ideal types, generalized models of how participants in the legal system think about justice and fairness. Their ultimate value is heuristic; instead of positing a single, universal model of the criminal trial (or the administrative proceeding) that various real trials either will or will not satisfy, the legal imaginary lets us see how each society has its own models. Uncovering the legal values of another society depends on the ability of an observer to make sense of the attitudes and expectations written into the laws, the courtroom behavior of lawyers and judges these laws inspire, and the public response to the ultimate fruit of this legal labor, the criminal trial. All the while the observer must, like the traveler, fall back upon her own preconceptions to make better sense of a foreign land. While some may call this unscientific, it is an unavoidable aspect of legal comparative work.

Explorations into foreign legal cultures share the burdens and benefits of travel literature.[19] On the one hand, they depend on a variety of idiographic factors. Different travelers not only go to different places, one visiting the cool heights of legal abstraction, the other preferring the torpid heat of trials, they view the same events differently. The best solution to this problem is to read multiple accounts of a foreign land before planning a trip. The accounts, however different, will agree on at least some points. It is from this overlap that our knowledge of other countries (and other legal systems) grows. At its best, the good travel book prevents the reader from making the mistakes of a tourist. Let us assume the public in a foreign land is outraged because an unpopular defendant has been acquitted. The tourist will be tempted to take this popular outrage at face value and assume the judge was, in fact, biased in favor of the accused, especially if the judge's behavior would be seen as biased in the tourist's home country. The traveler, by contrast, will look behind the scenes. Forearmed with a rudimentary knowledge of how the locals decide cases, she will be better able to understand why the judge's ruling caused such a furor.

III.

To show how legal imaginaries work in practice I have studied the response of the German, French, Canadian, and American legal systems to Holocaust denial.[20] The message of the deniers—that Holocaust never happened—is as close as a secular age comes to blasphemy. This is especially true for Germany, eager to transcend its Nazi past, and for Holocaust survivors for whom denial is a defamation of the dead. Holocaust denial has also become a rallying call of the extreme right, which would like nothing better than to cleanse fascism of its worst crime. These pressures have led to prosecutions of deniers (mostly in France and Germany) under laws outlawing group libel, racial hatred, and the spread of false news.[21] In the United States, where the First Amendment forecloses prosecutions, Holocaust survivors have brought civil lawsuits against deniers.[22]

If liberal democracies ignore denial at their own risk, the path of criminal prosecution has been fraught with difficulties. For one thing, Holocaust deniers are especially unpopular defendants. While this explains the popularity of legal sanctions, it raises a problem. Whenever a denier is acquitted, given a suspended sentence, or otherwise wins the court's praise, legal victory of the defendant risks becoming a political victory for Holocaust denial. The risk is especially great in France and Germany where the Holocaust is an extremely sensitive topic. Not only that, because the penalties for Holocaust denial are relatively light (usually a fine; at most a few years in prison) Holocaust deniers are highly politicized defendants. Alongside the legal aim of securing an acquittal, most deniers add the propaganda aim of spreading their message. Consequently, deniers often use the criminal trial to spread their views, even at the risk of alienating the judge and/or jury, a risk ordinary defendants try to avoid.

Will the defense succeed in hijacking the trial for its own ends? The answer to this depends on the procedural tools at the disposal of the accused. In other words, it depends on what process is due. The critical questions in the Holocaust denial context involve the proof of disputed facts. Must a prosecutor prove the Holocaust happened? Can the accused present his or her "evidence" that the Holocaust was a Zionist hoax? From an abstract perspective there is an argument on both sides of the issue. If Holocaust deniers present a ludicrous view of history, one supported by no serious historian, the right to tell one's own side of the story is a core element of the criminal trial. What is more, most of the statutes under which the deniers are prosecuted allow the accused to use truth as a defense. Under these circumstances, it seems unfair to prevent the accused from presenting his or her own "revisionist" evidence.

The relevant legal doctrine for resolving these tensions is judicial notice. The basic idea is simple: Some facts are so well established that it is not necessary to prove them in a court of law.[23] Every legal system takes notice of certain statements such as: "Water boils at 212 degrees Fahrenheit," or "July 5, 2001 was a Thursday." The harder question arises with historical facts, like the Holocaust, that are equally obvious but far more complex. The more the judicial notice doctrine extends into the realm of factual complexity, the greater the danger judicial notice will deprive (or appear to deprive) the accused of his or her right to a fair trial. The danger is especially great in adversarial systems, where judicial notice usurps the role of the jury as the ultimate finder of facts.

Each of the four legal systems has its own concept of judicial notice. At one extreme stands Germany where inquisitorial norms are strong and the doctrine of judicial notice is given wide scope. German courts are quite willing to take notice of what look like political facts. In 1957 the Federal Constitutional Court took judicial notice of the fact that the Communist party stood opposed to the "regular constitutional order."[24] The critical question is whether the person against whom judicial notice is taken had an opportunity to participate in the process through which the fact was established as public knowledge. If the answer to that question is yes, the court will take notice of even relatively controversial facts.

The French legal system, while broadly inquisitorial, takes a markedly different approach to judicial notice. Recognizing that a court must notice some facts in order to function at all, French courts have nonetheless refused to apply the doctrine to judge historical disputes.[25] In a 1970 case a Paris court censored a film on World War I which it felt was historically inaccurate. The Court of Appeals reversed not because of censorship, but because the trial court by judging the film had passed comment on history. The logic behind the French position is separation of judicial and political powers. Courts must be strictly impartial. The court that takes sides in a historical dispute also takes the first step down the road to official history and totalitarianism.[26]

The differing views of judicial notice held in the German and French legal imaginaries carried over into Holocaust denial cases. German judges were quick to accept the idea that "on the basis of countless documents it stands beyond doubt in the Third Reich millions of Jewish people were . . . killed by violent means by the National Socialist power holders, especially in East and Southeastern Europe."[27]

They reached this conclusion without taking evidence. Like the statement "2 + 2 = 4," the Holocaust was an indisputable fact, a point reaffirmed by a series of German courts.[28] What is more, the German doctrine of judicial notice carries a considerable bite. Not only does it relieve the prosecution of its burden to prove the Holocaust happened; it prevents the defense from presenting any evidence whatsoever questioning the Holocaust. As a result, German Holocaust denial prosecutions have encountered few fact-related problems.

The situation was quite different in France. During the 1981 prosecution of Robert Faurisson for falsifying history, the defense was able to present its own version of history to the judges who sat on the case. And when it came time to issue a ruling the trial court equivocated. While finding Faurisson guilty, and criticizing him for lacking "the . . . prudence, objective circumspection, and neutrality . . . of the researcher he would wish to be," the court refused to say whether Faurisson had, in fact, falsified history. Aware that it lacked "the competence to judge History," the court based its finding of guilty on the language with which Faurisson presented his views.[29] The Paris Court of Appeals reached a similar conclusion, finding Faurisson guilty but explicitly refusing to call his work frivolous.[30] Neither decision was well received. Pierre Vidal-Naquet, a leading opponent of Holocaust denial in France, called the Court of Appeals decision "outrageous."[31] Meanwhile, Faurisson claimed victory.

Why did this happen? Why did the French courts treat the Faurisson case with such an apparent lack of sensitivity? One possibility is to fall back on general societal attitudes: The reason the French judges treated the Holocaust with less respect is that the Holocaust is a less important issue in France than in Germany. While this may contain an element of truth, it is not the entire story. For one thing, it does not explain why both courts reserved scathing criticisms for Faurisson himself. Nor does it explain why both courts expressed their "insensitivity" in a particular way, i.e., by a reasoned refusal to judge history. Equally important to understanding the case are the contours of the French legal imaginary. Judicial determinations of history strike at the core of the French ideal of trial fairness. While the French courts struggled mightily to find Faurisson guilty, they could not judge his ideas about history without violating this deep-seated legal norm.

Whatever the differences between France and Germany, these pale before the gap that divides inquisitorial legal systems from their adversarial counterparts in the United States and Canada, where the jury provides both an alternative model of trial legitimacy and an alternative model of judicial notice. In contrast to Germany, where the judicial determination of obvious facts is seen as a form of democratic decision making, in North America judicial notice is seen as a check on the democratic jury. The only role for judicial notice in such a system is to prevent the people's representatives from embarrassing themselves by reaching a verdict that flies in the face of well-established facts. In practice, courts apply the doctrine narrowly to cover the basic facts of science, the days of the week, and the location of state and provincial capitals.

Unlike France, however, neither Canada nor the United States excludes the notice of historical facts per se. This makes taking judicial notice of the Holocaust a close issue for American and Canadian courts, so close that American and Canadian courts have reached different conclusions on the issue. In *Mermelstein v. IHR*, the plaintiff, a Holocaust survivor, sued the California-based Institute for Historical Review in civil court for breach of contract. At issue was the IHR's offer to pay Mermelstein $50,000 for proof that Jews were gassed at Auschwitz. The case turned on whether the IHR's offer was a valid contract. While Mermelstein argued his judicial notice motion vigorously, supplying over 300 pages of expert testimony, the legal significance of judicial notice was relatively minor. It did not resolve the lawsuit. As a result, the trial court quietly took judicial notice of the Holocaust, thereby handing Mermelstein an important symbolic victory.[32]

The context of *R. v. Zundel*, the Canadian case, was rather different. Ernst Zundel was prosecuted under an archaic statute outlawing the knowing dissemination of false news for publishing a pamphlet entitled *Did Six Million Really Die?* The legal question was whether Zundel published the pamphlet knowing it was false. Trial judge Hugh Locke refused to take judicial notice of the Holocaust because it might be seen to eliminate the prosecution's burden to prove its case.[33] The fear was not simply that the prosecution would use the judicial notice ruling to prove that the Zundel's pamphlet was false. Judge Locke (and the Ontario Court of Appeals that affirmed him) feared that the prosecution would use the ruling to prove Zundel's state of mind. In other words, they feared that the jury would use the fact that the Holocaust was well-established to prove that Zundel must have known Holocaust denial was false when he published *Did Six Million Really Die?*[34]

In *Mermelstein* and *Zundel* we have two different outcomes to the same legal issue. In this instance, however, it makes more sense to attribute these outcomes to the different procedural postures of the cases rather than to differences in Canadian and American ideals of judicial notice. This raises an important methodological point. Spotting differences in legal imaginaries can never simply be a matter of comparing cases. It is critical to set each case against the background of ordinary litigation. Sometimes this context can be inferred from the cases and the legal commentaries on them. For instance, the commentaries on the Faurisson case contain a very useful discussion of reluctance of French courts to judge history. At other times, the legal context must be pieced together. The key is to explore the backroads of the legal terrain. Even if one gets lost, or taken in by an unscrupulous guide, the explorer will definitely learn more than someone who only visits the tourist sites.

IV.

The differing ideals of legal fairness, what I have called legal imaginaries, not only help us explain the willingness of judges to take judicial notice of the Holocaust, they also illuminate the outcome of individual Holocaust-denial cases and the frequency with which Holocaust deniers are prosecuted. In Germany the dilemma of proof is nonexistent. The Holocaust is easily subsumed under the broad conception of judicial notice favored in that country. As a result, Germans prosecute Holocaust deniers without much difficulty and do so fairly frequently.[35] The prosecutor's task in France was not as easy. The Faurisson case led to a reluctance to prosecute Holocaust deniers. This changed in 1990 when the French passed the Gayssot Law, which resolved the problem judicial determinations of history by making the very act of questioning of the Holocaust a crime. Freed of the obligation to assess the truth or falsity of Holocaust denial, French courts enforced the new law vigorously. By shifting the fact-finding from the courts to the legislature, the Gayssot Law was ideally suited to French circumstances.[36]

The prosecution of Holocaust deniers posed far greater problems in Canada. (There have been no criminal prosecutions in the United States.) To make its case that Ernst Zundel disseminated false news, the prosecution relied on the evidence of Holocaust survivors, historical documents, and expert testimony. This led to two difficulties. First, the rule against hearsay made it extremely difficult for the prosecution to make a coherent case. Holocaust survivors could only testify as to what they saw; the moment they tried to describe what they heard, or worse yet, what they knew about the Holocaust, they were interrupted. Thus one survivor was prevented from saying that, among the inmates at Auschwitz, Birkenau was known as the death camp.[37] The problems only multiplied when the prosecution sought to admit written documents about the Holocaust (by definition hearsay) and expert testimony. Second, the interruptions and arguments over the hearsay rule played into the defense strategy of using the prosecution to put the Holocaust on trial. It created the appearance that the Holocaust was subject to debate, an appearance reinforced by the defense's sharp cross-examination of Holocaust survivors and experts. While the resulting trial ended with a legal victory for the prosecution, it was a political victory for the defense.

R. v. Zundel stands alone as the only Holocaust denial prosecution in the common law world. By contrast, prosecutions of Holocaust denial are fairly common in Continental Europe. In addition to France and Germany, there have been a series of prosecutions in Austria, and scattered reports of prosecutions in Switzerland, Belgium, and the Netherlands.[38] This raises an important point, not simply about legal imaginaries in general, but about the interrelationship of two legal imaginaries, one governing criminal procedure, and the other governing freedom of speech. The libertarian American position on hate speech regulation carries over to Holocaust denial. Even the most hardened American opponents of Holocaust denial such as Deborah Lipstadt and Alan Dershowitz oppose prosecutions.[39] They oppose prosecutions even as they excoriate college newspapers for "refusing to censor" the deniers, a position not without logical inconsistencies.[40]

Lipstadt, Dershowitz, and other American opponents of denial oppose prosecutions because they know in their bones that prosecutions of Holocaust denial can only backfire. They will backfire by making the deniers into free speech martyrs. (In other words, adversarialism is not the only reason Americans refuse to prosecute deniers.) But they also backfire because they lead to cases like *R. v. Zundel*, cases that give the deniers a platform to spread their views. And why does this happen? It doesn't happen because common law judges are anti-Semitic or biased in favor of the deniers. It happens because the adversarial norms of criminal procedure—especially the rule against hearsay and the right of cross-examination—give the defendant willing to accept a guilty verdict a great chance to put the Holocaust on trial.

Stated more generally, adversarial norms allow a defendant at a speech trial to turn the tables on her accusers. By contrast, inquisitorial norms concentrate power in the hands of the judge, making it harder for the accused to convert the trial for propaganda ends. In other words, speech defendants tried under inquisitorial procedures can only make their case by refusing to recognize the legitimacy of the court, much as American Vietnam War protesters did during the 1960s. By contrast, common law speech defendants used the law itself to undercut the legitimacy of the prosecution. Therefore, we would expect norms of free speech to be stronger in common law societies, where the logic of the criminal trial makes speech prosecutions extremely difficult, than in civil law societies, where speech prosecutions can be processed with far less difficulty.

I do not want to overstate the causal connection. The inquisitorial versus adversarial divide is not the only factor influencing freedom of speech. Even though Germany's criminal procedure is strongly inquisitorial, it has a more robust concept of freedom of speech than France. Here the scope of judicial review, much broader in Germany than in France, provides a key difference.[41] Likewise, the United States and Canada, both adversarial countries, have different attitudes towards freedom of speech. While the United States has over the past thirty years protected most political speech, the Canadian Supreme Court has upheld the constitutionality of hate speech regulation.[42] Clearly the influence of adversarialism must be supplemented with historical and cultural factors. Cultural and historical factors are also needed to explain the shift in the United States from McCarthyism to its current near-absolutist position.[43]

Still, the connection between adversarial procedures and enhanced freedom of speech is a strong one. France and Germany prosecute Holocaust deniers; with one exception (*R. v. Zundel*) Canada and the United States do not. As such, it stands as a useful rebuke to the tendency of Americans to criticize prosecutions as ineffective and self-defeating. While this may be true of adversarial trials, it is not as true of their inquisitorial counterparts. In Germany (and in France after the Gayssot Law) the prosecution of deniers has become routine. To be sure, these measures still raise questions about their efficacy as censorship, especially as the Holocaust deniers in those countries learn to speak in coded language. But the prosecutions themselves generally run smoothly. This makes speech act prosecutions less controversial.

V.

The interrelationship between norms of free speech and criminal procedure demonstrates the added power political theory (in this case political theories of law) can give to comparative research. Too often comparativists act as if one political theory is valid for all times and places. The diversity of the legal imaginaries suggests the opposite—different societies have different norms, and comparativists ignore these differences at their own risk. The legal imaginary idea will assist political scientists and those lawyers who write about comparative law. We will better understand high-profile litigation and have a better sense of the links between different doctrinal areas. But, to be used, these norms must be uncovered. This will only happen when we get our fingernails dirty and dig into real cases and the doctrines legal professionals use to resolve them. If the work is hard, and the results always tentative, the rewards are great. Not only do we learn how other liberal democracies understand basic legal norms such as freedom of speech, the rights of the accused, and equality before the law, we also remind ourselves how our own set of legal norms, our own American legal imaginary, is contingent. Ours is one way to operationalize legal fairness, but it is not the only way.

Notes

1. I would like to thank my wife, Jacqueline Baronian, for her insightful comments on this work.

2. For an excellent case book on German criminal procedure see John Langbein, *Comparative Criminal Procedure: Germany* (St. Paul, Minn: West Publishing Co., 1977), 3–60.

3. For a brief overview, see John H. Merryman, *The Civil Law Tradition* (Palo Alto, Calif.: Stanford University Press, 1984), 124–33. Merryman also discusses the difference between "common law" and "civil law" countries, a difference centered on how the legal system develops rules of private law (property, contracts, and torts). In common law countries these rules are fashioned by judges through a system of legal precedent. In civil law countries these rules are set forth in codes. While judges may interpret the codes, their interpretations have little precedental value. Although most civil law countries are inquisitorial, and most common law countries adversarial, the two distinctions are separate.

4. See Peter Westen, "The Empty Idea of Equality," *Harvard Law Review* 95, (1982): 537–96.

5. See, e.g., Nico Jörg, Steward Field and Chrisje Brants, "Are Inquisitorial and Adversarial Systems Converging?" in Phil Fennell and Christopher Harding, eds., *Criminal Justice*

in Europe: A Comparative Study (Clarendon Press: Oxford, 1997), 41–56.

6. For an American lawyer's critique of adversarialism as contrary to the search for truth, see Franklin Strier, *Reconstructing Justice: An Agenda for Trial Reform* (Chicago: University of Chicago Press, 1994). See also Ellen E. Sward, "Values, Ideology and the Evolution of the Adversary System," *Indiana Law Journal* 64, (1989): 301–55. The classic defense of adversarialism is Stephan Landsman, *The Adversary System: A Description and Defense* (Washington, D.C.: American Enterprise Institute, 1984).

7. Torture was not only used in the Medieval and Spanish Inquisitions; it was also a staple of secular legal powers, which used it to extract confessions from common criminals. See Edward Peters, *Torture* (Philadelphia: University of Pennsylvania Press, 1996), 40–73.

8. Mirijan Damaska, *The Faces of Justice and State Authority* (New Haven: Yale University Press, 1986); Max Weber, *Economy and Society, Vol II.* (Berkeley: University of California Press, 1978). Given his belief that "capitalistic interests will fare best under a rigorously formal system of adjudication" and that the common law exhibited a "degree of legal rationality essentially lower than, and of a type different from, that of Continental Europe," Weber faced the problem of why the common law did not impede the development of capitalism in England (814, 890–2).

9. Many of the discipline's early luminaries studied the subject, among them Carl Friedreich and Hans Morgenthau.

10. Theodore L. Becker, *Comparative Judicial Politics: The Political Functionings of Courts* (Chicago: Rand McNally & Company, 1970).

11. Martin Shapiro's *Courts: A Comparative and Political Analysis* (Chicago: University of Chicago Press, 1981), in which the author compares the legal systems of Great Britain, Continental Europe, China, and the Islamic world, is one notable exception to this trend. Yet, in keeping with the times, Shapiro was concerned with establishing the functional commonalities among these systems—their "courtness"—and so less willing to stress how differences of the systems shaped the legal and political lives of the people who lived and worked under them.

12. See, e.g., A.E. Dick Howard, "The Essence of Constitutionalism," in Kenneth W. Thompson and Rett R. Lodwikowski, eds. *Constitutionalism and Human Rights: America, Poland, and France*, (Lanham, Md.: University Press of America, 1991), 3–41.

13. For an exception, see Louis Greenspan and Cyril Levitt, eds., *Under the Shadow of Weimar: Democracy, Law, and Racial Incitement in Six Countries* (Westport, Conn.: Praeger, 1993).

14. Samuel Walker traces America's free speech absolutism and its departure from the European norm of hate speech regulation to divergent historical experiences. While American were learning through the civil rights and antiwar protests of the 1950s and 60s to tolerate increasingly seditious political speech, the rise of neo-Nazism taught the Europeans (and to a lesser extent, the Canadians) the opposite lesson. Walker, *Hate Speech: The History of an American Controversy* (Lincoln: University of Nebraska Press, 1994).

15. I owe the idea that comparativists should be able to explain the vagaries of American politics to Professor Richard S. Katz of Johns Hopkins University.

16. The term "legal imaginary" derives from Lacanian psychoanalysis. For Lacan an imaginary is "the world, the register, the dimension of images, perceived or imagined." Translator's Note, *The Four Fundamental Concepts of Psychoanalysis: The Seminar of Jacques Lacan, Book 9*, Jacques-Alain Miller ed., Alan Sheridan trans. (New York: W.W.

Norton & Co., 1978), 279–80. Drucilla Cornell, from whom I borrowed the term more specifically, refers to the "imaginary domain" as "an aesthetic idea that illuminates what freedom demands of creatures that inevitably are shaped by their own identifications." Cornell, *Just Cause: Freedom, Identity and Rights*, (Lanham, Md.: Rowman & Littlefield Publishers, Inc., 2000), 135. What an "imaginary domain" is to an individual, the legal imaginary is to a legal system—a place to engage in "self-evaluation through moral reflection" (136) It is, in effect, a place to engage in the Rawlsian reflective equilibrium, with the understanding that different legal systems (and societies) have different equilibriums. It is the yearning for justice that distinguishes the legal imaginary (governed by what should be) from legal culture (governed by what is).

17. For an insightful study of the origins of the jury and the role of jury selection in American society, see Marianne Constable, *The Law of the Other: The Mixed Jury and Changing Conceptions of Citizenship, Law and Knowledge* (Chicago: University of Chicago Press, 1994).

18. Canadian Civil Code §§ 648–49; Robert Martin & G. Stuart Adam, *A Sourcebook of Canadian Media Law* (Ottawa, Canada: Carelton University Press, 1994), 302–04.

19. Indeed, some of the best works of comparative law are travel literature. In *The Faces of Justice* (London: Collins, 1961), Sybille Bedford recounts her travels through England, Austria, Germany, France, and Switzerland during which she interviewed judges and sat in on trials. Her book is a classic.

20. The material in this section comes from my doctoral dissertation, "The Limits of Legal Fairness: Holocaust Denial and the Law in France, Germany, Canada and the United States," (Ph.D diss., Johns Hopkins University, 2000), which I am currently preparing for publication under the title *Holocaust Denial, the Law, and the Dilemmas of Liberal Legalism.*

21. In Germany prosecutors relied on Penal Code § 130 (incitement of racial hatred) and § 185 (group insult). In France deniers were charged with group libel, falsifying history under § 1382 of the Civil Code (a general provision establishing tort liability), and, later, under the Gayssot Law, which made it illegal to question the Holocaust. The sole Canadian prosecution was brought under a thirteenth century law which made it a crime to knowingly disseminate false news.

22. The most notable of these is *Mermelstein v. IHR*, which we shall discuss below.

23. The standard under the Federal Rules of Evidence (U.S.) § 201(b) is that the fact be "generally known within the territorial jurisdiction of the trial court" or "capable of accurate and ready determination by resort to sources whose accuracy cannot reasonably be disputed." Graham C. Lilly, *An Introduction to the Law of Evidence*, 3rd ed. (St. Paul, Minn.: West Publishing Co., 1996), 13–20.

24. Dr. Ranier Keller, "Offenkundigkeit und Beweisbedürfigkeit im Strafprozeß," in *Zeitschrift für die gesamte Strafrechtwissenschaft* 39, (1989): 380–418.

25. Bernard Edelman, "Note," *Recueil Dalloz Sirey, Jurisprudence* (1982): 60–4.

26. This reluctance to judge history has historical roots. During the *ancien regime* the French parliaments served as both courts and fonts of aristocratic power. As a consequence the French Revolution fostered a narrowly circumscribed conception of the judicial role. Merryman, *The Civil Law Tradition*, 14–8.

27. Koblenz District Court (May 2 1978), reported in *Kritische Justiz* 13, (1978).

28. Thus in the 1994 *Deckert* case, the Federal Supreme court held that taking judicial

notice of the Holocaust was in "agreement with the precedents," which it generously supplied. Federal Supreme Court (April 13, 1994), reprinted in *Neue Juristische Wochenschrift* 14, (1994): 1421.

29. Decision of Paris Trial Court (July 14, 1981) reported in *Recueil Dalloz Sirey, Jurisprudence* (1982), 59. The court drew particular attention to Faurisson's lack of sensitivity toward survivors and those who lost family members in the Holocaust.

30. Decision of the Paris Court of Appeals (April 26, 1983), 9.

31. Pierre Vidal-Naquet, *Assassins of Memory: Essays on the Denial of the Holocaust* (New York: Columbia University Press, 1992), 137.

32. I discuss the *Mermelstein* case at length in my dissertation and upcoming book.

33. Trial Transcript of *R. v. Zundel*, 2181–91.

34. This comes out most clearly in the appellate decision, see *R. v. Zundel*, 35 D.L.R. (4th) 338 (1987).

35. The difficulty of German Holocaust denial litigation lies elsewhere, with the written verdict and the obligation of the judge to describe the criminal and the crime in sympathetic terms. While this creates a dilemma for the judges, it does not interfere with the litigation per se. See Robert A. Kahn, "Who Takes the Blame? Scapegoating, Legal Responsibility and the Prosecution of Holocaust Revisionists in the Federal Republic of Germany and Canada," *Glendale Law Review* 16, (1998): 17–64.

36. For more on the Gayssot Law, see Robert A. Kahn, "Holocaust Denial Prosecutions in a Liberal Society: France Under the Gayssot Law," (paper presented at the Annual Meeting of the Law and Society Association, Miami, Florida, May 2000).

37. Testimony of Arnold Friedman, Trial transcript of *R. v. Zundel*, 317.

38. See Kenneth S. Stern, *Holocaust Denial* (New York: American Jewish Congress, 1992), ch. 2.

39. Deborah Lipstadt, *Holocaust Denial: The Growing Assault on Truth and Memory* (New York: Basic Books, 1993), 17, 220; Alan Dershowitz, *The Vanishing American Jew: In Search of Jewish Identity for the Next Century* (Boston: Little, Brown & Co., 1996), 115.

40. I discuss these inconsistencies in Robert A. Kahn, "The Informal Censorship of Holocaust Revisionism in the United States and Germany," *George Mason University Civil Rights Law Journal* 9, (1998/99): 125–49.

41. In Germany individuals can raise constitutional claims during ordinary litigation. In France, such review is limited to groups of 60 or more members of parliament who raise the claim after the bill is passed but before it is signed by the president.

42. *R. v. Keegstra*, 61 C.C.C (3d) 1 (1990). The Canadian Supreme court, did, however, find the false news unconstitutional, an event that invalidated Zundel's conviction. *R. v. Zundel*, 95 D.L.R. (4th) 202 (1992). For a discussion of American and Canadian approaches to hate speech (and the distinctive political, cultural, and legal traditions behind them), see Robert A. Kahn, "How Americans and Canadians Justify Their Positions on Hate Speech," (paper presented at the Annual Meeting of the Law and Society Association, Vancouver, Canada, May, 2002).

43. The case of McCarthyism does not rebut the general thesis that adversarial systems prosecute speech offenses with difficulty. At its height McCarthyism was less about establishing the falsity of Communism than with rooting out Communists. In this regard, the anti-Communist crusade followed the same strategy as the framers of the Gayssot Law. By making the being of a communist the offense, the Internal Security Act of 1950 relieved the

courts of the duty to judge the subversiveness of individual communists. See Thomas I. Emerson, *The System of Freedom of Expression* (New York: Vintage, 1970), 129–48.

Conclusion

Bridging the Disciplinary Divide

Jennifer S. Holmes

All the contributions to this volume aim to demonstrate the usefulness of the incorporation of political theory to comparative politics, or vice versa. For the subfield of comparative politics, this approach offers an alternative to the stale debates between the quantitative, large sample size work and the qualitative, area studies approach and between the rationalists and the interpretivists. The authors use their particular theoretical framework because it delivers. The common aim of the authors is to demonstrate the usefulness of the incorporation of theory to provide new insights and perspectives to the substantive questions of politics.

This volume coincides with some larger movements within political science. Recently, political theorists such as Rogers Smith and others have encouraged political theorists to be more empirically engaged.[1] This recent paper follows up on the urging of other theorists, such as William Galston, to have political theory be connected to contemporary political controversies.[2] Other theorists, such as Susan Carroll and Linda Zerilli,[3] have discussed the implications of feminist theory to applied problems on inequality and other empirical research. Similar calls have been made by scholars such as Donald Green and Ian Shapiro in *Pathologies of Rational Choice Theory*, Jeffrey Isaac in his article "The Strange Silence of Political Theory" in *Political Theory*, and Terence Ball in *Reappraising Political Theory*. All these theorists support an incorporation of political theory into inquiry of substantive political problems. Others, such as Ian Shapiro, David Miller, Charles Taylor, William Galston, and Bruce Ackerman have moved in these directions. Rogers Smith notes that if we are to seek answers to pressing political questions, whether or not there are sufficient data to analyze the issue statistically, the question should be addressed. He states, "We seek to achieve genuinely scientific knowledge about politics, that is to say, descriptions, explanations, and arguments that are as well tested, logically rigorous and empirically accurate as possible. We also seek to provide substantive, useful normatively compelling answers to political questions that we, along with most other people, regard as extremely important in human life."[4]

In comparative politics, there has been a similar movement. In 1996, *World Politics* published a symposium about the "Role of Theory in Comparative Politics" with Atul Kohli, Peter Evans, Peter Katzenstein, Adam Przeworski, Susanne Hoeber Rudolph, James C. Scott, and Theda Skocpol contributing. There are two main divisions in the field: the old debate between the quantitative and the qualitative and another debate between the cultural relativists and the postmodernists on one side and those founded on nomothetic claims, such as some practicioners of rational choice.[5] Peter Katzenstein calls for a "cathedral" of scholarship, in which different approaches are welcome. "The church of scholarship accommodates many different sects often bent on fighting holy wars: behavioralists and nonbehavioralists then, rationalists and interpretivists now."[6] Kohli concludes that most of the scholars are in the "eclectic messy center" and are problem oriented.

In terms of the discipline as a whole, the Perestroika movement has challenged the dominance of a quantitative, scientific approach to politics and has encouraged scholars to embrace a less hegemonic approach to the study of politics. In the words of John Mearsheimer, "This is about the mathematicization of political science . . . I'm in favor of filling the zoo with all kinds of animals. But I'm concerned about them running us out of the business or making us marginal."[7] The movement asks for problem-driven research with a substantive focus, methodological pluralism, and an interdisciplinary approach.[8]

The fact that we have so many examples of calls for a reconciliation of political theory with the rest of political science signifies that there not enough scholars who have been willing to cross these boundaries. The contributors to this volume all do so, with the sophistication of eclectic approaches, substantive questions, and meaningful answers. The results of combining political theory with comparative politics are impressive, useful, and practicable. The different chapters in this volume have provided new perspectives and used diverse methodologies, asked relevant normative and practical questions, and are interdisciplinary.

This collection of essays does not represent a proposed unification of the discipline of political science in any particular way. However, what this collection of essays provides is a rich sampling of the ways in which political theory and comparative politics can be combined. Among these authors, there is no uniformity of approach. On the contrary, there is methodological pluralism and almost all of the authors proceed in an interdisciplinary manner. As James C. Scott admonishes the discipline, "If half of your reading is not *outside* the confines of political science, you are risking extinction along with the rest of the subspecies. Most of the notable innovations in the discipline have come in the form of insights, perspectives, concepts and paradigms originating elsewhere. Reading exclusively within the discipline is to risk reproducing orthodoxies or, at the very least, absorbing innovations far from the source."[9] The authors also address relevant normative and practical questions of real politics in a style of research that truly is problem driven.

Michaelle Browers assesses the subfields of comparative politics and political theory. She also engages the new comparative political theory approach, but challenges it to gain a "perspective on the interaction, contention, and negotiation that occur between and among different cultural or national contexts and within our increasingly global context."[10] Browers calls for interdisciplinary work among all the subfields, including political theory, comparative politics, and international relations. She states, "comparativists can and should benefit from both the insights and categories of analysis of both contemporary political theory and the history of political thought. Recent transformations within political science and the political world suggest the need and opportunity for comparatitivists and theorists to not only cross the subfield divides within political science, but to engage to incorporate a greater interdisciplinary perspective in general."[11] Browers highlights the focus of both comparative politics and political theory on areas of democracy, democratization, civil society, citizenship, sovereignty, constitutionalism, liberalism, and globalization. For example, she discusses her own previous work in which she addressed the question of how the concept of civil society crossed into the culture and language of Arab countries. She found that the necessary cultural and linguistic translation of the concept provided an opportunity for "political and conceptual transformation and contestation in Arab political thought."[12]

John Peeler incorporates twentieth-century pluralist theory, democratic theory in general, and models of democracy which focus on inclusion. Peeler specifically includes the work of democratic theorists such as Iris Marion Young and Seyla Benhabib to examine citizenship, inclusion, and difference in the experience of the indigenous peoples of Bolivia, Ecuador, Guatemala, and Peru. Peeler addresses how the indigenous peoples who have historically been powerless and excluded attempt to make their citizenship effective. He notes that the advent of democracy in much of Latin America over the last two decades makes issues of democratic theory fundamentally relevant to indigenous peoples as they attempt to gain meaningful inclusion in their democracies.

My own contribution uses an Aristotelian approach to create a concept of purposes of the state, instead of using the conventional concept of legitimacy, to allow an assessment of citizen support based on how well the state meets its purposes. This Aristotelian approach is appropriate for Colombian democracy, which appears to be procedurally stable, but is in effect a sick democracy with serious deficiencies in terms of maintaining control over its territory and in terms of achieving the rudimentary purposes of the state. I base my concept of the purposes of the state on the works of Aristotle and on contemporary Aristotelians, incorporating philosophy and political theory into comparative politics. The Aristotelian approach is used to assess the effects of drug-related violence, state violence, and guerrilla violence on democracy and the political community in Colombia. Also evaluated is the potential effectiveness of Plan Colombia on the problems in Colombian democracy as well as what aspects a successful plan would incorporate.

Kirk Bowman and Seán Patrick Eudaily use the perspective of radical political theory, specifically utilizing Richard K. Ashley's concept of "heroic practice," Michel Foucault's studies of "governmentality," and Karl Kautsky's theory of "ultra-imperialism." Utilizing this alternative framework, they generate different empirically testable expectations. Bowman and Eudaily stress the importance of the analysis of historical and regional contexts, the nature of the capitalist world system, and the intertext of internal militarization. Bowman and Eudaily examine the theoretical foundation and causal relationship of "Democratic Peace" by problematizing the assumptions, critically evaluating the conclusions, and exploring the potentialities of alternative lines of inquiry into the connection between democratic states and peace.

Robert A. Kahn incorporates the study of comparative law and comparative politics to urge the new constitutionalism to "descend from constitutional platitudes into the trenches."[13] The relationship between the norms of free speech and criminal procedures becomes clear by including political theory in this comparative research. Kahn examines the idea of a legal imaginary, which he defines as a set of values, experiences, and laws that guide how people conceptualize legal fairness, to operationalize competing images of legal fairness in different societies.

Ann Davies incorporates political theory, comparative politics, and history. Davies uses an assessment of the theories of political development and the historical experiences of the U.S. and French revolutions to examine the relationship between Enlightenment thinkers and the conflicts and problems of political life. She provides an example of a dynamic relationship in which theory informs practical politics which then informs theory. Davies examines the murkiness of the Enlightenment approach to political development, focusing specifically on rationalism, liberalism, power, and state building. In her conclusion, she notes that the "uneasy relationship between the Enlightenment and the state may say less about the Enlightenment's limits in acknowledging and grappling with the hard realities of politics and more about the difficulty of arriving at a straightforward or unqualified conclusions about any human phenomenon."[14] She considers what could become the basis of a model of the interactions between democracy and the state that has the implications for scholars of political development, liberalism, and the state.

Zeric Kay Smith discusses how democratic theorists have debated the normative nature of democratic politics, with some taking a substantive view of democracy and others arguing for a minimalist definition of democracy. This debate is reflected in practice of the international development community. Smith links insights of political theory and tests their relative importance through comparative political analysis and to democracy promotion efforts in Mali. Specifically, he examines impact of democracy promotion efforts on the poor in a situation to view the theoretical debate between process and outcomes. He concludes "by putting poverty first theoretically, the reciprocal nature of democratic outcomes and democratic process is dramatically highlighted."

All eight of us authors, in our own ways, combine political theory with comparative politics. Some utilize their applied scholarship to sharpen concepts and clarify arguments of political theory. Others utilize frameworks and perspectives gleaned from political theory to guide analysis. By bridging the disciplinary divide, we provide examples of a fruitful collaboration among subfields, suggesting answers to interesting questions, gaining clarity, and gaining better understanding of the subject matter.

Notes

1. Rogers Smith, "Reconnecting Political Theory to Empirical Inquiry, or a Return to the Cave?" Paper presented at the September 2001 American Political Science Association's annual meeting in San Francisco, 2.

2. William Galston, "Political Theory in the 1980s: Perplexity Amidst Diversity" in A.W. Finifter ed., *Political Science: The State of the Discipline II* (Washington D.C.: APSA, 1993), 40–1.

3. Susan Carroll and Linda Zerilli, "Feminist Challenges to Political Science" in A. W. Finifter ed., *Political Science: The State of the Discipline II* (Washington D.C.: APSA, 1993).

4. Smith, 14.

5. Atul Kohli, "Introduction: The Role of Theory in Comparative Politics: A Symposium." *World Politics* 48:1, 2.

6. The Role of Theory in Comparative Politics: A Symposium." *World Politics* 48:1, 2, 11.

7. D. W. Miller, "Storming the Palace in Political Science." *The Chronicle of Higher Education,* Vol. 48, Issue 4.

8. Mr. Perestroika "On Globalization of the APSA and APSR: A Political Science Manifesto" The letter is as follows

> Questions to ponder over:
>
> 1) Why do people like Benedict Anderson and James C. Scott find APSA and *APSR* irrelevant? These are probably the most famous political scientists in the world. They are equally famous abroad and in other disciplines compared to the "stars" of Political Science: Hey, Hey, Vee (look at their classic book on literary methodologies).
>
> 2) Related to above is the question: Why do a majority of political scientists who do comparative politics ignore APSA and APSR and go to their regional meetings and read regional association journals—such as those associated with East Asia, Latin America, Hispanic Studies, etc.?
>
> 3) Why does a "coterie" of faculty dominate and control APSA and the editorial board of APSR—I scratch your back, you scratch mine. I give award to your student from Harvard and you give mine from Duke or Columbia. In short why do the "East Coast Brahmins" control APSA?
>
> 4) Why are a few men who make poor game theorists and who cannot for the life of me compete with a third grade Economics graduate student—WHY are these men allowed to represent the diversity of methodologies and areas of the world that APSA "purports" to represent?
>
> 5) Why are FAILED Africanists and Economists allowed to dominate a discipline which has a rich history of intellectual contributions from the likes of James Scott, Charles Tilly, Aristide Zolberg, Leanard Binder, Benedict Anderson, R. Bendix, Susanne Rudolph, Theda Skocpol, etc.
>
> 6) Have we learned any lesson from the thousands of pages of research that were funded by APSA in the name of political science to examine the former Soviet Union and make "predictive" models? What happened to those models and why did they fail? How is it that those esteemed colleagues failed to predict the collapse of the Soviet Empire while Sovietologists from Korea, Japan, India, and even one from Tanzania could predict the fall of the empire?

Are we making the same mistake by ignoring diverse knowledges and methodologies present in the study of politics?

7) Why isn't APSR subscription made separate from the APSA membership so that APSR becomes truly representative of a "coterie" that rules APSA while the rest of the true political scientists can devote their money to buying the more important regional journals. Either reform the *APSR* board and have more political historians, area specialists, political sociologists and constructivists on the board or let the market decide—you will find a sharp drop in *APSR*'s subscription as soon as *APSR* is delinked from the membership of APSA.

8) Why are the overwhelming majority of Presidents of APSA or editorial board members of *APSR* WHITE and MALE? Where are the African-Americans, Hispanics, women, gays, Asians—in short, where is the diversity of United States and the world that APSA "pretends" to study—is somebody afraid that APSA will slip out of their hands???

9) Why are all the articles of APSR from the same methodology—statistics or game theory—with a "symbolic" article in Political Theory that is often a piece that has been rejected by the journal *Political Theory*. Where is political history, international history, political sociology, interpretive methodology, constructivists, area studies, critical theory, and last but not the least—postmodernism. Why can't you have 5 percent of the articles in *APSR* allocated under the category: incomprehensible. Then just go ahead and publish game theory, statistics and postmodernism under the category.

10) At a time when the free market models of economics are being challenged in IMF and World Bank, discredited in much of Asia, and protested by numerous groups; why are simple, baby-stuff models of political science being propagated in our discipline. If these pseudo-economists know their math so well—let them present at the University of Chicago's Economics Workshop—I assure you every single political science article will be trashed and thrown into the dustbin. Then why are these people allowed to throw their weight around based on undergrad math and stats—an Econ 101. We are in the business of Political Science and not failed Economics. Lastly,

11) When are you going to offer the APSA presidentship to Benedict Anderson or Charles Tilly or Richard Falk or Susanne Rudolph or Ari Zolberg or James C. Scott or Theda Skocpol who are more representative of our discipline than the "coterie" that runs APSA. I hope this anonymous letter leads to a dismantling of the Orwellian system that we have in APSA and that we will see a true Perestroika in the discipline.

Mr. Perestroika

9. James C. Scott, "The Role of Theory in Comparative Politics: A Symposium." *World Politics* 48:1, 37.

10. Michaelle Browers, "The Reconciliation of Political Theory and Comparative Politics," in *New Approaches to Comparative Politics: Insights from Political Theory*, ed. Jennifer S. Holmes (Lanham, Md.: Lexington Books, 2003), 8.

11. Browers, p. 18. This sentiment is strongly stated by James Scott: "If half your reading is not *outside* the confines of political science, you are risking extinction along with the rest of the subspecies. Most of the notable innovations in the discipline have come in the form of insights, perspectives, concepts, and paradigms originating elsewhere. Reading exclusively within the discipline is to risk reproducing orthodoxies or, at the very least, absorbing innovations far from the source." (Kohli et al. 1996, 37)

12. Browers, 16.

13. Robert A. Kahn, "Imagining Legal Fairness: A Comparative Perspective," in *New Approaches to Comparative Politics: Insights from Political Theory*, ed. Jennifer S. Holmes (Lanham, Md.: Lexington Books, 2003), 134.

14. Ann Davies, "Modernity and the State: Enlightenment, Liberalism and Political Development in the United States" in *New Approaches to Comparative Politics: Insights from Political Theory*, ed. Jennifer S. Holmes (Lanham, Md.: Lexington Books, 2003), 37.

Selected Bibliography

Ackerman, Bruce. *We the People*. Cambridge, Mass.: Belknap Press, 1991.

Adams, David, and Paul de la Garza. "EU Backs Colombian Peace." *St. Petersburg Times,* May 3, 2001.

Adams, Richard N. "A Report on the Political Status of the Guatemalan Maya." 155-86 in *Indigenous Peoples and Democracy in Latin America*, ed. Donna Lee Van Cott. New York: St. Martin's, 1994.

Agrawal, Arun and Jesse Ribot. "Accountability in Decentralization: A Framework with South Asian and West African Cases." *The Journal of Developing Areas* 33, (Summer 1999) 473–502.

Albó, Xavier. "And from Kataristas to MNRistas? The Surprising and Bold Alliance between Aymaras and Neoliberals in Bolivia." In *Indigenous Peoples and Democracy in Latin America,* ed. Donna Lee Van Cott. New York: St. Martin's, 1994.

Albó, Xavier. "Bolivia: Making the Leap from Local Mobilization to National Politics." In "Gaining Ground: The Indigenous Movement in Latin America." *NACLA Report on the Americas* 29, no. 5 (1996) 15–20.

Amnesty International. *Annual Report Colombia* 1998.

Amnesty International. *Annual Report Colombia* 2001.

Andreski, Stanislav. *Military Organization and Society.* Stanford, Calif.: Stanford University Press, 1968.

Arendt, Hannah. *On Revolution*. New York: Pelican Books, 1986.

Aristotle. *Nicomachean Ethics.* Translated by David Ross. Oxford, England: Oxford University Press, 1980.

Aristotle. *Politics.* Translated by Earnest Barker. London: Oxford University Press, 1958.

Aruquipa, José Antonio. "Indigenous Groups Enter Politics." *Latinamerica Press* (April 23, 2001) 4–5.

Ashley, Richard K. "Untying the Sovereign State: A Double Reading of the Anarchy Problematique." *Millenium: Journal of International Studies* 17, (Summer 1988) 227–62.

Bacon, David, "The Coca-Cola Killings." *American Prospect* 13, no. 2 (January 28, 2002)13–6.

Bagley, Bruce. "Drug Trafficking, Political Violence and U.S. Policy in Colombia in the 1990s." *Mama Coca* 2001.

Barber, Benjamin. *Strong democracy: Participatory politics for a new age.* Berkeley: University of California Press, 1984.

Barometro Iberoamericano. *Informe de Opinión de Latinoamerica y de la Peninsula Ibérica Enero 2001.* Consorcio Iberoamericano de Empresas de Investigación de Mercados y Asesoramiento December 2000–January 2001.

Bastos, Santiago, and Manuela Campos. *Quebrando el Silencio: Organizaciones del Pueblo Maya y Sus Demandas (1986–1992).* Guatemala City: FLACSO, 1993.

Bates, Robert H. "Area Studies and the Discipline." *APSA-CP: Newsletter of the APSA Organized Section in Comparative Politics* 7 no. 1 (1996) 1–2.

Bates, Robert. "Area Studies and the Discipline." *PS: Political Science and Politics,* 30, no. 2 (1995) 166–9.

Becker, Theodore L. *Comparative Judicial Politics: The Political Functionings of Courts.* Chicago: Rand McNally & Company, 1970.

Bedford, Sybille. *The Faces of Justice.* London: Collins, 1961.

Bellamy, Richard. *Liberalism and Modern Society: A Historical Argument.* University Park: Pennsylvania State University Press, 1992.

Benhabib, Seyla. "Toward a Deliberative Model of Democratic Legitimacy." 67–94 in *Democracy and Difference: Contesting the Boundaries of the Political,* ed. Seyla Benhabib. Princeton, N.J.: Princeton University Press, 1996.

Berryman, Phillip. *Liberation Theology.* New York: Pantheon, 1987.

Black, George. "Garrison Guatemala." *NACLA Report on the Americas,* 27, no.1 (1983) 2–35.

Bliss, Henry and Bruce Russett. "Democratic Trading Partners: The Liberal Connection." *Journal of Politics* 58, no. 4 (November 1998) 1126–47.

Bowman, Kirk. *Militarization, Democracy, and Development: The Perils of Praetorianism in Latin America.* University Park: Pennsylvania State University Press, 2002.

Browers, Michaelle L. "The Politics of Translation: Civil Society's Travels and Travails in Arab Political Thought." Doctoral Thesis in Political Science. Twin Cities, University of Minnesota, 2001.

Brown, Michael and Eduardo Fernández. *War of the Shadows: The Struggle for Utopia in the Peruvian Amazon.* Berkeley: University of California Press, 1991.

"Building Peace in the Midst of War: Civil Society Initiatives in Colombia: Introduction." An edited transcript of a seminar sponsored by George Washington University Andean Seminar and Washington Office on Latin America on May 3, 2000.

Bureau for International Narcotics and Law Enforcement Affairs. "Fact Sheet." April 23, 1999.

Bureau of Democracy, Human Rights and Labor, U.S. Department of State. *1999 Country Reports on Human Rights Practices.* Accessed 15 December 2002.
www.state.gov/www/global/human_rights/1999_hrp_report/colombia.html

Burt, Jo-Marie. and Fred Rosen. 1999. "Truth-Telling and Memory in Postwar Guatemala: An Interview with Rigoberta Menchú." *NACLA Report on the Americas* 32, no. 5 (1999) 6–10.

Carothers, Thomas. *Aiding democracy abroad: The learning curve.* Washington, D.C.: Carnegie Endowment for International Peace, 1999.

Carter, Lynn, Michael Lund, and Zeric Smith. "USAID REDSO/GHA Conflict Assessment Protocol: Pastoralist Conflicts." Washington, D.C.: Management Systems International, 2001.

Castillo, Fabio. *Los nuevos jinetes de la cocaína.* Bogotá, Colombia: Oveja Negra, 1996.

Ceaser, Mike. "Expressions of the Indigenous Majority." *Latinamerica Press* (April 23, 2001) 4–5.

Cederman, Lars-Erik. "Modeling the Democratic Peace as a Kantian Selection Process." *Journal of Conflict Resolution* 45, no. 4 (August 2001) 470–502.

Chan, Steve. "In Search of Democratic Peace: Problems and Promise," *Mershon International Studies Review* 41, no. 1 (May 1997) 55–91.

Chan, Steve. "Mirror, Mirror on the Wall . . . Are Freer Countries More Pacific?" *Journal of Conflict Resolution* 28 (December 1984) 617–48.

Constable, Marianne. *The Law of the Other: The Mixed Jury and Changing Conceptions of Citizenship, Law and Knowledge.* Chicago: University of Chicago Press, 1994.

Cornell, Drucilla. *Just Cause: Freedom, Identity and Rights.* Lanham, Md.: Rowman & Littlefield Publishers, Inc., 2000.

Crook, Richard C. "Making Law Matter: Rules, Rights and Security in the Lives of the Poor. Editorial Introduction." *IDS Bulletin.* 32 no. 1 (January 2001) 1–7.

Crook, Richard C. and J. Manor. *Democracy and Decentralisation in South Asia and West Africa: Participation, Accountability and Performance.* Cambridge, U.K.: Cambridge University Press, 1998.

Cubides, Fernando. "The Paramilitaries." 127–150 in *Violence in Colombia 1990–2000 Waging War and Negotiating Peace.* eds. Charles Bergquist, Ricardo Peñaranda, and Gonzalo Sánchez. Wilmington, Del.: SR Books, 2001.

d'Entreves, Alexander Passerin. *The Notion of the State.* Oxford, England: Clarendon Press, 1967.

Dahl, Robert. *A Preface to Democratic Theory.* Chicago: University of Chicago Press, 1956.

Dahl, Robert. *Polyarchy: Participation and Opposition.* New Haven, Conn.: Yale University Press, 1971.

Dallmayr, Fred R. "Introduction: Toward a Comparative Political Theory." *The Review of Politics* 59 (1997) (Non-Western Political Thought) 421–7.

Dallmayr, Fred R. *Alternative Visions: Paths in the Global Village.* Lanham, Maryland: Rowman & Littlefield, 1998.

Dallmayr, Fred R. *Beyond Orientalism: Essays on Cross-Cultural Encounter.* Albany, N.Y.: SUNY Press, 1996.

Dallmayr, Fred R., ed. *Border Crossings: Toward a Comparative Political Theory.* Global encounters: studies in comparative political theory. Lanham, Md.: Lexington Books, 1999.

Damaska, Mirijan. *The Faces of Justice and State Authority*. New Haven, Conn.: Yale University Press, 1986.

Dante, Idrissa, Jean-François Gautier, Mohamed Ali Marouani, and Marc Raffinot. "'Gagner l'argent' ou formuler une politique de développement? Le Cadre Stratégique de Lutte contre la Pauvreté au Mali." Mimeo, 2001.

Dante, Idrissa, Jean-François Gautier, Mohamed Ali Marouani, Marc Raffinot. "Chapter 6: Institutionalising the PRSP approach in Mali." PRSP Institutionalisation Study: Final Report. Paris: DIAL, 2001.

Dean, Mitchell. *Critical and Effective Histories: Foucault's Methods and Historical Sociology*. London: Routledge Press, 1994.

Degregori, Carlos Iván, et al. *Las rondas campesinas y la derrota de Sendero Luminoso*. Lima, Peru: Instituto de Estudios Peruanos, 1996.

Degregori, Carlos Iván. "After the Fall of Abimael Guzmán: The Limits of Sendero Luminoso." 179–91 in *The Peruvian Labyrinth: Polity, Society, Economy*, eds. Maxwell Cameron and Philip Mauceri. University Park, Pa.: Penn State University Press, 1997.

Degregori, Carlos Iván. Ethnicity and Democratic Governability in Latin America: Reflections from Two Central American Countries. 203–36 in *Fault Lines of Democracy in Post-Transition Latin America,* eds. Felipe Agüero and Jeffrey Stark. Miami, Fla.: North-South Center, 1998. 203–36.

"La democracia en peligro: Los alcaldes como objetivo military" Bogotá, Colombia: CIDEC (August 2000).

Dershowitz, Alan. *The Vanishing American Jew: In Search of Jewish Identity for the Next Century*. Boston: Little, Brown & Co., 1996.

Díaz Polanco, Héctor. *Indigenous Peoples in Latin America: The Quest for Self-Determination*. Boulder, Colo.: Westview, 1997.

Docking, Timothy. "Mali: The roots of democracy's success" *L'Afrique Politique: Revindications Populaires et Recompositions Politiques.* Bordeaux, France: Editions Karthala/Centre d'Etude d'Afrique Noire, 1997.

Dudley, Steven. "David Stoll on Rigoberta, Guerrillas and Academics." *NACLA Report on the Americas* 32, no. 5 (1999) 8–9.

Dunkerley, James. *Rebellion in the Veins: Political Struggle in Bolivia, 1952–1982*. London: Verso, 1984.

Dyson, Kenneth. *The State Tradition in Western Europe*. New York: Oxford University Press, 1980.

Easton, David *A Framework for Political Analysis*. Englewood Cliffs, N. J.: Prentice-Hall, 1965.

Easton, David *The Political System: An Inquiry into the State of Political Science*. New York: Knopf, 1953.

Eckstein, Harry. *Regarding Politics: Essays on Political Theory, Stability and Change*. Berkeley: University of California Press, 1992.

Edelman, Bernard. "Note." *Recueil Dalloz Sirey, Jurisprudence* (1982) 60–4.

Elliot, Jonathan, ed. *The Debates in the Several State Conventions, on the Adoption of the Federal Constitution*, vols. 1–4. Philadelphia, Pa.: J. B. Lippincott Co., 1901–11.

Emerson, Thomas I. *The System of Freedom of Expression.* New York: Vintage, 1970.

Euben, Roxanne. "Islamic Fundamentalism and the Limits of Modern Rationalism." Doctoral Thesis in Politics, Princeton, N. J.: Princeton University, 1995.

Euben, Roxanne. *Enemy in the Mirror: Islamic Fundamentalism and the Limits of Modern Rationalism, A Work of Comparative Political Theory.* Princeton, New Jersey: Princeton University Press, 1999.

Farber, Henry S., and Joanne Gowa. "Common Interests or Common Polities? Reinterpreting the Democratic Peace." *Journal of Politics* 59, no. 2 (May 1997) 393–418.

Farrand, Max, ed. *Records of the Federal Convention of 1787*, vols. 1–3. New Haven, Conn.: Yale University Press, 1966.

Ferrer, Yadira. "Gov't Takes FARC Terrorism Charges to UN." *Inter Press Service,* April 10, 2002.

Field, Les. "Ecuador's Pan-Indian Uprising." *NACLA Report on the Americas* 25, no. 3 (1991) 39–44.

Foucault, Michel. "Governmentality," in *The Foucault Effect: Studies in Governmentality.* eds. Graham Burchell, Colin Gordon, and Peter Miller. Chicago: University of Chicago Press, 1991.

Foucault, Michel. "The Eye of Power," in *Power/Knowledge: Selected interviews and other writings, 1972–1977.* ed. Colin Gordon. New York: Pantheon Books, 1980.

Foucault, Michel. "Questions of Method in *The Foucault Effect: Studies in Governmentality.* eds. Graham Burchell, Colin Gordon, and Peter Miller. Chicago: University of Chicago Press, 1991.

GAD (Support Group for Displaced People Organizations), "Report of Forced Displacement in Colombia 1999." Bogotá, Colombia.

Gadamer, Hans-Georg. *Truth and Method.* New York: Continuum, 1993.

Gasiorowski, Mark J. "An Overview of the Political Regime Change Dataset." *Comparative Political Studies* 29, no. 4 (August 1996) 469–83.

Gay, Peter. *The Enlightenment: An Interpretation*, vol. 2. New York: Alfred A. Knopf, 1969.

Gepp, Charles. "Colombia's Kidnapped Candidate." *Christian Science Monitor,* March 12, 2002.

Giraldo, Javier. "Corrupted Justice and the Schizophrenic State in Colombia." *Social Justice* 26, no. 4 (1999) 31–55.

Gowa, Joanne. *Ballots and Bullets: The Elusive Democratic Peace.* Princeton, N.J.: Princeton University Press, 1999.

Greenspan, Louis, and Cyril Levitt, eds. *Under the Shadow of Weimar: Democracy, Law, and Racial Incitement in Six Countries.* Westport, Conn.: Praeger, 1993.

Gunnell, John G. *Between Philosophy and Politics: The Alienation of Political Theory.* Amherst, Mass.: University of Massachusetts Press, 1986.

Haggard, Stephan, and Robert Kaufman. *The Political Economy of Democratic Transitions.* Princeton, N.J.: Princeton University Press, 1995.

Hahn, Dwight. *The Divided World of the Bolivian Andes: A Structural View of Domination and Resistance.* New York: Crane Russak, 1992.

Halliday, Terence C., and Lucien Karpik. *Lawyers and the Rise of Western Political Liberalism: Europe and North America from the Eighteenth to Twentieth Centuries*. Oxford: Oxford University Press, 1997.

Hamilton, Alexander, James Madison, and John Jay. *The Federalist Papers*. ed. Clinton Rossiter. New York: New American Library, 1961.

Handelman, Howard. *Struggle in the Andes: Peasant Political Mobilization in Peru*. Austin: University of Texas Press, 1975.

Handy, Jim. "'A Sea of Indians': Ethnic Conflict and the Guatemalan Revolution, 1944–1952." *The Americas* 46, no. 2 (October 1989) 189–204.

Hardt, Michael, and Antonio Negri. *Empire*. Cambridge, Mass.: Harvard University Press, 2000.

Hartlyn, Johnathan. "Colombia: The Politics of Violence and Accommodation." in *Democracy in Developing Countries* Vol. 4, eds. Juan Linz, Larry Diamond, and Jonathan Hartlyn. Baltimore, Md.: Johns Hopkins University Press, 1993.

Hartz, Louis. *The Liberal Tradition in America*. New York: Harcourt, Brace, Jovanovich, 1991.

Hefner, Robert W. "Multiple Modernities: Christianity, Islam and Hinduism in a Globalizing Age." *Annual Review of Anthropology* 27 (1988).

Hegre, Havard, Tanja Ellignsen, Scott Gates, and Nils Petter Gleditsch. "Towards a Democratic Civil Peace? Democracy, Political Change, and Civil War, 1816–1992." *American Political Science Review* 95, no. 1 (March 2001) 33–48.

Holmes, Jennifer S. *Terrorism and Democratic Stability*. Manchester, England: Manchester University Press, 2001.

Holmes, Stephen. *Passions and Constraint: On the Theory of Liberal Democracy*. Chicago: The University of Chicago Press, 1995.

House of Representatives, Committee on International Relations. *U.S. Narcotics Policy Toward Colombia.* 104th Cong. 2d. sess., 47.

Howard, A. E. Dick. "The Essence of Constitutionalism." 3–41 in *Constitutionalism and Human Rights: America, Poland, and France*. eds. Kenneth W. Thompson and Rett R. Lodwikowski. Lanham, Md.: University Press of America, 1991.

Huntington, Samuel. "American Ideals vs. American Institutions." *Political Science Quarterly* 97, no. 1 (Spring 1982).

Huntington, Samuel. *American Politics: The Promise of Disharmony*. Cambridge, Mass.: Belknap Press, 1981.

Huntington, Samuel. *Political Order in Changing Societies*. New Haven, Conn.: Yale University Press, 1968.

Ibarra, Alicia. *Los indígenas y el estado en el Ecuador*. Quito, Ecuador: Abya-Yala, 1992.

Iliffe, John. *The African Poor: A History*. Cambridge, U.K.: Cambridge University Press, 1997.

International Confederation of Free Trade Unions. *Colombia: Annual Survey of Violations of Trade Union Rights 2001.*

Irish, Marian "Introduction: Advance of the Discipline?" *Journal of Politics* 30, no. 2 (1968) 291–310.

Jackson, Robert H. *Quasi-states: Sovereignty, International Relations, and the Third World.* Cambridge, U.K.: Cambridge University Press, 1990.

Janowitz, Morris. *The Military in the Political Development of New Nations.* Chicago: University of Chicago Press, 1964.

Jonas, Susanne. *The Battle for Guatemala: Rebels, Death Squads, and U.S. Power.* Boulder, Colo.: Westview, 1991.

Jörg, Nico, Steward Field, and Chrisje Brants. "Are Inquisitorial and Adversarial Systems Converging?" In *Criminal Justice in Europe: A Comparative Study.* eds., Phil Fennell and Christopher Harding. Oxford, England: Clarendon Press, 1997.

Kahn, Robert A. "How Americans and Canadians Justify Their Positions on Hate Speech." Paper presented at the Annual Meeting of the Law and Society Association, Vancouver, Canada, May, 2002.

Kahn, Robert A. "Holocaust Denial Prosecutions in a Liberal Society: France Under the Gayssot Law." Paper presented at the Annual Meeting of the Law and Society Association, Miami, Florida, May 2000.

Kahn, Robert A. "The Informal Censorship of Holocaust Revisionism in the United States and Germany," *George Mason University Civil Rights Law Journal* 9 (1998/99) 125–49.

Kahn, Robert A. "The Limits of Legal Fairness: Holocaust Denial and the Law in France, Germany, Canada and the United States." Ph.D. diss. Johns Hopkins University, Md., 2000.

Kahn, Robert A. "Who Takes the Blame? Scapegoating, Legal Responsibility and the Prosecution of Holocaust Revisionists in the Federal Republic of Germany and Canada." *Glendale Law Review* 16 (1998) 17–64.

Kant, Immanuel. "To Perpetual Peace: A Philosophical Sketch," in *Perpetual Peace and Other Essays*, ed. Ted Humphry. Indianapolis, Ind.: Hackett Publishing, 1983.

Kasza, Gregory. "Perestroika: For an Ecumenical Science of Politics (Forum)." *PS: Political Science and Politics* 34, no. 3 (2001) 597–9.

Keller, Ranier. "Offenkundigkeit und Beweisbedürfigkeit im Strafprozeß." *Zeitschrift für die gesamte Strafrechtwissen schaft* 39 (1989) 380–418.

Kim, Soo Yeon. "Ties That Bind: The Role of Trade in International Conflict Processes" Ph.D. diss., Yale University, Conn., 1998.

Kline, Harvey. *State Building and Conflict Resolution in Colombi.* Tuscaloosa, Ala.: University of Alabama Press, 1999.

Kohli, Atul, Peter Evans, et al. "The Role of Theory in Comparative Politics: A Symposium." *World Politics* 48, no. 1 (1996) 1–49.

Kramnick, Isaac, ed. *The Portable Enlightenment Reader.* New York: Penguin, 1995.

Kramnick, Isaac. *Republicanism and Bourgeois Radicalism.* Ithaca, N. Y.: Cornell University Press, 1990.

Krasner, Stephen D. *Sovereignty: Organized Hypocrisy*. Princeton, N.J.: Princeton, 1999.

LaFeber, Walter. *Inevitable Revolutions: The United States in Central America*. New York: Norton, 1984.

Landsman, Stephan. *The Adversary System: A Description and Defense*. Washington, D.C.: American Enterprise Institute, 1984.

Lane, Jan-Erik, and Svante Ersson. *Comparative Politics: An Introduction and New Approach*. Cambridge, Mass.: Polity Press, 1994.

Langbein, John. *Comparative Criminal Procedure: Germany*. St. Paul, Minn.: West Publishing Co., 1977.

Larson, Gerald James. "Introduction." 3–18. *Interpreting Across Boundaries: New Essays in Comparative Philosophy*. Gerald James Larson and Eliot Deutsch. Princeton, N. J.: Princeton University Press, 1988.

Lenin, V. I. *Imperialism: The Highest Stage of Capitalism*. New York: International Publishers, 1979.

Li, Chenyang. *The Tao Encounters the West: Explorations in Comparative Philosophy*. Albany, N. Y.: State University of New York Press, 1999.

Lichbach, Mark Irving, and Alan S. Zuckerman. "Preface." *Comparative Politics: Rationality, Culture, and Structure*. Mark Irving Lichbach and Alan S. Zuckerman. New York: Cambridge University Press, 1997.

Lilly, Graham C. *An Introduction to the Law of Evidence*. 3d ed. St. Paul, Minn.: West Publishing Co., 1996.

Linz, Juan, ed. *The Breakdown of Democratic Regimes*. Baltimore, Md.: Johns Hopkins University Press, 1978.

Lipstadt, Deborah. *Holocaust Denial: The Growing Assault on Truth and Memory*. New York: Basic Books, 1993.

Lowi, Theodore. *The End of Liberalism: The Second Republic of the United States,* Second Edition. New York: W. W. Norton & Co., 1979.

MacIntyre, Alasdair. *After Virtue*. Notre Dame, Ind.: University of Notre Dame Press, 1984.

Mair, Peter. "Comparative Politics: An Overview." 309–35 in *A New Handbook for Political Science*. Robert E. Goodin and Hans-Dieter Klingmemann. Oxford, England: Oxford University Press, 1996.

Malloy, James. *Bolivia: The Uncompleted Revolution*. Pittsburgh, Pa.: University of Pittsburgh Press, 1970.

Malloy, James. *Revolution and Reaction: Bolivia, 1964–1985*. New Brunswick, N.J.: Transaction, 1988.

Mansbridge, Jane J. *Beyond Adversary Democracy*. New York: Basic Books, 1980.

Marquis, Christopher. "New Drug Plan Shifts Focus in Latin America." *New York Times* May 17, 2001.

Martin, Robert, and G. Stuart Adam. *A Sourcebook of Canadian Media Law*. Ottawa, Canada: Carelton University Press, 1994.

Martinez, Margarita. "Colombia Paramilitary Boss Speaks Out." Associated Press, February 12, 2002.

Martz, John D. *Politics and Petroleum in Ecuador*. New Brunswick, N.J.: Transaction, 1987.

May, Henry F. *The Enlightenment in America*. New York: Oxford, 1976.

McClintock, Cynthia, and Abraham Lowenthal, eds. *The Peruvian Experiment Reconsidered*. Princeton, N.J.: Princeton University Press, 1983.

McClintock, Cynthia. *Peasant Cooperatives and Political Change in Peru*. Princeton, N.J.: Princeton University Press, 1981.

McClintock, Cynthia. *Revolutionary Movements in Latin America: El Salvador's FMLN and Peru's Shining Path*. Washington D.C.: United States Institute of Peace Press, 1998.

Menchú, Rigoberta. *I, Rigoberta Menchú*. London: Verso, 1984.

Merryman, John H. *The Civil Law Tradition*. Palo Alto, Calif.: Stanford University Press, 1984.

Meyer, Donald H. *The Democratic Enlightenment*. New York: G. P. Putnam's Sons, 1976.

Miller, David. *Principles of Social Justice*. Cambridge, Mass.: Harvard University Press, 1999.

Ministerio de Defensa Nacional. *La fuerza pública y los derechos humanos en Colombia*. (March 2000) Bogota, Colombia.

Montejo, Víctor. *Testimony: Death of a Guatemalan Village*. Willimantic, Conn.: Curbstone Press, 1987.

Moore, Mick, and James Putzel. "Politics and poverty: A background paper for the World Development Report 2000/1." (August 7, 2002). www.worldbank.org/poverty/wdrpoverty/dfid/synthes.pdf

Morgan, Edmund. *Inventing the People: The Rise of Popular Sovereignty in England and America*. New York: W. W. Norton & Co., 1988.

Morrow, James, Randolph Siverson, and Tessa Tabares. "The Political Determinants of International Trade: The Major Powers, 1907–90." *American Political Science Review* 92, no. 3 (September 1998) 649–61.

Nader, Laura. "The underside of conflict management in Africa and elsewhere." *IDS Bulletin* 32, no. 1 (January 2001) 19–27.

Nakamura, Hajime. *Parallel Developments: A Comparative History of Ideas*. New York: Harper & Row, 1975.

Nettl, J. P. "The State as a Conceptual Variable." *World Politics* 20, no. 2 (July 1968).

Nielsen, Greg. "Backhtin and Habermas: Toward a Transcultural Ethics." *Theory and Society* 24, no. 6 (1995) 803–36.

Nkruma, Kwame. *Neo-Colonialism: The Last Stage of Imperialism*. New York: International Publishers, 1969.

O'Donnell, Guillermo, and Philippe Schmitter, eds. *Transitions from Authoritarian Rule: Tentative Conclusions about Uncertain Democracies*. Baltimore, Md.: Johns Hopkins University Press, 1986.

Organization of American States. "OAS Inter-American Human Rights Commission 2000 Report: Colombia."

Otzoy, Antonio. "Guatemala: The Struggle for Maya Unity." *NACLA Report on the Americas* 29, no. 5 (1996) 33–5.

Pacari, Nina. "Ecuador: Taking on the Neoliberal Agenda." *NACLA Report on the Americas* 29, no. 5(1996) 23–32.

Padilla Castro, and Nelson Fredy. "Toxic Rain Kills More than the Coca." *UNESCO Courier* (May 2001), 10–1.

Palmer, David Scott. ed. *Shining Path of Peru.* New York: St. Martin's, 1992.

Pardo, Rafael. "Colombia's Two Front War." *Foreign Affairs* 79, no. 4 (July/August 2000) 64–74.

Parel, Anthony, and Ronald C. Keith. *Comparative Political Philosophy: Studies Under the Upas Tree*. New Delhi, India; Newbury Park, Calif.: Sage, 1992.

Parrish, Geov. "Call This a Plan?" WorkingForChange.com, February 11, 2002.

Pateman, Carole. *Participation and democratic theory.* Cambridge, U.K.: Cambridge University Press, 1970.

Peeler, John. *Building Democracy in Latin America.* Boulder, Colo.: Lynne Rienner, 1998.

Perera, Víctor. *Unfinished Conquest: The Guatemalan Tragedy.* Berkeley: University of California Press, 1993.

Peters, Edward. *Torture*. Philadelphia: University of Pennsylvania Press, 1996.

Petras, James. "The FARC faces the Empire." *Latin American Perspectives* Issue 114, Vol. 27, No. 5 (September 2000) 134–43.

Pole, J. R. "Enlightenment and the Politics of American Nature" in *The Enlightenment in National Context*. eds. Roy Porter and Mikulas Teich. New York: Cambridge, 1981.

Pomper, Miles. "Leaders Push Trade Aid for Colombia." *CQ Weekly*, September 2, 2000, 2037.

Pratt, Mary Louise. *Imperial Eyes: Travel Writing and Transculturation.* London: Routledge, 1992.

"Primer Congreso de Nacionalidades Quechuas, Aymaras, y Nativas de la Selva. Segunda Plenaria, Transcripción" (mimeo). Cuzco, Peru: Centro Bartolomé de las Casas, 1980.

Ray, James Lee. "The Democratic Path to Peace." *Journal of Democracy* 8, no. 2 (April 1997) 49–64.

Ray, James Lee. "Does Democracy Cause Peace?" *Annual Review of Political Science* 1 (1998) 27–46.

Reich, Otto. "Crucial Battle for Colombia." *Washington Times*, July 19, 2002.

Remy, María Isabel. "The Indigenous Population and the Construction of Democracy in Peru." 107–130 in *Indigenous Peoples and Democracy in Latin America,* ed. Donna Lee Van Cott. New York: St. Martin's, 1994.

Republic of Colombia. "Plan Colombia and U.S. Support for Democracy, Peace and Economic Prosperity in Colombia." June 2001.

Reyes, Alejandro. "Drug Trafficking and the Guerrilla Movement in Colombia" in *Drug Trafficking in the Americas* eds. B. M. Bagley and W. O. Walker. Coral Gables, Fla.: North-South Center, University of Miami Press, 1995.

Rivera Cusicanqui, Silvia. "Aymara Past, Aymara Future." *NACLA Report on the Americas* 25, no. 3 (1991)18–23.

Rodee, C. C., T. J. Anderson, and C. Q. Christol. *Introduction to Political Science*. New York: McGraw-Hill, 1957.

Ross, Dorothy. *The Origins of American Social Science*. New York: Cambridge University Press, 1991.

Ruben, Mauricio. "La violencia en Colombia: dimesionamiento y políticas de control." Serie de documentos de trabajo R 345, Interamerican development bank. Washington, D.C. (October 1998).

Rueschemeyer, Dietrich, Evelyne Huber Stephens, and John Stephens. *Capitalist Development and Democracy*. Chicago: University of Chicago Press, 1992.

Russet, Bruce, and Harvey Starr. "From Democratic Peace to Kantian Peace: Democracy and Conflict in the International System." in *Handbook of War Studies*, 2nd ed. ed. Manus Midlarsky. Ann Arbor: University of Michigan Press, forthcoming.

Salinger, Lynn, and Dirk Stryker. "Comparing and evaluating poverty reduction approaches: USAID and the evolving poverty reduction paradigm. Assessment prepared for USAID/PPC/CDIE/POA." July 28. Associates for International Resources and Development (AIRD) and Management Systems International (MSI), 2001.

Salkever, Stephen. "Aristotle's Social Science." *Political Theory* 9, no. 4, (November 1981) 479–508.

Sánchez, Francisco. and Flavia Freidenberg. "El Proceso de Incorporación Política de kos Sectores Indígenas en el Ecuador: Pachakutik, un Caso de Estudio." *América Latina, Hoy* 19 (July 1998) 65–80.

Scheingold, Stuart. *The Politics of Rights*. New Haven, Conn.: Yale University Press, 1974.

Schoultz, Lars. *Beneath the United States: A History of U.S. Policy toward Latin America*. Cambridge, Mass.: Harvard University Press, 1998.

Schoultz, Lars. *Human Rights and United States Policy toward Latin America* . Princeton, N.J.: Princeton University Press, 1981.

Schoultz, Lars. *National Security and United States Policy toward Latin America*. Princeton, N.J.: Princeton University Press, 1987.

Seely, Jennifer C. "A political analysis of decentralization: Coopting the Tuareg threat in Mali." *Journal of Modern African Studies*. 39 no. 3 (2001) 499–524.

Selmeski, Brian. *Transformational Politics: The Development and Effect of Indigenous Organizations in Ecuador*. Lewisburg, Pa.: Bucknell University Program in Latin American Studies, Honors Thesis, 1992.

Selverston, Melina H. "Pachacutik: Indigenous People and Democracy in Ecuador." *Native Americas* (Summer 1998) 12–20.

Selverston, Melina H. "The Politics of Culture: Indigenous Peoples and the State in Ecuador." 131–52 in *Indigenous Peoples and Democracy in Latin America* , ed. Donna Lee Van Cott. New York: St. Martin's, 1994.

Sen, Amartya. *Development as Freedom*. Alfred A. Knopf: New York, 1999.

Shapiro, Ian. *Democratic Justice*. New Haven, Conn.. Yale University Press, 1999.

Shapiro, Ian and Casiano Hacker-Cordon. *Democracy's Value.* Cambridge, U.K.: Cambridge University Press, 1999.

Shapiro, Martin. *Courts: A Comparative and Political Analysis.* Chicago: University of Chicago Press, 1981.

Sheridan, Alan. Translator's note to *The Four Fundamental Concepts of Psychoanalysis: The Seminar of Jacques Lacan, Book 9.* Edited by Jacques-Alain Miller. New York: W.W. Norton & Co., 1978.

Shifter, Michael. "Colombia on the Brink," *Foreign Affairs* 78 no. 4 (July/August 1999) 14–21.

Shklar, Judith N. *After Utopia.* Princeton, N.J.: Princeton University Press, 1957.

Skinner, Quentin. *The Return of Grand Theory in the Human Sciences.* Cambridge, U.K.: Cambridge University Press, 1985.

Skowronek, Stephen. *Building a New American State.* New York: Cambridge University Press, 1982.

Smith, Rogers M. *Reconnecting Political Theory to Empirical Inquiry, or, A Return to the Cave?* American Political Science Association Annual Meeting, San Francisco, CA, 2001.

Smith, Zeric Kay with Bakary Doumbia. "USAID/Mali Democratic Governance Strategic Objective Fourth Annual Performance Measurement Survey Data Analysis Presentation." March 7, 2001: MSI and InfoStat, 2001.

Smith, Zeric Kay. *Democracy and Civic Community in Mali.* Masters thesis, University of North Carolina at Chapel Hill, 1993.

Smith, Zeric Kay. "The Rhythm of Everyday Politics in Mali." In *This is How We Flow: Rhythm and Black Culture.* ed. Angela Nelson. Columbia: University of South Carolina Press, 1999.

Snyder, Jack. *From Voting to Violence: Democratization and Nationalist Conflict.* New York: W.W. Norton, 2000.

Steiner, Roberto. "Hooked on Drugs: Colombian-U.S. Relations." in *The United States and Latin America: The New Agenda.* eds. Victor Bulmer-Thomas and James Dunkerley. London: Institute of Latin American Studies, University of London, 1999.

Stepan, Alfred. *State and Society: Peru in Comparative Perspective.* Princeton, N.J.: Princeton University Press, 1978.

Stern, Kenneth S. *Holocaust Denial.* New York: American Jewish Congress, 1992.

Stoll, David. *Between Two Armies in the Ixil Towns of Guatemala.* New York: Columbia University Press, 1993.

Stoll, David. *Rigoberta Menchú and the Story of All Poor Guatemalans.* Boulder, Colo.: Westview, 1999.

Strauss, Leo. *Natural Right and History.* Chicago: University of Chicago Press, 1965.

Strier, Franklin. *Reconstructing Justice: An Agenda for Trial Reform.* Chicago: University of Chicago Press, 1994.

Ströbele-Gregor, Juliana. "Culture and Political Practice of the Aymara and Quechua in Bolivia." *Latin American Perspectives* 23, no. 2 (1996) 72–90.

Sward, Ellen E. "Values, Ideology and the Evolution of the Adversary System." *Indiana Law Journal* 64 (1989) 301–55.

Taylor, Charles. "Modes of Civil Society." *Public Culture* 3, no. 1 (Fall 1990).

Thoumi, Francisco. "Why the Illegal Psychodelic Drug Use Industry Grew in Colombia" in *Drug Trafficking in the Americas.* eds. B. M. Bagley and W. O. Walker. Coral Gables, Fla.: North-South Center, University of Miami Press, 1995.

U.S. Department of State. "On the Record Briefing: Andean Regional Initiative" May 18, 2001.

United States Government. *International Narcotics Strategy Report*, 1999.

USAID. *Conducting a DG Assessment: A Framework for Strategy Development.* Technical publication series. Center for Democracy and Governance/Bureau for Global Programs, Field Support, and Research, 2000.

Van Cott, Donna Lee. ed. *Indigenous Peoples and Democracy in Latin America.* New York: St. Martin's Press, 1994.

Verba, Sidney. "Comparative Politics: Where have we been, where are we going?" 26–38 in *New Directions in Comparative Politics.* eds. Howard J. Wiarda and Douglas A. Chalmers. Boulder, Colo.: Westview, 1985.

Vidal-Naquet, Pierre. *Assassins of Memory: Essays on the Denial of the Holocaust.* New York: Columbia University Press, 1992.

Violence in Colombia: Building a Sustainable Peace and Social Capital. World Bank: Washington D.C, 2000.

Walker, Samuel. *Hate Speech: The History of an American Controversy.* Linclon, Nebr.: University of Nebraska Press, 1994.

Warren, Kay, ed. *The Violence Within: Cultural and Political Opposition in Divided Nations.* Boulder, Colo.: Westview, 1993.

Warren, Kay. *Indigenous Movements and Their Critics.* Princeton, N.J.: Princeton University Press, 1998.

Webb, Jason. "Colombia Warlord to Free Venezuelan, Quit AUC Role." Reuters, July 12, 2002.

Weber, Max. "Politics as a Vocation." in *From Max Weber: Essays in Sociology.* eds. H. H. Gerth and C. Wright Mills. New York: Oxford University Press, 1946.

Weber, Max. *Economy and Society, Vol. II.* Berkeley: University of California Press, 1978.

Westen, Peter. "The Empty Idea of Equality." *Harvard Law Review* 95 (1982) 537–96.

Wickham-Crowley, Timothy. *Guerrillas and Revolution in Latin America: A Comparative Study of Insurgents and Regimes since 1956.* Princeton, N.J.: Princeton University Press, 1992.

Wills, Garry. *Inventing America.* New York: Doubleday, 1978.

Wilson, Richard. *Maya Resurgence in Guatemala: Q'eqchi Experiences.* Norman: University of Oklahoma Press, 1995.

Wilson, Scott. "U.S. Drug Chief Tries to Boost Colombian Resolve." *Washington Post,* November 21, 2000, A22.

Wilson, Scott. "Colombia's Rights Cleaning Campaign." *Washington Post,* April 17, 2001.

Wood, Gordon. *The Creation of the American Republic, 1776–1787.* New York: W. W. Norton & Co., 1969.

World Values Survey, 1997.

Yashar, Deborah. "Contesting Citizenship: Indigenous Movements and Democracy in Latin America." *Comparative Politics* 31, no. 1 (October 1998) 23–42.

Young, Iris Marion. *Inclusion and Democracy.* New York: Oxford University Press, 2000.

Index

About the Editor and Contributors

Kirk Bowman is Assistant Professor in the Sam Nunn School of International Affairs at the Georgia Institute of Technology. He has published articles on democratization, inequality, development, and the Latin American military in various journals and books, including *World Development*, *Journal of Peace Research*, and the *Journal of Latin American Studies*. Dr. Bowman has conducted extensive fieldwork in Argentina, Brazil, Costa Rica, Cuba, Honduras, and Uruguay. His book, *Militarization, Democracy, and Development: The Perils of Praetorianism in Latin America*, is published by the Pennsylvania State University Press (2002). His current research project explores tourism ministries in six Latin American countries in an effort to better conceptualize and understand state capacity.

Michaelle Browers is Assistant Professor of Political Science at Wake Forest University who writes on Arab and Islamic Political Thought. A volume she has coedited with Charles Kurzman, entitled *An Islamic Reformation?*, will be published by Lexington Books.

Ann Davies is Associate Professor of Political Science at Beloit College, where she teaches courses in political theory, American politics, and constitutional law. She has written on religious tolerance and the development of the state, as well as the Supreme Court's approach to children in its jurisprudence.

Seán Patrick Eudaily is Assistant Professor of Politics and History at the North Dakota State College of Science. His Ph.D. is from the University of Maryland and he has taught at George Mason University. He has published articles on contentious politics and democratic theory. Currently, he is working on a book analyzing the normative challenges posed to liberal governmentality by indigenous land claims.

Jennifer S. Holmes is Assistant Professor of Government and Politics and Political Economy at the University of Texas at Dallas. Dr. Holmes received her Ph.D. in Political Science from the University of Minnesota in 1998. Her major area of research is regime change and democratic stability with an emphasis on the consequences of violence, repression, and the drug trade. She is the author of *Terrorism and Democratic Stability* (Manchester University Press, 2001) and has had articles published in *Terrorism and Political Violence* and the *Latin American Research Review.*

Robert A. Kahn holds a Ph.D. from the Johns Hopkins University Department of Political Science and a J.D. from the New York University School of Law. His dissertation, which he is preparing for publication, shows how differences in the way American, Canadian, French, and German legal systems view legal fairness helped shape the response of those societies to the legal challenges posed by Holocaust denial. Dr. Kahn is currently an Instructor of Law at Brooklyn Law School.

John Peeler is Professor of Political Science at Bucknell University. He is the author of *Building Democracy in Latin America* (Lynne Rienner, 1998) and other publications.

Zeric Kay Smith is a Senior Research Associate at Management Systems International. He received his Ph.D. from the University of North Carolina, Chapel Hill. He has twelve years experience in international development, education, and consulting. He has been published in *The Journal of Democracy* and *The Journal of Modern African Studies*. Currently, he is writing a book about the role of civil society–based groups in democratic transitions in Africa.